Eternal Hostility

The Struggle Between Theocracy and Democracy

Frederick Clarkson

Common Courage Press

MONROE, MAINE

First edition, first printing

Copyright ©1997 by Frederick Clarkson

Common Courage Press
Box 702
Monroe, Maine 04951
Phone: (207) 525-0900
Fax: (207) 525-3068

Cover design by Matt Wuerker

Library of Congress Cataloging-in-Publication Data
Clarkson, Frederick.
Eternal hostility: the struggle between theocracy and democracy
p. cm.
Includes index.
ISBN 1-56751-089-2 (cloth). ISBN 1-56751-088-4 (pbk.)
1. Conservatism--Religious aspects--Christianity--Controversial literature.
2. Conservatism--United States--History--20th century. 3. Christian Coalition.
4. Theocracy--Controversial literature. 5. United States--Church history--20th
centruy. 6. United States--Politics and government--1993- I. Title.
BR526.C57   1996
320.5'5'0973--dc20   96-41262
CIP

To Kate Cornell

Whose love and companionship saw me through this project
just as in everything else.

Thank you, Kate.

Contents

Introduction

As a Presbyterian (USA) clergy with a life-long zeal for both my Christian religion and our democratic country, *Eternal Hostility* has illuminated my mind and sensitized my heart like nothing I have read in recent times. This is exactly what is needed to help us secure the health of our democracy and preserve true religious liberty. Its honest and intelligent investigative journalism embodies some of the most in-depth research and reporting on the religious right in print. An encounter of my own with the religious right may serve to illustrate the need for this book.

In the spring of 1994, I gave a sermon to our 7,600 member congregation, introducing the personnel, theology, and goals of the radical religious right. The text was subsequently published locally and then in the *Sunday New York Times*. This drew the wrath of religious right leader James Dobson of Focus on the Family in the form of a full page ad in the *Kansas City Star*. This was just the tip of a large iceberg of stealth campaigns by the religious right to take over the Republican Party and run for public office in our area. It was then that a local grassroots Mainstream Coalition was formed to challenge the religious right.

I first met Fred Clarkson when we shared the podium at a public forum a few months later in July, 1994, titled "Exposing the Agenda of the Radical Religious Right" and sponsored by Planned Parenthood. The event turned out to be a benchmark in the growing struggle with the religious right in our suburban community outside of Kansas City.

The Planned Parenthood Forum drew extensive coverage from television, radio, and out of town newspapers. Fred spent all day before the evening forum doing interviews. So concerned had the community become that more people had to be turned away than those who packed the large auditorium. On that unforgettable evening, Fred detailed with clarity, and with good humor essential to civil discourse, the imminent threat of the radical religious right to our democratic institutions. This was especially significant in that there were many religious right activists present. It is evident that people are starved for accurate information and analysis about the radical religious right as it affects our communities.

Now Clarkson has drawn on the themes of that address and more, to create a very readable and well-documented book. In bringing out the facts, he is discerning, and not judgmental—a true investigative journalist.

From his critique of authors dealing with the so-called "culture wars," to his first-hand observation of the founding meetings of the Christian Coalition, much of his writing comes of personal experience, not hearsay. Everything he reports is carefully documented.

Clarkson exposes the distorted use of American colonial history—as some use statistics, interpreting as they will in an attempt to prove whatever they want—and the misreading of the Constitutionby the leadership of the religious right. Pat Robertson and his fellow generals in the army do the same with holy Scripture to give their narrow sectarian views the authority of "thus says the Lord." Clarkson eliminates any confusion; he clearly demonstrates that the Constitution and Bill of Rights were purposefully designed to preserve this democracy and forever save it from being made a theocracy.

Eternal Hostility introduces many important players who receive little media attention, from the anti-democratic "reconstructionist" theologians to James Dobson, long-hailed hero of family values who has been building a prime political empire for a decade. He may well influence more people than the Christian Coalition. His "Focus On The Family" brings in annual revenues of more than $100 million. But while Clarkson issues a warning about these groups and others such as the Unification Church and the Promise Keepers, the author makes clear that apathy on the part of mainline Christians and other centrists is more to be feared. Clarkson insists that "Political participation must not be limited to the voting booth, but active participation in political and electoral life must span the calendar year."

Too many wonderfully good citizens upon hearing the religious right stand back and say, "They certainly don't speak for me." But they do speak for you if you are not doing anything to keep our democracy from being converted to a theocracy!

This book is a masterpiece for God and country!

—Robert H. Meneilly

Robert H. Meneilly founded and then pastored the Village Presbyterian Church (USA) for more than 47 years in Prairie Village, Kansas. It is the second largest mainstream Presbyterian Church in the country. He is one of the founders of the Interfaith Alliance and the Mainstream Coalition, organizations of mainstream religious leaders who oppose the agenda of the religious right.

Acknowledgements

There are many who made this book possible in more ways that I can ever adequately acknowledge.

First, thanks to Mom and Dad who provided a quiet place to work when I needed one. Then thanks the people who have over the years provided invaluable research materials and insights. I am greatly in their debt. These include Lois Bell, Russ Bellant, Bill Berkowitz, Chip Berlet, Rob Boston, Priscilla Coates, Joe Conn, Glenn Davis, Sara Diamond, Ford Green, Kathy Frasca and the Mainstream Voters Project, Jean Hardisty, Steve Hassan, Leon Howell, Richard Kanegis, Barbara Rochelle, Al Ross, Jerry Sloan, Skipp Porteous, James Ridgeway, Barbara Simon, Louis Wolf, and Lenny Zeskind. To the many others who have been helpful in this work-in-progress but who, for reasons of space, discretion, or forgetfulness, cannot be named here, also go my heartfelt thanks.

Additionally, I want to thank my former colleagues at Planned Parenthood Federation of America, and the many exceptional people who staff and lead Planned Parenthood affiliates around the country. I especially want to acknowledge my friends and colleagues of the former Public Policy Institute. I benefited greatly from their knowledge and experience during my tenure.

Special thanks to Bill Bradford of the law firm of Hogan and Hartson, and to Bob Alley for providing valuable documents on the Smith v. Mobile School Board case, and to Claire Lewis for her valuable research assistance.

Many thanks especially to those who patiently read some or all of these chapters and provided thoughtful comments, criticisms, and corrections: Anne Bower, Chip Berlet, Rob Boston, Kate Cornell, Joe Conn, Glenn Davis, Jerry Sloan, and Mel Wulf of Beldock, Levine and Hoffman. Naturally, I am responsible for any further errors of fact or analysis here.

Greg Bates at Common Courage Press encouraged me to write

this book and contributed editing and ideas that made this a much better and more readable work. Tara Townsend's patient "book building" made it happen.

Earlier versions of some of the material in this book first appeared in *Church & State*, *Christianity & Crisis*, *Covert Action Quarterly*, *The Freedom Writer*, *Extra!*, *Front Lines Research*, *In These Times*, *Mother Jones*, *Public Eye*, the *St. Louis Journalism Review*, and the *Washington City Paper*. Portions of chapters 4 and 5 were anthologized in *Eyes Right: Challenging the Right Wing Backlash*, South End Press, 1995. Chip Berlet, ed.

—Frederick Clarkson
Northampton, Massachusetts

CHAPTER 1

Eternal Hostility

The Born-Again Struggle

Pensacola, Florida: a man shoves a shotgun in the window of the cab of a truck and blasts away, killing a doctor and an escort, and seriously wounding another escort.

Virginia Beach, Virginia: a law school graduates a man whose thesis argued that the murder of doctors who perform abortions is justifiable homicide.

Bowie, Maryland: a minister publishes a book advocating armed theocratic revolution—titled *A Time To Kill.*

The men in these vignettes, Paul Hill the shooter, Michael Hirsch the lawyer, and Michael Bray the minister, are all public figures, if not all household names. The media often portray these people as lone actors, zealots, or extremists who justify violence against abortion providers. Hill is also described as a convicted murderer and Bray as a convicted clinic bomber. However, there is much more to these men, their tactics, their worldview and their political goals, than they would like people to know. They are, in fact, key theorists, spokesmen and activists for the armed wing of the Christian Right.

Similar discrepancies between popular understanding and the somewhat hidden, larger purposes of Christian Right leaders occur in every area—from the meaning of "family" to electoral politics. The stakes are far larger than the question "how do we deal with fringe elements?" The agenda of the Christian Right is more astounding and dangerous to democracy than most of us are prepared to believe. The scale of change in American politics is more serious than has been generally reported. Political violence is growing. Armed paramilitary groups are forming.

Behind the media's portrayal of "fringe elements," a vital but little discussed struggle is unfolding centered on the issue of whether the

United States should be a democracy, or a theocracy governed by "Biblical law." To many, this struggle appears only on the distant horizon of political discourse, if at all. Even the term "theocracy"— the rule of government by a God and God's representatives, who may be priests, ministers, or non-clerical individuals, with citizenship generally limited to members of the governing sect[1]—has an antiquated feel to it. But it would be a mistake to believe that the relative obscurity of the concept indicates that the theocratic movement is a thing of the past. As the events described above and many others indicate, the time has come to re-think the situation. The time has come to get to know the opposition.

How can a critique and response to the Christian Right be developed without trampling on their religious freedom? How can the tricky problem of "labels" be avoided to prevent effective responses from being slowed, skewed, or stuck in terminological gridlock? The task of understanding and responding is not straightforward and begs many questions.

The winners in history have tended to be those that capture the flag of nationalism and the robe of religious justification and authority. The Christian Right is dramatically striving for both under the banner of the "Christian Nation." Its leaders have cleverly reinterpreted American history and constitutional law to accommodate their contemporary religious and political goals and to animate their movement. Those who would defend and advance democratic values must understand what the Christian Right is about. Keeping or regaining the moral, intellectual, and historical high ground is part of this.

The struggle between democracy and theocracy, which seemed to have been settled when the U.S. Constitution was ratified, is far from over. As Christian Right theorist Gary North writes, "For the first time in over 300 years, a growing number of Christians are starting to view themselves as an army on the move. This army will grow." Taking this metaphor a step farther, North declared that, "We are self-consciously firing the first shot."[2]

Although the Christian Right is a formidable force in American politics, it is also vulnerable. Although they are ideologically driven, their numbers are relatively small. Although they have achieved considerable power, it is precarious and their influence extends disproportionately throughout the electorate. Most importantly, their agenda, the family-values gloss not withstanding, is unacceptable to most Americans. How to respond to the paradoxical nature of a movement that is powerful, and yet has not captured the sentiments of the majority, is a central theme to which we will return.

The Christian Right's War of Aggression

A certain despair about the future of democracy and civil discourse in the United States nags our political plans, our institutions, and our conversations. Some speak darkly of the possibility of civil war. But the urgency born of a media culture that feeds on conflict is in some respects overblown, or at least misdirected. Without in any way underestimating the significance of the multifaceted Christian Right political movement and its growing militant, revolutionary wings, there is actually good news.

The strategy of the Christian Right, as we will see in subsequent chapters, is based on the mobilization of a self-conscious minority that is arguably the best organized faction in American politics. It is a faction that has also been misunderstood by opponents across the political spectrum. The narrow lens of specific issues, or even party politics, tends to cramp and skew our understandings of the larger threat of the Christian Right. This segmented perspective limits effective political response. The Christian Right knows that it does not really have the numbers to control American politics—unless most Americans remain politically asleep and uninvolved. Their strengths are often based on stealth, the illusion of strength, and the seeming moral high ground of religious authority. The various components of stealth strategy are discoverable. Accurate assessments of the strengths and weaknesses of the Christian Right are obtainable. And the supposed moral high ground occupied by the Christian Right is built on quicksand.

Although the United States was the first nation in history founded without the sanction of an official God or an official church, the national ethos of religious pluralism and equality is under attack. It is an attack rooted in struggles between advocates of democratic values and the established theocracies of 17th and 18th century colonial America. Much of the contemporary Christian Right is looking back to what their religious and political ancestors lost when the Constitution was ratified—now they seek a different outcome. We can hear this agenda lurking in the speeches of political leaders, like Pat Robertson, when they claim that America was founded as a "Christian Nation," and that they aim to restore that heritage. Unfortunately, the idea that this past is but a prologue to the politics of today is taken seriously by few outside of the Christian Right itself.

The notion that there is a "culture war" underway in the U.S. is thus a paradigm that results in a great deal of misdirection. Issues are presented individually, or as a package of social issues about which the so-called culture war is supposedly being fought. The politically sophisticated refer to some of these as "wedge issues." But a wedge towards what? For 350 years, the struggle has been about power, about beliefs, about the definition of what it is to be human. It is about the definition of democracy and religious freedom, and how to avoid religious warfare. These issues are not side dishes to the main meal of politics; they are at the center of the country's identity.

None other than Pat Buchanan, in his speech at the 1992 Republican convention, said there is a "religious war" going on in the U.S. He is right. But not in the sense that he probably meant. It is a war of aggression by the Christian Right against beliefs of which they do not approve and against the expression of those beliefs.

The issues arising from the politics of theocracy are many, leading some to protests, others to politics. Still others openly advocate armed theocratic revolution in the United States. Some are actively engaged in a low level guerrilla war, waiting for their moment in the sun.

Most extraordinarily, the theocratic right has successfully appropriated the themes of religious freedom and individual conscience to support its agenda of intolerance. These values of religious freedom and individual conscience—which were among the very reasons for *dismantling* the colonial theocracies and ratifying the Constitution—have been turned on their heads. How did we get here?

From Colonial Culture War to the Second Comeback

From the persecution of Quakers, Jesuits, and "witches" in the Massachusetts Bay Colony during the 1600s through the bitter Presidential election campaign of 1800, and the advent of the Christian

Right in the 1980s, an animating, underlying theme of the American experience has been the struggle between democratic and theocratic values. The descendants of the losing side have not forgotten. Self-proclaimed "orthodox" Christians have opposed democracy, pluralism, and religious freedom for hundreds of years. Having regrouped after losing most of the major battles since the ratification of the Constitution, they are attempting a comeback.

Historian John Wilson observes that the historic "tensions between temporal and spiritual life in America" were far from settled with the adoption of the First Amendment.[3] The religious diversity of the U.S. today would astound the framers of the Constitution. Wilson believes this diversity exacerbates the issues of the proper relationship between church and state. Issues like the right to an abortion, or even the rights to freedom of speech, of association, and freedom from unwarranted search and seizure, appear settled to most Americans, but Constitutional rights are fragile things and subject to the prevailing mood of enforcement, or the interpretation of the latest majority on the Supreme Court. In the 19th century, there was a de facto Protestant establishment in the U.S. However, the Christian Right of the day, according to author Robert Boston, "acknowledged the secular nature of the Constitution, and called for amending it to include references to God or Christianity. The Christian Right of today has generally abandoned this strategy and in the face of all available evidence, insists that the Constitution was somehow written to afford special protection to Christianity."[4]

This change in political strategies over time reflects the regrouping of the theocrats after a steady two century decline. A principal catalyst is the advent of the politically oriented theology of Christian Reconstructionism—the effort to replace Constitutional law with "God's law." However outlandish it appears, it is one of the most significant, but least remarked-upon events in modern politics —and it is the driving ideology of the resurgent Christian Right. Not only is Reconstructionism explicitly anti-democratic and anti-pluralist, but adherents of other religions are viewed as heretics at best, and unfit to hold public office. So narrowly intolerant is the movement of Reconstructionism that even those who profess Christianity but hold differing religious or theological views are often castigated as "anti-Christian" and agents of Satan.

Thomas Jefferson and Bill Clinton: God's Little Atheists?

During the election of 1800, candidate Thomas Jefferson was viciously attacked by the Protestant clergy of New England who were concerned that the political power they enjoyed as the established churches would erode if Jefferson ascended to the presidency. Jefferson was well known for his determined efforts to disestablish the state churches and his advocacy of religious equality.

Jefferson held deep religious beliefs, yet he was called "anti-Christ,"[5] "atheist," and a "French infidel"—because of his supposedly anti-religious views, and because of his association with the French Enlightenment philosophers during his tenure as U.S. Ambassador to France. (Nominally a member of his local Anglican church, theologically, he was an early Unitarian.)

"Numerous sermons were preached," writes Jefferson scholar Charles Sanford, "warning that if Jefferson was elected he would discredit religion, overthrow the church and destroy the Bible."[6] When the news came that Jefferson had been elected, people in New England actually hid their Bibles, certain that agents of Jefferson would come to seize them. These preachers, aligned with the Federalists, "warned that electing a 'deist or infidel' to the presidency would be 'no less than rebellion against God,' and would end in the destruction of the churches and a reign of infamy."[7]

Jefferson, who did not publicly answer the many attacks upon his religious character, believed that it was useless to argue about it in the newspapers. He understood that these politically motivated attacks came from theocrats seeking to establish or re-establish their version of Christianity in the new nation.[8] During the tumultuous fall campaign season, he wrote to his friend Dr. Benjamin Rush about these attacks—which Jefferson understood were central to the meaning of religious freedom, pluralism and religious bigotry. He stated: "I have sworn upon the altar of God, eternal hostility against every form of tyranny over the mind of man."[9] This sentence, so emblematic of Jefferson's life and career, is engraved inside the rotunda of the Jefferson Memorial in Washington, DC. Generally forgotten is how it also evokes the nature of the struggle that brought about a secular and republican form of government to the former colonies, and the fierce democratic sensibility that underlies the ethos of pluralism in the United States.

Most Americans, including most informed and politically involved Americans, are unaware of the context, meaning and contemporary relevance of this declaration. However, it is a benchmark in the history of the struggle between the creation of democratic institutions and the Christian Right of the 18th century, a movement which had to be dragged kicking and screaming into the era of democracy and pluralism.

At a time when the modern Christian Right had assembled considerable political power, Bill Clinton suffered some of the same treatment at the hands of the theocratic right in 1992 as candidate Jefferson did during the campaign of 1800. Militant anti-abortion activist Randall Terry and a group of Christian Right leaders issued pamphlets claiming, among other things, that a vote for Clinton was a sin against God. Terry's church, of which he is an elder, also placed full page newspaper ads in the *Washington Times* and in *USA Today*.

Terry's organization, Operation Rescue, then distributed some 140,000 copies of the pamphlet titled, "Christian beware...To vote for Bill Clinton is to sin against God." Among the endorsers of the pamphlet was Rev. Lou Sheldon, Chairman of the California-based Traditional Values Coalition, who argued that the Clinton campaign was an attack on Christianity itself. He claimed to be "contacting thousands of ministers across America and challenging them concerning this attack against the Church and the Kingdom of God. The shepherds must warn the sheep," he concluded, "not to vote for the wolf, Bill Clinton."[10]

The pamphlet and its endorsers specifically attacked Clinton's religious sincerity, although he has been a practicing Baptist for many years. "Clinton has a veneer of Christianity" they argued, and claimed that the theme of Clinton's "new covenant," as expressed in his acceptance speech at the 1992 Democratic convention, was a "frightening... humanistic pact that has nothing to do with Biblical Christianity. What would his sacraments be?" they asked rhetorically. "The body and blood of dismembered babies?"

They further questioned the authenticity of Clinton's faith by attacking his political views on such matters as abortion, divorce, and women in the military—views which are well within his own, and many other, religious traditions. "[I]f Bill Clinton is elected," they concluded, "he will help destroy three centuries of Christianity in America." Theocratic activist George Grant added, "I fear for the future of our nation should Bill Clinton ever reach the White House. The Bible is very clear about national leaders that have blood on their hands: it's the whole nation that suffers. I believe this election may ultimately determine the destiny of our nation."

Grant's political hyperbole is characteristic of conservative Christian doctrines that assert that God punishes nations that do not adhere to their notion of Biblical law. The profound religious bigotry that animates such political hyperbole is one of the major, if under-appreciated themes of the contemporary Christian Right.

One of the results of the full page ads taken out against Clinton by Randall Terry's home church in Vestal, New York, was that the Internal Revenue Service revoked their 501(c)(3) non-profit tax status. This was probably precisely what Terry and his political allies were seeking. Randall Terry declared, "Our tax status be damned if it prevents us from proclaiming God's truths." Elsewhere he has described IRS tax exemptions for churches as a way to compel churches to "keep their mouths shut about politics."[11]

Acting on a complaint filed by Americans United for Separation of Church & State, the IRS determined that the church violated the rules which prohibit tax-exempt organizations from endorsing or opposing a candidate for office. Pat Robertson's American Center for Law and Justice (ACLJ) subsequently filed suit claiming that the IRS rules against church politicking were a violation of the Religious Freedom Restoration Act, and an unconstitutional infringement on the First Amendment rights of churches. Jay Sekulow, the ACLJ's chief litigator (who has represented Terry in other matters) claimed that churches should have the right to tax exemption and still be able to endorse candidates. Rev. Daniel Little, pastor of the Church at Pierce Creek, said "We have the word of God... Principle sometimes takes precedent over silly laws."[12] Little was subsequently featured as a speaker at a Christian Coalition conference in Syracuse, New York, along with Sekulow, Syracuse Mayor Roy Bernardi, state Attorney General Dennis Vacco, and U.S. Rep. Bill Paxon (R-NY), among others. Little was portrayed as a hero for having "the courage to print what the press would not."[13]

This episode epitomizes the seriousness of the challenge theocratic elements pose to the constitutional order, as increasingly they seek more space within the existing system to exert political influence as a self-identified Christian political movement.

"Christian Bashing" (Or, What Happens When You Let Your Opponents Define the Terms of Debate)

Two years into Clinton's Presidency, the Democratic Party launched a political counterattack on the "Radical Right" that fell flat. The context and fallout from it reveals much about the Christian Right and can inform response strategies.

The actual attack was on the GOP which, they said, was being "taken over" by the Radical Right. The Democrats thought that by hanging the albatross of the Christian Right around the neck of the Republicans, they could bounce back from the string of losses they had suffered in the by-elections held after Clinton's election, as well as such problems as the lingering Whitewater scandal and the awkward health care debate. At a press conference, Rep. Vic Fazio, Chairman of the Democratic Congressional Campaign Committee, spoke of the "fire breathing Christian Radical Right."[14] Democratic National Committee chairman David Wilhelm offered similar denunciations. The speeches were met with cheers by the Democrats and with outrage by the Christian Right, Congressional Republicans, and their allies among the conservative columnists[15] that dominate the op-ed pages of the nation's newspapers. The Democrats were charged with "religious bigotry," and "Christian bashing."[16]

The Democrats had no effective answer to this. What could have been an effective counter-offensive sputtered to an embarrassing halt—even though the Democrats correctly assessed that the Christian Right's agenda and tactics were unacceptable to most Americans most of the time.

The Christian Right's use of the term "bigotry" reveals how the meaning of the term has been inverted. Religious bigotry is defined and measured by the standard of religious equality and mutual respect. Religious bigotry, or intolerance, with which it is often used interchangeably, is a deviation from this principle. Religious equality is not merely a matter of people who happen to inhabit a religious majority "tolerating" those who do not. It is a matter of upholding the values of democracy which respect and defend the right of difference. The Christian Right has cynically and successfully turned the value of religious freedom into a "wedge issue." The very movement whose intellectual and political leaders seek a "Christian Nation," and publicly assert that adherents of other religions ought to submit to the rule of their (Christian) betters are the very ones claiming religious discrimination! That moderate and progressive elements in both major parties have failed to effectively respond to this claim is one of the most remarkable lapses in American politics of the late 20th century.

Conservative strategist Paul Weyrich wrote in his newsletter for movement insiders[17] that the 1994 Democratic strategy was "a simple one. Make the Christian Right radioactive to the point where Republican candidates will either disavow their support or be forced to defend the Christian Right, thus driving away moderate suburban voters. The Democrats," he continued, "have counted on the Republican establishment to walk away from such a fight, knowing that many of them feel about the Religious Right about the same way that many Democrats feel. However, that hasn't happened." Weyrich says he advised Republican leaders to describe Clinton's attack on the Christian Right as an attack on religion itself.

Democrats and moderate Republicans rarely argue effectively against the religious bigotry and theocratic agenda of the Christian Right in American political life. What's more, Republicans increasingly rely on the Christian Right for votes, and many will take every opportunity to rally to their defense.

In a letter to Clinton, then-Senate minority leader Bob Dole and 43 GOP Senators demanded that Clinton "join with us in repudiating" criticism of Americans who "happen to go to church and go to the polls." Similarly, Haley Barbour, chairman of the Republican National Committee, told the *Washington Times* that the Democrats "think Christian-bashing is the only acceptable form of religious bigotry left… It's offensive to every religious group in the country."[18]

The late Art Kropp, executive director of People for the American Way, said that Dole's comments rang hollow because the Christian Right had for years "characterized opponents as un-Christian, anti-Christian and godless for stands on political issues ranging from the Panama Canal to federal taxes."

Weyrich felt that Clinton's run at the Christian Right was precipitated by Democratic losses in special elections in Oklahoma and

Kentucky which were "won by conservative Republicans with the help of Christian activists." If the trend continued, he reasoned, Democrats could lose "working control" of Congress. This is, of course, exactly what happened in 1994. While the loss of both houses to the GOP may not have been attributable solely to the Christian Right, it was clear that the movement had come of age and the Democrats had failed to derail its growing claim to moral authority.

The Democrats had not resorted to religious bigotry as much as they had failed to know how to answer the charge. Weyrich claimed that the situation led to a "major internal debate inside the Clinton camp as to how far these attacks should go." Thus William Jefferson Clinton, the leader of the Democratic Party, who symbolically began his presidential inaugural motorcade at Thomas Jefferson's home, Monticello, two hours outside Washington, had no answer to the charge of "religious bigotry"—the standard response from religious conservatives to criticisms of their role in American political life. What's more, the Democrats, who had so much to gain and so much to lose have not made the Christian Right an effective issue at the national level.

This situation plays itself out at all levels of American political life. While Jefferson, as the founder of the Democratic Party, served as Clinton's symbolic political ancestor, Clinton and his advisors seemed to have lost touch with what Jefferson actually represents in the American history of religious freedom and religious bigotry.

That the Christian Right has been able to occupy the moral high ground on religious bigotry represents a seismic shift in their ability to define the framework of the debate over tolerance. Historically, it is progressives who have led opposition to bigotry in all of its forms, including race, gender, sexual orientation, and especially religion. Christian conservatives have, in the main, been on the other side. Their success in defining issues of religious bigotry has helped them gain moral leverage in re-defining other areas of human and civil rights.

The challenge for those who politically engage or write about the Christian Right and other theocratic political movements is to know the difference between bigotry and fair criticism. Belief in and knowledge of what religious freedom means is essential to the advocacy and defense of freedom and democracy. Knowledge of the beliefs, goals and practices of religious based political movements is necessary as well. The loaded charge of "Christian bashing" is a frequently used ace in the rhetorical poker of American politics. The defense of religious freedom and democracy requires an effective response.

Defending fair criticism against the charge of religious bigotry means, for starters, not relying on labels to carry the argument. As will be discussed below, it is the substance, not the slogan, that persuades. For example, to argue that religion has no place in politics is to fall into the trap of being pegged as anti-religion. Whatever one's view of religion, it is an integral part of the lives of most Americans. The only question is how it is used. Religiously animated groups have always been involved in political life. Mainline Protestants, Unitarians, Evangelicals, and Quakers worked in opposition to slavery. Rev. Dr. Martin Luther King Jr., epitomized the religious community's leadership of the civil rights movement. Protestant, Catholic and Jewish religious institutions played a decisive role in ending the war in Vietnam. Such things are normal in a pluralistic society.

Fair criticism must be accurate and not based solely on the religious identity of a person or group. However, to the extent that a religiously motivated political entity is using a religious identity as the source and ultimate authority for political beliefs and matters of public policy, religious beliefs may fairly become part of the discussion. This said, people have a *right* to their beliefs, no matter how unusual or heinous they appear to the critic. That is the meaning of religious equality. When these beliefs are put out into the public square to advance political objectives, however, they may very well be criticized, challenged, and debated. No one should be subjected to religious bigotry. Neither should religious faith be cheapened by use as a political tool, or worse, a political shield. The misuse of the accusation of religious bigotry or "Christian bashing" to answer political opponents cheapens the special value that we place on religious freedom in the United States. In the case of many Christian Right leaders, the source of their apparent insensitivity to the religious sensibilities of others is their lack of belief in religious freedom for anyone but themselves and their followers.

It is not religious bigotry, for example, to charge the Christian Coalition with deliberately conflating Christianity with a right-wing or Republican political agenda. To charge Pat Robertson with religious bigotry because he says that Christians are more fit to hold public office than Moslems or Hindus is fair. To charge him further with demagoguery by suggesting that a Christian Coalition backed candidate is more Christian than another Christian whom they politically oppose, is fair. To say that Robertson stoops to anti-Semitic conspiracy theories in his books, as Michael Lind exposed so effectively in *The New York Review of Books*, is fair.[19] To say that one of Robertson's closest longtime advisors has been a supporter of former Nazi, former Ku Klux Klansman David Duke,[20] is fair. To charge the Christian Coalition with hypocrisy because they are now saying that they are not an explicitly Christian organization, and welcome people of all faiths who agree with their political goals, is fair. To say that Robertson's argument that the U.S. is a "Christian Nation" (from the Christian Coalition's first organizing video) is an affront to religious equality and the spirit and letter of Constitutional government in the U.S., as the Anti-Defamation League has done, is fair. (Some of these points will be discussed further in chapter 2.)

Serious criticism often requires strong words. But to have a chance at prevailing, such things must be said with the person-to-person persuasiveness that comes from knowledge and conviction. Anything less leaves one open to the charge of religious bigotry. Worse, sometimes the charge may even be true.

It's the Substance, Not the Slogan
(Before We Give it a Name, Let's Figure Out What it Is)

While the forces of Reconstructionism have been gathering to lay down Biblical law, progressives and moderates have been scattered by a continuing debate over what to call their opponents. Of course, many of these enemies are really just neighbors, and on most days are just other people at the supermarket, the workplace, the Little League game, or the beach. Demonization is a two-way street, and is engaged in by demagogues for purposes of their own. Sometimes it simply adds a B-horror-movie excitement to the normalcy of politics. Whatever the outcome of the political struggles of the day, people still need to live in the same communities when it is over. This does not mean that debate and political mobilizations need be meek and mild—only that those who would speak for democratic values need to effectively and forcefully speak for those values, in ways that demonstrate those values in action.

What happened to Vic Fazio and company epitomizes what happens when political "messages" substitute for actual understanding of the political strategies and beliefs of the Christian Right. Conversations throughout progressive and mainstream politics are often dominated by whether the term "Christian Right" is offensive to Christians. Some people find it so. Some people think it too positive because it suggests that they are representative of Christianity.

For matters of public discourse, some people seek an accurate term. Others seek something more pejorative, to undermine the credibility of the opposition. Still others are concerned about offending some or all people of religious faith. In any case, enormous amounts of time and money are spent on polls and focus groups to determine the most effective labels for this movement and its various components. For example, Paul Weyrich noted in his internal strategy newsletter in 1994, that polling by the Democrats indicated that attacks on the Christian Right had the potential to backfire, so they made a terminological shift to the "radical right."[21] Much of this has worked to the strategic advantage of the Christian Right, since their opponents stay scattered, unable to agree on even what to call them, let alone what to do about them.

While mainstream and progressive communities and journalists have been catching up with the Christian Right, definitional issues remain. Sociologist Sara Diamond takes mainstream organizations to task for name calling, and painting as "extremists" those who oppose them, for purposes of political marginalization and direct mail fundraising. This is a "disservice to the general public," she states and believes that it contributes to a "faulty analysis of their political opponents." Diamond disparages labeling the right "radical," in part because much of the right's agenda supports the status quo in terms of economic and foreign policy. Pat Robertson, and his related organizations, for example, have sometimes played roles as political partners with the U.S. in foreign policy objectives, notably in Central America.[22] However, it is also true that elements of the Christian Right are "radical" by one of the Webster dictionary's definitions: "favoring fundamental or extreme change" specifically "in the social structure."

Nevertheless, the labeling of political opponents often debases political understanding and civil discourse. While the drive to label, as Diamond correctly points out, is a problem, the avoidance of naming out of fear of offense is another problem in the continuing bi-polar political disorder. Many are afraid to use just about any term for fear of offending someone—particularly someone's (usually hypothetical) religious sensibilities. This is particularly true of the terms "Christian Right," and even "Religious Right." While it is essential to respect people's beliefs, confidence in one's own commitment to and knowledge of the meaning of religious freedom allows one to distinguish between religious bigotry and fair criticism and to defuse the charge—the Christian Right's skillful exploitation of such matters not withstanding. There is no one word or phrase that will resolve these concerns.[23]

Whatever it's called, there is a new political reality that has to be addressed. Actual knowledge and understanding of the ideology and institutions of the Christian Right is at least as important, if not more important, than what to call it. Only such knowledge will dissolve the terminological gridlock.

One effective term proposed by Chip Berlet, the senior analyst with Political Research Associates, and the late Margaret Quigley is "theocratic right." They write that "the central threat to democracy posed by the theocratic right is not that its leaders are religious or fundamentalist or right-wing—but that they justify their political, legislative, and regulatory agenda as fulfilling God's plan."[24] The term theocratic right also allows one to discuss the character of a range of allied movements in the U.S., notably certain conservative groups of Catholics and Protestants, and even the Unification Church of Sun Myung Moon. This does not, of course, encompass all of the political right, but it does address the most animated and growing section of the right, and in a way that identifies in two words the main agenda of the Christian Right without being tripped up by the innumerable connotations in the term "Christian." Another useful term is "anti-democratic," because it refers not to religious motivations, but to the values that they oppose, as distinct from the ones they claim to hold.[25]

While it is possible that "theocratic" is not the kind of word or concept that will be widely understood, or play well in polls and focus groups, it is at least necessary for political leaders and journalists to understand this element, lest political analysis be skewed or dumbed down.

In this regard, wondering if, when, and which labels may offend, it is the tradition of the Enlightenment, inherent in our constitutional system, that is offensive to the Christian Right—whatever names we give to their movement out of fear, respect, or political spin. This stance against the Enlightment values embodied in reason, equality, and democracy is the underlying theme throughout the subsequent chapters.

The End of (Secular) History

Historical understanding is essential because the Christian Right's attack is not limited to the religious character of politicians, but includes any aspect of American history which does not support their contemporary aims. In fact, the Christian Right embraces a wholesale attack on the constitutional doctrine of separation of church and state.

One Christian Right leader, John Whitehead of the Rutherford Institute, wrote an influential book, *The Separation Illusion*, in which he attacks Thomas Jefferson's notion of the "separation of church and state" as the key phrase grounding the Supreme Court's understanding of the religion clauses of the First Amendment. Whitehead claims that Jefferson's views are irrelevant because Jefferson was not present when the First Amendment was written.[26] Christian Right activist David Barton, among others, makes the same point in his book *The Myth of Separation: What is the Correct Relationship Between Church and State?*[27]

While it is true that Jefferson was, at the time, President Washington's Ambassador to France and was not personally present for the drafting of the Constitution and the First Amendment, his influence is generally acknowledged by historians. In fact, the preponderance of evidence demonstrates the centrality of Jefferson's views in shaping the framers' view of the proper relations between religion and government. In 1777, Jefferson drafted the Virginia Statute for Religious Freedom which was ultimately pushed through the Virginia legislature by his close colleague, then-Governor James Madison, in 1786. This law provided the theoretical basis for the First

Amendment. Jefferson believed that it was, along with authoring the Declaration of Independence and founding the University of Virginia, one of his most important accomplishments. (Madison, in turn, is generally credited with being the principal author of both the Constitution and the First Amendment.)

Historical distortions are a key ingredient in the success of the Christian Right to date. This effort to somehow discredit the historical relevance of Jefferson is part of a larger effort to revise American history to suit their contemporary religious and political objectives—a point which will be discussed further in a later chapter.

There are many deceptive propaganda ploys, such as Whitehead's, to fire up the prospective constituents of the Christian Right. They are often difficult to address, not only because they can be such a tangle of lies and distortions, but because few outside their primary intended audience pay much attention. The effect of all this is the systematic alienation of conservative Christians from mainstream society and the creation of a counterculture which believes that somehow "the truth" has been kept from them through various conspiracies. Thus when those indoctrinated by the likes of Whitehead and Barton turn up at school board meetings, or run for office, their premises about American history and contemporary political reality are profoundly at odds with everyone else's.

Such views are the rule, rather than the exception, in Christian Right circles. Patricia Hoffman, who is a leader of both the Christian Coalition and Concerned Women for America in Worcester, Massachusetts, has written that "'separation of church and state' is a bogus phrase. Our country was founded on Biblical principles and we need to turn back to God and His precepts."[28]

David Barton, who rarely reaches the national radar screen we call the media, is probably the leading spokesman for revisionism of this sort. He frequently appears at official functions as an expert on the Constitution and American history. In 1994, he spoke at an inaugural function for Virginia Governor George Allen and was the featured speaker at the "Commonwealth Prayer Breakfast" sponsored by Pennsylvania State legislators. In 1995, he gave a series of lectures on American history to conservative freshman Congressional Republicans and was featured at a Christian Coalition forum in Tennessee, along with Tennessee Governor Don Sundquist. Barton is also a popular speaker at both state and national Christian Coalition events, and his books and videos are in wide circulation. Christian Coalition leader Bob McClellan of El Cajon, California, says, "David Barton's products have been invaluable in furthering the principles of the Christian Coalition in San Diego."[29] Emblematic of his growing role in political life, Barton was a Texas delegate to the 1996 GOP presidential nominating convention in San Diego, and served on the platform committee.

Whether one is seeking to understand the Christian Right for purposes of accurately reporting on the movement, or for politically engaging the Christian Right from the framework of democratic values, success depends on knowing when the Christian Right is distorting the meaning of religious bigotry and the facts of American history for partisan political advantage.

CHAPTER 2

Neither a Juggernaut nor a Joke

How Overestimating and Underestimating Helps the Christian Right

If American democracy is threatened by the theocratic right, how big is the threat? While the answer is difficult to measure (there's no official roster, as there is with political party membership, and individuals often belong to more than one group, making a tabulation of memberships meaningless), size may not be what counts. The political success of the Christian Right in recent years is derived in part from how others perceive it. In the late 1980s the Christian Right was treated as a joke. The televangelist scandals involving Jim and Tammy Bakker and Jimmy Swaggart, among others, became the stuff of late-night TV comedy. Swaggart was caught with a prostitute. Jim Bakker procured sex with a church secretary, bilked his followers out of millions of dollars and went to jail. In 1989, the Moral Majority of Rev. Jerry Falwell folded, and the unsuccessful 1988 GOP presidential bid of Pat Robertson left many people (including most of the political community) believing, prematurely as it turned out, that the religious right was dead. Journalists who covered the Christian Right faced considerable skepticism that this was a movement of lasting political consequence. Even after the 1992 Republican national convention, when the prominent role and inflammatory rhetoric of Pat Buchanan and Pat Robertson shocked the nation during prime time, many still dismissed the Christian Right as a flash in the pan.

The Christian Right quickly rebounded into a significant political force with apparent staying power. This was effectively demonstrated at the 1996 GOP convention where Robertson, claiming 575 delegates were Christian Coalition members, enjoyed ideological control of the convention. The exercise of this power was apparent in its influence over the Dole campaign. Pro-choice GOP leaders, such as Massachusetts governor William Weld and California governor Pete Wilson, who had been scheduled to speak declined to do so because of content restrictions. The Christian Right also sought to avoid the embarrassing spectacle of 1992, and generally cooperated with Dole efforts to homogenize the event. In fact, Ralph Reed, with a platoon of floor deputies equipped with walkie-talkies deployed at all times, kept firm control of his people. The restraint shown by the Christian Right was not, as suggested by the media, a muzzling by Dole's convention managers. Rather it was a confident and disciplined exercise of power. Having won every battle worth winning, there was no need to humiliate the candidate, nor show off in victory.

More typically, there is a tendency among both the media and opponents to treat the Christian Right, and the Christian Coalition in particular, as a "juggernaut." Instead of treating the Christian Right as a distinct political movement with comprehensible characteristics and definable strengths and weaknesses, both political opponents and elements of the media routinely inflate the actual strength of the Christian Right—and in doing so play into their hands.

By looking at how this movement has managed to achieve many electoral victories, it becomes clearer what the nature of the threat is, and why aggrandizing the Christian Right as an unstoppable force, or conversely, writing it off as a fringe element, is a grave mistake.

Small Numbers, Pivotal Power

A brief look at the Christian Right's own analyses shows that they are making up in strategy and a disciplined use of resources what they lack in numbers. At the first national strategy conference of the Christian Coalition, held in November 1991 at Robertson headquarters in Virginia Beach, Virginia, then National Field Director Guy Rogers, explained that their task was simple: "We don't have to worry about convincing a majority of Americans to agree with us," he declared. "Most of them are staying home and watching *Falcon Crest* on television."

Although the leading TV shows have changed since 1991, the organizing principle has not. Even in high turn-out presidential election years, Rogers explained, only 15 percent of the eligible voters determine the outcome. Of all eligible adults, only about 60 percent are actually registered. Only half of those cast ballots. "So," he continued, "only thirty percent of the eligible voters actually vote. Therefore only fifteen percent of the eligible voters determine the outcome…In low turn out elections," he concluded, "city council, state legislature, county commissions—the percentage of the eligible voters who determine who wins can be as low as six or seven percent."[1]

Such thinking did not originate with Ralph Reed, who was in elementary school when his political mentors began the long march to political power. (Although, thanks to spin doctors and a pliant media, the legend that he did develop the idea may be forever fixed in the popular political imagination.)[2] Two years before the Coalition was founded, Christian Right theorist George Grant (who later became a featured speaker at Coalition events) presciently showed how a theocratic minority can begin to seize political power. "Since only about 60% of the people are registered to vote and only about 35% of those actually bother to go to the polls," wrote Grant, "a candidate only needs to get the support of a small, elite group of citizens to win. It only takes 11% of the electorate to gain a seat in the House or the Senate. It only takes about 9% to gain a governorship. And it takes a mere 7% to gain an average mayoral or city council post."[3] Grant further declared that the purpose of "Christian political action is therefore an acknowledgment of the theocracy of heaven and earth."[4]

Grant and others credit Larry Pratt, a former employee of direct mail entrepreneur Richard Viguerie, with pioneering in the 1980s the use of computerized mailing lists for low turn-out local elections and issue campaigns—a key component of what the Christian Coalition is now doing on a national scale.[5] Pratt, who heads the Gun Owners of America lobby, made news in 1996 when he was ousted as a co-chairman of Pat Buchanan's campaign for the Republican presidential nomination after public exposure of his links to white supremacist groups. There are many others, of course, who have also contributed important elements to this strategy, some of whom will be discussed further.

A second wing of the new strategy arose from a bitter lesson. Two Republican presidents over twelve years were unable or unwilling to deliver much of the social agenda the Christian Right thought they would get in return for their support. Abortion remained a constitutional right, gay rights were advancing, and there was still no prayer in the schools. The Christian Right decided to establish their own power base in the party instead of serving merely as a delivery system for conservative evangelical votes which would later be taken for granted. Thus the first two national strategy conferences of the Christian Coalition were dominated by 'how-to' discussions of the mechanics of party takeover—from how to get to be a GOP national convention delegate to how to take over the state and local party apparatus. Since then, the Christian Right, led by the Christian Coalition, has become deeply integrated into the party infrastructure. Their "Road to Victory" national conferences, now held at the Washington Hilton in Washington, D.C., are no longer serious strategy meetings. Rather they are displays of political clout where GOP leaders and presidential candidates troll for support.

How They Do It:
The Covert Operations of the Christian Right

Many of the tactics that the Christian Coalition would develop into a national plan were used elsewhere and were coming to fruition at the same time the Coalition was in its formative stages. Christian Right activists in San Diego, California effectively used the tactics that the Coalition and other groups would fine tune and replicate nationally.

"The San Diego Surprise" of November 1990 epitomized the efficacy of county-level organizing. Candidates were quietly recruited, primarily by local activists Steve Baldwin and Dan Van Tiegham, of the California Pro-Life Council, the state affiliate of the National Right to Life Committee. Most of the candidates were political unknowns, pre-screened for political reliability, and did no campaigning. Membership lists of sympathetic churches were obtained and compared with voter registration lists. This was followed by phoning voters to turn out the "Christian vote." Then the California Pro-Life Council endorsed the candidates, by obvious pre-arrangement, and distributed 200,000 endorsement flyers in church parking lots on Sunday before the Tuesday election. Many pastors used the pulpit to urge their members to vote. On election day, 60 of the 90 candidates for such local offices as rural fire district boards, school boards, and town councils won, demonstrating that there was a significant Christian Right constituency in the county with a deliverable voting bloc. Thus the now famous (or infamous) "stealth campaign," was born.

Over the long run, these political novices could also be groomed for higher office. "The people we recruit will be like our farm league," Baldwin told the *Southern California Christian Times*. Baldwin himself went on to serve in the state legislature.

Van Tiegham wrote that an earlier effort in June 1990 "resulted in the takeover of the San Diego Republican party by pro-family activists." Most of those winners also did no campaigning except to distribute flyers in churches.[6] Tactics like these are carried out because the Christian Right is a self-conscious minority aware that their views will not prevail in most of America, most of the time. The vast majority do not share their views, when given the opportunity to hear them, and the Christian Right itself does not have enough voters to prevail.

Contrary to some published reports, it was not the Christian Coalition behind the San Diego Surprise. While some of the people involved later became leaders of the local Christian Coalition, there was, in fact, no Christian Coalition organized in San Diego at the time. But the method has since been adopted by the Christian Coalition in many areas, as the organization has systematically sought to take over the GOP from the bottom up and the inside out. The Coalition's first statewide mass distribution of voter guides in churches and church parking lots was pivotal to the narrow 1990 reelection of Sen. Jesse Helms (R-NC).[7]

Helms, according to Ralph Reed, called Pat Robertson a week before the election to ask for help. Reed claimed, "I had access to the internal tracking, and I know [Helms] was down by eight points. So Pat called me up and said, 'We've got to kick into action.' Bottom line is... five days later we put three quarters of a million voters' guides in churches across the state of North Carolina and Jesse Helms was re-elected by 100,000 votes out of 2.2 million cast." "We," said Reed, "also made over 30,000 phone calls."[8] It later came out that the Republican Senatorial Committee contributed $64,000 to the Christian Coalition, in October 1990—just prior to the November election. "The press had no idea what we were doing," bragged then-Coalition Southern Regional Director Judy Haynes, in 1991. "And they still don't know what we did." [9] (The Helms campaign is at the center of a 1996 lawsuit filed by the Federal Election Commission which charges that the Christian Coalition illegally assisted the campaigns of George Bush, Newt Gingrich, and Oliver North as well as that of Senator Helms. The FEC also cited a speech by Ralph Reed in which he advised the Montana Christian Coalition to heed the advice of ancient Chinese military philosopher Sun Tzu. "The first strategy and in many ways the most important strategy for evangelicals is secrecy. Sun Tzu says that's what you have to do to be effective at war and that's essentially what we're involved in, we're involved in a war. It's not a war fought with bullets, it's a war fought with ballots.")[10]

There is nothing new about these half-page, inexpensive guides that are highly biased comparisons of positions of the candidates on selected issues. But the Christian Coalition has perfected mass distribution through networks of churches. More importantly, the voter guides would not have been successful without the two decades of political consciousness developed in the conservative churches—from which many, if not most of the candidates, campaign workers, and other activists emerge. We will review more on how this came about in Chapters 4 and 5.

The Silent Minority

Although the Christian Coalition and the wider Christian Right have made effective tactical use of technology, political legwork, and stealth, the underlying premise of the strategy remains that they are a small minority of the registered and eligible voters. Their successes are at once a testimony to their political skill, and to the failure of other groups in society, particularly GOP moderates, to match the Christian Right's disciplined registration of new voters and strategic mobilization on behalf of conservative candidates. In one outstanding example, the Massachusetts delegates to the 1996 Republican party convention in San Diego were chosen at party caucuses after the winner-take-all presidential primary which was won by Bob Dole. Christian Right anti-abortion forces packed the district caucuses and won election as Dole delegates and dominated the delegation. This was an embarrassment to Governor William Weld, a prominent Republican voice for choice. In fact, several people going to the convention as Dole delegates had been leaders in the campaign of the leading anti-abortion candidate, Pat Buchanan.[11] Weld ultimately retained ideological control of the delegation through at-large appointments.

Nevertheless, Weld's caucus defeat is of a piece with the Christian Right takeover strategy in the party. In this case, Christian Right activists became convention delegates for a candidate that they did not support, by packing the party caucuses. They did this in order to be able to control the agenda of the party, the selection of the vice-presidential candidate, the tenor of the convention, and the presidential candidate himself. It worked. Dole was unable to deliver on his promise to party moderates that he would insert language in the platform that would urge respect for differences on abortion.

Far Out Politics, Mainstream Power

A closer examination of the new strategy of the Christian Right, which carefully maximizes their strengths, reveals at least three major weaknesses.

The first weakness is that many in the Christian Right have unpopular views on everything from public education to birth control, and are often required to run as conventional conservatives instead of distinctly Christian Right candidates, which leaves them open to the charge of having a hidden agenda or running as a stealth candidate.[12]

Although abortion remains a polarizing issue, Christian Right leaders rarely talk about birth control and family planning. An exception is Randall Terry, who does not stop at abortion; he is more anti-birth control than the Catholic Church. Terry admonishes "anyone using the pill or an IUD" to "stop immediately" because "they are abortifacients." (Terry and many of his colleagues, such as Joe Scheidler of the Pro-Life Action Network (PLAN), believe that the use of these forms of birth control is also a form of infanticide.) Terry further urges people to stop using "any kind of birth control" and to "leave the number of children you have in God's hands."[13] While the Catholic Church endorses various "natural" forms of birth control, Terry opposes any conscious interference in procreation. Similarly, Rev. Michael Bray, a convicted and published proponent of anti-abortion violence, says that the notion of contraception is a "false doctrine" and that the job of God's creatures "is to obey his commands, which includes bountiful procreation."[14]

A second major weakness is that the Christian Right does not have the numbers to carry elections without the help of moderate Republicans. Given the threat to the stability of democratic institutions posed by the Christian Right, it may be short-sighted on the part of Democrats and independents to enjoy the defeat of GOP moderates at the hands of the Christian Right in party primaries and caucuses. In many states non-Republicans have the legal opportunity to vote in GOP primaries, and could help to defeat the Christian Right candidates before they reach the general election. Non-Republicans could still vote as they choose in the general election. However, few opponents of the Christian Right seem to take advantage of this strategic opportunity.

A third, and perhaps most important major weakness is the often genuinely repulsive views behind the well-crafted public relations images of the leadership, particularly of the Christian Coalition. Pat Robertson, for example, has been repeatedly exposed for anti-democratic, crackpot, and even anti-Semitic views. Although he and some of his neo-conservative allies argue that he cannot be anti-Semitic because he is a supporter of Israel, former conservative insider Michael Lind demonstrated that Robertson repeatedly trots out classic anti-Semitic conspiracy theories in his books, and relies on classic works of anti-Semitism to support those views. Although Ralph Reed has been dispatched to Jewish organizations and the media to make the right noises about pluralism, and to oppose the Christian Nation doctrine,[15] Pat Robertson's books—which contain offensive material, are still promoted and sold by the Christian Coalition.

The New World Order, for example, was distributed to every new member of the Christian Coalition for several years after its founding. Thus if there is a doctrinal guide for the Coalition, this is it. In this book, Robertson invokes the Massachusetts Bay Colony as a model for Christian governance. "The founders of America—at Plymouth Rock and in the Massachusetts Bay Colony—felt that they were organizing a society based on the Ten Commandments and the Sermon on the Mount,…and they tried their best to model their institutions of government after the Bible." As a result, Robertson concludes, the United States has "the finest concept of ordered liberty the world has ever known," because "for almost two hundred years prior to our Constitution, all of the leadership of this nation had been steeped in the biblical principles of the Old and New Testaments."[16] Indeed—it was precisely this period Robertson is talking about that the Constitution's framers shook off. They had learned from the mistakes of the colonial theocracies.

Given his celebration of this theocratic period, it is no small irony that Robertson, who resigned his Baptist ministry to run for president in 1988, ignores the fact that two and a quarter centuries earlier his home state of Virginia actively persecuted and jailed Baptists—especially preachers. The established church in Virginia was the Anglican church, the colonial wing of the Church of England. "The decade of the 1760s was one of violent persecution of the dissenters, especially the Baptists who were very active in the Piedmont," writes historian Ralph Ketcham. "They were stoned out of Culpepper County in 1765 and jailed in Spotsylvania County in 1768."[17]

Beyond the extraordinary—and extraordinarily public—views of Robertson, and often lost in the discussion is that among the more zealous of the Christian Right constituency which he leads there is overlap with the racist constituency of former Nazi, former Ku Klux Klansman David Duke. Within the Christian Coalition this is epitomized by Rev. Billy McCormack—a founder and top leader of the Christian Coalition although he has been repeatedly exposed as a prominent Duke supporter during Duke's rise to prominence in Louisiana politics.[18] McCormack told a reporter in response to inquiries about the Duke connection that if he really wanted to do a story he should investigate "the Jewish element in the ACLU which is trying to drive Christianity out of the public place, and I'd like to see you do something objective there. Because the ACLU is made up of a tremendous amount of Jewish attorneys." McCormack further claimed that "there is, isn't there, the same kind of thing happening on the other end of the spectrum that can be just as prejudiced and just as mean as what David Duke does." McCormack concluded that neither David Duke nor Nation of Islam leader Louis Farrakhan was as much of a threat as the ACLU.[19] McCormack, one of Robertson's longest and closest political colleagues, remains one of only four national board members of the Coalition.

McCormack is not the only Christian Coalition leader to have expressed such a preference. Then Massachusetts Coalition director Al Fitzsimmons of Braintree told the *Springfield Advocate* in 1992 that "Duke's message isn't that far off the mark, it's just that people are trying to cloud it with the [background] of the messenger." "That's unfortunate," he continued. "We have a governor in Massachusetts [William Weld] who is kind of off the wall on some issues that Christians are concerned about—abortion, gay rights, and Sunday blue laws. He's more of a drawback than a David Duke would be."[20]

Despite these significant obstacles—that electoral candidates from the Christian Right must often hide their views, that they depend on Republican moderates to win elections, and that their views are antithetical to mainstream politics—the movement has gained considerable ground. With the integration of the Christian Coalition into the GOP an apparent fait accompli, and with the media's portrayal of the Coalition as moderates, the temptation to believe that they must represent a constituency that is broad and deep remains strong. In an imperfect democracy, power is not necessarily proportional to numbers. As we shall see, it's certainly a point of confusion for the media.

The Christian Coalition Membership Figures and Other Media Myths

One of the extraordinary myths promulgated by the media is the Christian Coalition membership figures. The Christian Coalition's 1996 claim of 1.7 million members or more is wildly exaggerated and certainly undocumented. Nevertheless, these numbers are routinely reported as fact—even though there is compelling evidence that their numbers are not nearly so large, and may even be declining. *Church & State* magazine revealed that the Coalition's officially reported paid circulation figures for its membership magazine *Christian American* actually dropped from 353,703 to 310,296 from 1994 to 1995. "Even allowing for some duplication," *Church & State* concluded, "such as married couples who may receive one magazine, it seems likely that dues-paying Coalition membership does not top half a million and may be well below that.[21]

Similarly, following the second national strategy conference, Ralph Reed declared that they would have 3,000 "delegates" at the next conference in Washington, DC in 1993. They only got 2,300. Unimpressive for an organization that was, at the time, claiming 10,000 new members a week. And since there was no criteria for being a "delegate" other than paying the entrance fee, this was an especially dubious turnout. Similarly, the 4,000 person turn-out for the 1995 conference was unimpressive for a Washington national convention. "Hell, even the car dealers get 10,000" remarked one GOP activist. But the Christian Coalition routinely gets away with this inflation.[22]

Even the best political reporters sometimes unwittingly serve as runners in the Christian Coalition's numbers game. In a cover story profile of Ralph Reed in the *Washington Post Magazine,* for example, Dan Balz of the *Washington Post* and Ronald Brownstein of the *Los Angeles Times* wrote that since its beginning, "the coalition has grown exponentially in numbers and impact and now aspires to occupy the political mainstream…The Christian Coalition today is an army of 1.7 million members from more than 1,700 local chapters in all 50 states—and it is expanding at the rate of a chapter a day."[23] Later in the same story, they wrote that "by last year, the Texas chapter alone claimed 60,000 members—and had taken control of the state GOP party apparatus." In this case they used the standard hedge and wrote "claimed." While the Christian Right had indeed, by 1995, taken over the GOP apparatus in 18 states, and gained considerable sway in another 13, it was not the Christian Coalition alone. Attributing all of the strength of the Christian Right to one organization is inaccurate at best, and contributes to the inflation of public perceptions of the actual strength of the Christian Coalition.

This has been going on for many years, according to former top Christian Right strategist Colonel V. Doner (this is his name, not his rank). "It was true," he writes of the late 1970s and early 1980s, "that the Christian Right… was viable and growing; but the media consistently gave the few national Christian Right organizations credit for larger budgets, more memberships, and more 'muscle' than actually existed. Memberships and financial strengths were routinely inflated by both the media and the Christian Right organizations themselves. But the media needed a good story in 1980," he concluded, "and the emergence of the Christian Right seemed to be as good as any."[24]

The numbers game gains in importance as the Coalition seems to be crumbling in some places. In Pennsylvania, for example, the Coalition has split into two groups and efforts to take over the state GOP have failed.[25] In fact, the Christian Right has further splintered in the state. Peg Luksik, a former Republican, ran as the gubernatorial candidate of the Constitution Party of Pennsylvania (the state affiliate of the U.S. Taxpayers Party) and received over 400,000 votes in the 1994 election.(She served as the manager for the 1996 campaign of USTP presidential candidate Howard Phillips.) The *New York Times* reported that in response to the Christian Coalition's major effort in the 1994 district school board elections in New York City, pro-democracy groups essentially fought them to a draw. As a result, there has been little change in New York education policies, and the Christian Coalition seems to have largely withdrawn. When the *Times* went looking for the Coalition, they discovered that it had shut down its office, and the volunteer city coordinator was unreachable.

Still, the Coalition's work in New York City has not been without impact. The Catholic archdiocese plans to continue to use the Christian Coalition's candidate information survey data to produce their own guide for distribution in Catholic churches.[26] The Coalition's relationship with the Catholic hierarchy is generally more uneasy. Their Catholic outreach arm, the Catholic Alliance, has been met with considerable skepticism and resistance by those Catholic bishops who are at odds with the Christian Coalition on a range of issues including welfare reform, capital punishment, and health care reform. According to a statement by the three bishops of Colorado, "The most significant difference between the Catholic Church and the Christian Coalition is what is not the Coalition's agenda—legislation and polices to protect poor children and families, immigrants, and the active pursuit of international peace."[27]

Meanwhile, the Christian Coalition and its allies have accomplished much of what they have set out to do over the past few years. That the media has gone along with the Christian Coalition's new "image" as moderate or mainstream, is certainly a reflection of growing political power. Ralph Reed expressed it well at the 1995 Christian Coalition convention in Washington at which a parade of GOP presidential hopefuls appeared before several thousand Coalition members: "We are not about endorsing candidates, we are about candidates endorsing our agenda." Indeed the 1995 Christian Coalition conference was an extraordinary display of GOP presidential contenders competing to demonstrate who more completely conformed to the group's views. Political pandering by such major figures as Newt Gingrich and Bob Dole, (as well as Senators Phil Graham and Richard Lugar) gave the appearance that the group was actually mainstream, while ignoring the actual goals of the Christian Right—particularly those of leader Pat Robertson.

At the Coalition's 1995 national conference, Robertson characteristically acknowledged with mock incredulity that critics describe the Christian Coalition's agenda as "theocratic." By raising the issue in this way he seems to have inoculated himself against it. He suggested the charge was preposterous because his opponents say it. He did not, however, bother to deny or explain it, and the hundreds of reporters covering the event said nothing about it. Most Christian Right activists do not see themselves as moving towards theocracy, and are unaware that their intellectual, theological and political leaders often are headed in that direction. One of the main reasons for this discontinuity between membership and the leadership is that the media has gone along for the public relations ride with Ralph Reed.

This is particularly stiking considering the media's long and unforgiving memory for mistakes and excesses by progressive leader Rev. Jesse Jackson. In contrast, the mainstream media largely ignored the racist and anti-Semitic views of Pat Buchanan—until he nearly knocked Bob Dole out of the running for the GOP nomination for president in the New Hampshire primary.[28] The media's double standard could be overcome by simply applying the same or at least a similar yardstick to any other pubic figure.

Fault Lines Everywhere (Waiting for a Quake)

The media's increasingly deferential treatment of the Christian Coalition is one sign of long-range change in the configuration of American politics that the Coalition itself has sparked. However, there is also every indication that the Christian Coalition's growth has peaked, and that whatever its actual numbers, they are seeking to fast-track the consolidation and institutionalization of its role in the Republican Party and national affairs. "My model," Reed told Balz and Brownstein, "would be a cross between the NEA (National

Education Association) and the Chamber of Commerce: grassroots, permanent, well-funded, with a lobbying presence at every level of government. It's what the social historians call professionalization."[29] With the media focused on how "mainstream" and "legitimate" the Christian Coalition is seeking to be, or may even be becoming, they may well achieve this status.

Reed's methods and goals have not, however, been well received in many conservative Christian circles, and there are fractures and fault lines all over the Christian Right. In 1994, in the wake of a highly critical report by the Anti-Defamation League of B'nai B'rith which detailed some of the anti-democratic and anti-Semitic views of Christian Right leaders, especially Robertson, the Christian Coalition went on the defensive. Reed sought to defuse the problem by saying all the right pluralist things. In one speech to the National Press Club he went so far as to paraphrase the sixth article of the Constitution which bars "religious tests" for public office, in an effort to demonstrate that he does not favor the Christian Nation doctrine.

Reacting to Reed's comments, a special issue of the *Christian Statesman* magazine, was devoted to assessing "just how Christian is the Christian Coalition?" The president of the forthrightly theocratic National Reform Association, Andrew Sandlin, denounced Ralph Reed's statement that "We believe in a nation that is not officially Christian, Jewish, or Muslim." Reed's view is "precisely" what Christian theocrats seek to combat. Sandlin writes that his wing of Christian conservatism is not "interested in 'an ethic of democratic fairness,' but in a 'requirement of theocratic authority.'" Sandlin acknowledges that there are many on the Christian Right who do not share this view, and he does not intend to track them down to expose "what we believe to be their errors." However, he sees the Christian Coalition as a particular "menace" because they have "not only refused to support explicitly Christian candidates, but actively discouraged their support."[30] Another writer finds it a "mystery" as to why "unbelievers, Jews, Mormons, and Muslims... can be part of a 'Christian' coalition" and questions whether the Coalition "really deserves to be called Christian" when Reed advocates "religious pluralism."[31]

Christian theocrats are appalled by the Christian Coalition's support for "liberal" or pro-choice Republicans—such as 1994 U.S.

Senate candidates Kay Bailey Hutchison in Texas and Paul Coverdell in Georgia, while the Coalition has been unwilling to list "Christian third-party candidates in the voters guides."[32] Like many other critics, they don't buy the Christian Coalition's disingenuous claim that their "voter guides do not endorse candidates, [when] it is clear by the selection and presentation of issues which candidates have the organization's blessing."[33]

Epitomizing the growing gulf between Christian Right purists and the Christian Coalition, Randall Terry has gone so far as to describe the Christian Coalition as the "mistress of the Republican Party," and advocates support for the U.S. Taxpayers Party, headed by Howard Phillips.[34] The USTP promotes an uncompromising version of the Christian Right's agenda. In 1996, Terry served as the Northeast regional co-chairman of USTP.

Behind the Flip-Flopping on Christianity:
Eyes on the Prize—of a Theocratic State

The tack taken by Reed is a flip-flop from Robertson's explanation of the origins of the Christian Coalition at the organization's first national strategy conference in 1991. Robertson told of meeting with his senior colleagues to discuss the new organization they were forming. He said that they didn't choose the name according to politically fashionable emphases on "traditional values" or a "pro-family agenda." Robertson was not going to shade his convictions. "I said no!" he shouted. "I am a Christian! I am not ashamed of Jesus! And we will call this the *Christian* Coalition. And if other people don't like it, that's just tough luck."[35]

More recently, the Coalition has gone to great lengths to achieve the appearance, if perhaps not the fact, of inclusiveness, especially of Jews. National conferences of the Christian Coalition now routinely feature token rabbis, but no actual leaders of any other non-Christian religion.

The supposed moderation of the message does not mean that the goals have changed. Robertson made it clear in *The New World Order* that anyone who is not Christian or Jewish is not fit to hold public office. He specifically names Hindus, Moslems, Buddhists, atheists and "new age" adherents. He details his wistfulness for the colonial theocracies where, he claims "almost all were committed to the biblical worldview," and that, "They all shared the same language traditions, and political concepts about the nature of man and the will of God."[36] This nostalgia for a cultural homogeneity which never was tells us much about Robertson's contemporary bigotry and political ideals. He longs for the time "when this country started," when voting rights were restricted to "property owners," because "People had to have a stake in society before they were allowed to determine its laws." His implicit endorsement of these policies suggests that he too believes that only people who own property have a stake in society, and thus would deny voting rights to renters and tenants of public housing, along with the religiously incorrect, if he and his movement ever gain sufficient political power. However, so far, Reed has wisely ignored Robertson's endorsement of the Massachusetts Bay Colony or any of the related declarations detailed here. Given that Reed works for Robertson, this is not surprising, but the media does not enjoy the same excuse.

Silence is also Reed's reaction to Robertson's demagogic attacks on many of the premises of modern civil rights legislation, claiming that federal policies "force the citizens to bus their children away from their friends, hire by quota instead of aptitude, make loans to people who won't pay them back, go to doctors who secretly have deadly diseases, and rent their property to undesirables with aberrant sexual habits."[37] Nowhere in *The New World Order*, does Robertson praise a single advance in civil rights for women, minorities or anyone else. Instead he makes coded and base appeals to bigotry as the basis for public policy. He also makes the crackpot claim that "egalitarianism—meaning equality for women, races, religions, sex and the like—and a host of other liberal concerns" did not exist prior to World War II and exist now because of the collapse of socialism.[38] Robertson does not make clear how these matters connect in his fevered version of history. In the looming end-of-the-world scenario envisioned by Robertson, leaps of disconnected logic and distortions of fact are the "history" which serves as prologue to the coming cataclysm from which the Christian Nation may emerge. (See Chapter 7.)

By way of contrast, Robertson's ubiquitous proxy, Ralph Reed, is receiving media attention and political deference far out of proportion to the power that he actually commands. It is Pat Robertson who is, after all, the founder, the funder, and the unquestioned leader, who controls a large media empire, a university which includes a law school, and other business interests. The talented Reed has been successfully deployed to deflect or neutralize unwanted attention to the more unpalatable aspects of Robertson's views. The continuing failure of the media and the political parties to challenge the unstable and extreme views of Robertson is one of the factors enabling the Christian Right to sustain political momentum.

Out of the Limelight—But Just as Dangerous

The disproportionate focus on Reed and the Christian Coalition also obscures the complexity of the movement. A well-rounded understanding must include examination of significant political formations that are rarely covered by the media such as Concerned Women for America, (CWA), Focus on the Family, and Dr. D. James Kennedy's Coral Ridge Ministries, to highlight but a few in the forefront of the Christian Right's drive for political power. These major organizations have moved beyond single-issue campaigns, although these remain important as "wedge issues." They have also become more than mere conservative multi-issue organizations because they are increasingly ideological, animated by what is generally referred to as a "Biblical Worldview." Although it is usually only vaguely defined even by those who use the term, it is often a code word for theocracy.

Like the Christian Coalition, CWA's membership figures are unsubstantiated. They claim to be the largest women's political organization in America, though they also say that 100,000 of their *claimed* 600,000 members are men. CWA has an annual budget of $10-12 million and CWA chief Beverly LaHaye's radio talk show reportedly airs on about 100 stations. Like other Christian Right leaders, LaHaye opposes the separation of church and state. She has claimed "we are forbidden to speak, to pray aloud, to read our Bible, to even teach Judeo-Christian values in our public schools and other public places because of an imaginary 'wall of separation' conjured up by non-believers."[39] Consistent with this view, a guest on LaHaye's radio show, militia activist and U.S. Taxpayers Party leader Jeffrey Baker, attacked "the lie of separation of church and state."[40]

Focus on the Family, headed by radio psychologist James

Dobson, plays an increasingly influential role in politics through its 35 state-level think tanks and lobbying units located in or near state capitals. In Connecticut, Pennsylvania and Tennessee, they are called The Family Institute. Less obvious affiliates in other states are called, for example, The Alabama Family Alliance, North Carolina Family Policy Council, and the Capital Resource Institute (in California). Although they are separately incorporated, they are all vetted and approved by Focus on the Family and publish state-level editions of the national organization's political magazine *Citizen.* Like the Christian Coalition, some Family Institutes have distributed voter guides, often through *Citizen* magazine. In Pennsylvania, they claim to have distributed over one million voter guides in the 1994 elections.[41] Like the Christian Coalition, they hold political training schools (Community Impact Seminars), to motivate, recruit, train and inform Christian Right political activists to answer the question: "what do we, as Christians, have to do to take control of our society?"[42] Michigan Family Forum, an FOF unit, is the "major religious right organization" in the state, writes journalist Russ Bellant in his study of the religious right in Michigan.[43]

Dobson, who is known primarily as a radio psychologist and the author of books on child rearing such as *Dare To Discipline*, has been quietly building a political empire for a decade. Focus on the Family's annual revenues now exceed $100 million. Although he has often been portrayed in the press as apolitical, Dobson made his agenda clear at the 1994 annual convention of the National Religious Broadcasters—the trade association of television and radio evangelists. He said that "the church has not just the right but the duty" to challenge a governmental leader who "acts contrary to God's will" and to "call him to biblical fidelity." Dobson predicted persecution for the church, and according to Joe Conn's account in *Church & State* magazine, with "voice breaking and appearing near tears, Dobson stated 'I want to tell you folks, I'm prepared to pay with my life…'"[44]

Televangelist D. James Kennedy, of Ft. Lauderdale, Florida, has a growing role in the Christian Right. His weekly TV program reportedly airs on 360 stations and five cable networks in the U.S. and in the former Soviet Union, as well as on the Armed Forces Network. His 30-minute radio show, "Truths That Transform," is heard six days a week on over 300 stations. His church, which is affiliated with the conservative splinter denomination, Presbyterian Church in America, sponsors a seminary in Ft. Lauderdale which has a branch in Colorado Springs, Colorado.

Since 1994, he has hosted a national political conference— "Reclaiming America"—aimed largely at his white, upper middle class conservative Presbyterian audience. The first, held at his Ft. Lauderdale headquarters, received little media attention. What news coverage there was focused largely on the featured speech given by former vice president Dan Quayle. However, there was much more that was newsworthy and worth knowing. The conference drew over 2,000 people, including such top Christian Right leaders as Gary Bauer of the Family Research Council, Beverly LaHaye of Concerned Women for America, Bob Dugan of the National Association of Evangelicals, Bob Simonds of Citizens for Excellence in Education, and Rus Walton of the Plymouth Rock Foundation. Reconstructionist George Grant, the former vice president of Coral Ridge Ministries, repeatedly invoked images of armed revolution. He told the conferees that the "country gentlemen" who signed the Declaration of Independence, were "reluctant revolutionaries," who were driven, as Patrick Henry put it, to demand liberty or death. Grant hoped the conference would "raise up patriots who will say it's time to stop quoting the Founding Fathers. It's time to *be* the Founding Fathers." The revolutionary message was coded, but clear. And he received a standing ovation. For his part, Gary Bauer said that he would never again vote for a candidate who did not "share our values" and suggested that "maybe neither major party deserves to be the governing party of the United States." Beverly LaHaye urged conferees to pray for God to "help remove" government officials who are "standing in the way." [45]

Quayle's speech was unremarkable, except for his presence during the recitation of the pledge of allegiance—to the "Christian flag," which preceded his remarks. The Christian flag, white with a gold cross on a blue field in the upper left corner, flies outside Kennedy headquarters. The assemblage recited together: "I pledge allegiance to the Christian flag, and to the Saviour, for whose Kingdom it stands. One Saviour, crucified, risen and coming again, with life and liberty for all who believe." [46]

Since this conference, Bauer has emerged as the prototypical Christian Right Washington lobbyist and, along with Ralph Reed, is one of those most sought out for personality profiles in major magazines and newspapers. But there is still little serious reporting about the seriousness of the agenda of the Christian Right—which is far greater than the sum of its annual legislative agenda, its intriguing personalities, and its posturing within the national electoral sweepstakes.

Wildmon's Kingdom of (Self)Censorship

Another major organization that has been the beneficiary of much misdirected press attention is Rev. Don Wildmon's American Family Association—the scourge of TV, movies, and the arts. He is credited, for example, with making (in collaboration with Sen. Jesse Helms) "obscene" and "blasphemous" art a major issue. However, his reputation rests more on his pressuring of TV to censor programs he doesn't like and pressuring advertisers who sponsor publications of which he does not approve.

Wildmon has had many successes. In the late 1980s for example, he forced such major advertisers as Ralston Purina, General Mills, Domino's Pizza, Clorox and Noxell to drop sponsorship of the "offensive" TV shows on his hit list. In 1989 he cost NBC $1 million by leaning on would-be sponsors for a docudrama about the *Roe v. Wade* Supreme court decision that legalized abortion. Nevertheless, there has been debate about the effectiveness of Wildmon's operations. Some argue that his bark is worse than his bite, that his power is overrated, that companies actually have little to fear.[47] While the American Family Association's staff of 35 and a $6 million budget (mostly from direct mail) is not insignificant, his real clout comes from his direction of CLeaR-TV (Christian Leaders for Responsible Television), a large coalition of some 1,600 ministers, including some mainstream clergy, notably, many bishops of the United Methodist Church, and such Roman Catholic leaders as John Cardinal O'Connor of New York, and Tom Minnery, vice president of Focus on the Family.

Wildmon changed the name of his organization from the National Federation for Decency (NFD) to the American Family Association in 1987. A larger NFD-led alliance called the Coalition for Better Television collapsed in 1982 after Jerry Falwell's Moral Majority pulled out. Wildmon updated and refashioned his modus operandi with AFA and CLeaR -TV, and achieved new heights of censorship.[48] Specifically, he provided the catalyst for the far-right attacks on the arts, and a critical change in the political climate regarding tolerance for cultural diversity.

Through the AFA Law Center, for example, a nationally watched lawsuit against a California school district's use of the *Impressions* textbook may have sent a chill of self-censorship down the spine of publisher Holt, Rinehart, and Winston, which did not republish the well-regarded series. (The suit was based on the idea that the reading series violated the constitutional separation of church and state because some of the stories referred to witches, and witches are part of a recognized religion known as Wicca.)

Part of the problem with the reporting on Wildmon, as in the case of Ralph Reed, is the reductionism of "personality driven stories" which continues to be the trend in both print and electronic journalism. Such stories tend to inflate or distort the importance of their subjects, or fail to appropriately demonstrate how a Wildmon epitomizes a wider movement.

Joan DelFattore, a professor of English at the University of Delaware and an expert on textbook censorship notes, for example, "I don't see Wildmon as an isolated phenomenon. I see him as part of a wider far-right movement."[49] Indeed, Wildmon himself has been a leader in several far-right groups—including Christian Voice, American Coalition for Traditional Values, and the Coalition on Revival. He is a member of the Council for National Policy, a secretive leadership group of the conservative movement. His son and heir apparent, Tim Wildmon, is also a member.[50]

DelFattore points out that other Christian Right groups around the country also attacked the *Impressions* curriculum, notably Focus on the Family, Concerned Women for America, Eagle Forum, and Citizens for Excellence in Education. Although AFA lost in federal district court, Holt, Rinehart, and Winston's and other publishers' future reading series may well have to pass the Wildmon test, lest the publisher and its public school customers face further expensive "controversies."

Wildmon, like the Christian Coalition, exaggerates his membership and chapter list. (He also uses ridiculously unscientific methods to "survey" sex, violence, and anti-Christian views on TV.) His anti-Semitic remarks about the role of Jews in the media have been roundly denounced, though not widely publicized. In 1989, the Institute for First Amendment Studies and People for the American Way each released detailed reports charging Wildmon with anti-Semitism. Wildmon had insisted, for example, that the problem with the media is not immorality per se, but the "secular humanist value system" of those who own the media. And who are these people? Mostly Jews, who, according to Wildmon, "intentionally and by design" produce "anti-Christian" shows and films. Consequently, Wildmon lost some supporters, notably Catholic archbishop John May of St. Louis. He has gotten away with a lot, while his conservative and mainstream religious allies have looked the other way,[51] as have most of the media, most of the time. This has helped preserve his influence.

Wildmon continued as a co-chair of the 1996 Buchanan campaign for president even after fellow co-chair Larry Pratt was driven from the campaign by revelations of his association with white supremacist and militia groups. Curiously, Wildmon did not become an issue—even though the Anti-Defamation League of B'nai B'rith had earlier pointed out "Wildmon's Jewish problem" in a major report on the religious right and concluded that no major figure of the Christian Right "has made anti-Semitic thinking more central to his or her agenda than has Wildmon."[52]

The Cost of Jumping to Jokey Conclusions

A classic example of the media's underestimating Wildmon's power is a story which first appeared in *Mother Jones* and in expanded form later in *Penthouse,* in which Wildmon is depicted as a fringe player with no real clout.[53] Bill Dedman, a Pulitzer Prize winning journalist, successfully infiltrated the annual meeting of Wildmon's American Family Association. He exposed AFA as a right-wing fringe group, and ridiculed corporate advertisers who were afraid of Wildmon. However, nowhere in the story was there a discussion of CLeaR-TV—Wildmon's real source of power.

Wildmon has used the tool of boycotting companies that sponsor programming of which he disapproves to considerable effect. However, boycott threats are based on smoke and mirrors and bluffing on all sides. Some companies, such as Holiday Inn and Johnson &

Johnson, stood up to Wildmon and seemed to be unaffected. Others, such as Burger King, caved in completely. One recent example of a local boycott failure was a 1995 effort by the AFA of Texas to discourage businesses from advertising in a statewide weekly gay newspaper. The campaign not only caused few advertisers to bolt, but the attendant publicity apparently resulted in new advertisers. This happened not because the AFA did not have some strength, but because community groups and advertisers rallied around the embattled paper and denounced the bigotry of the AFA.[54]

Interestingly, the *Mother Jones* report took companies at their word that Wildmon had nothing to do with advertising policy changes that they had made—and that Wildmon had taken credit for changing. Since when are corporate PR departments the best source of information about the efficacy of citizen boycotts? Corporations faced with a boycott will usually claim that it has no impact—whether it does or not. Boycotts don't always make an obvious dent in sales, but may, for example, retard planned growth and cost a company millions in public relations, research, and lobbying. Boycotts can also give would-be investors pause.[55] On the other hand, advertisers may make crude cost/benefit analyses in which their commitment to freedom of expression withers before the relentless pursuit of the bottom line. Thus it can be difficult for outsiders and even companies themselves to measure the actual effectiveness of Wildmon's or anyone else's campaigns. Self-censorship, of course, rarely makes news. All this works to Wildmon's advantage. The AFA takes stands on far more targets than they can possible win. (Not all AFA targets are simultaneously targeted by CLeaR-TV.)

"There is no denying that Wildmon and his followers have had some impact," the *Mother Jones* piece acknowledged, "But is he a real power, and who is his active constituency?" The conclusion that "he's just a Bible Belt Blowhard,"[56] was cute, but a classic case of treating a serious phenomenon as a joke by reducing it to its most extreme element, while completely ignoring the larger coalition of censors which Wildmon also directed.

A better focus for the story would have been learning how it was that the AFA, given its actual status, was able to muster the support of such a wide range of religious leaders to sustain clout with advertisers, the networks and Hollywood. It would have been far more illuminating to learn how much the leaders on Wildmon's letterhead actually support his views and act on his initiatives.

Meanwhile, the threat of letter-writing campaigns, boycotts and the attendant bad publicity from CLeaR-TV has been compelling to corporate advertisers. The best targets for consumer boycotts are consumer-products companies selling items such as cars, cosmetics, hamburgers and computers because their market tends to be so large, and they tend to advertise on television. Thus it can be difficult for a company to evaluate the risks of challenging Wildmon's coalition. And of course, fear of the unknown is perhaps greater than fear based on knowing exactly what one is up against.

Wildmon has often benefited from being underestimated as an ignorant right-wing vigilante. In fact, Wildmon has made a career out of the failure of his opponents to accurately assess his strengths. Earlier in his career as a censor, he held his own with talk show hosts like Phil Donahue, and in debates with TV network executives. In recent years Wildmon has been less available to the media, and following a heart attack, has been considerably less influential. However, he and his organization continue to play an important role in advocating content restrictions in television, movies, and the arts.

On the plus side, Bill Dedman's *Mother Jones* story effectively debunked Wildmon's AFA chapter and membership figures, and skewered the mainstream press for serving as a conveyor belt for these unsubstantiated, unquestioned figures. Wildmon's claim that the AFA "is supported by 450,000 members in 640 chapters nationwide," had "appeared in nearly every newspaper story about him." However, Dedman reported that for $25 anybody can start a chapter, as *Mother Jones* did. Many chapters were inactive, "and the typical AFA chapter has 5 to 12 people. Wildmon's [1992] annual conference for chapter leaders drew from fewer than 40 chapters, including *Mother Jones'* and *Playboy*'s"[57] Unfortunately, few reporters and few political opponents of the Christian Right have followed this example of questioning and researching the actual numerical strength of Christian Right groups.

Moving Beyond the Psychology of Defeat

That most of us did not know that the religious right was not really dead in the late 1980s is an important lesson. But overreaction to their rebounding political successes remains a problem. A major progressive conference in 1996 had a panel titled "The Right-Wing Juggernaut." The dictionary defines 'juggernaut" as an "irresistible force." Like other aspects of the terminological gridlock discussed in Chapter 1, how the Christian Right is characterized, just as what it is named, can play a significant role in the psychology of how to deal with it. It is not necessary to make monsters out of movements in order to take them seriously. By way of contrast, a 1995 article by Jean Hardisty referred to "the resurgent right," and better captured in a phrase the seriousness of the situation without overreaction.[58]

Knowledge—that is, factual and sound analyses of the Christian Right and the cultures and communities that support it—combined with seriousness of purpose, is more likely to lead to empowerment, effective civil discourse, good reporting, and well crafted strategies to defend democratic institutions. Ignorance, exaggeration and laughing it off, lead to business as usual and risk political defeat.

CHAPTER 3

Americans for Theocratic Action

Rev. Sun Myung Moon, "Family Values," and The Christian Right—One Dangerous Theocrat

Theocratic political movements are, of course, not unique to Christianity. Jewish and Islamic theocratic movements, for example, have been much in the news in recent years with the assassinations of Israel's Prime Minister Rabin and Egyptian President Anwar Sadat, and with the rise of the theocratic state of Iran and the civil wars in Afghanistan. In the U.S., there is another important theocratic movement besides the Christian Right—the Unification Church of Sun Myung Moon. This small church has played an historic and pivotal role in the development of the conservative movement. Church front-organizations have engaged in an extraordinary range of activities—from high profile lobbying for the Gulf War against Iraq, to attacks on sex education in the public schools. The Unification Church has also played a pivotal role in the development of the Christian Right—helping, for example, to develop the theme of religious persecution as the response to criticism of their political activities, and helping to finance and to develop some of the political techniques that define the contemporary Christian Right and the Republican Party.

Mainstream Fascism

Best known as a so-called religious cult nicknamed "the Moonies," the Korean-based Unification Church of Sun Myung Moon has been the subject of ongoing controversies involving deceptive and unethical recruiting and indoctrination practices. This controversial group does not leap immediately to mind when mention is made of the religious right, or anti-democratic movements generally. However, the theocratic movement called the Unification

Church—and its myriad front groups—has played a significant, if generally under-appreciated role in American politics for a generation.

In the controversial "cult" model, young people enter the church through one of its recruiting fronts and are suddenly cut off from their previous lives and family, having turned themselves over to the church in as little as a weekend seminar. Come-ons are often pegged to current events. In the 1980s, presentations on international hot spots from Nicaragua to Afghanistan were the hook used on college campuses by CARP (Collegiate Association for the Research of Principles), a Moon recruiting front, while now in the 1990s, AIDS is often the attention-grabber.[1] Although the "cult mind control" issue still defines the public identity of the Unification Church, the church's greatest significance rests more with its mysterious financial backing, its theocratic agenda, its domestic alliance with the Christian Right and the Republican Party, its foreign entanglements with notorious fascists, links to intelligence agencies, and its surprising political power.

Since the first Unification Church missionaries arrived on the west coast from Japan in the late 1950s, the church seems to have never had more than a few thousand members at a time in the U.S. Thus the surprising influence of the church needs to be examined in the context of those activities not directed toward cult recruitment. The church's early history is murky and subject to debate. Despite extraordinary controversies the church has engendered over the years and the information turned up by news coverage and congressional and criminal investigations, the church is still not widely understood.

The biggest scandal was the church's central role in Koreagate scandal of the 1970s in which the Korean government was exposed as having engaged in a pattern of bribery and espionage aimed at involving the White House, the Congress, and other government agencies.[2] Additionally, Korean agents routinely spied on and harassed Korean dissidents in the U.S. and generally sought to promote the image and interests of the South Korean military dictatorship. Several of the top Korean agents were leading members of the tiny Unification Church.[3]

There is a plethora of Moon-controlled nonprofit groups, for-profit businesses, media outlets, and international conferences which function as a multifaceted empire. Congressional investigators have called it the "Moon organization." Although Moon front groups are usually outspokenly "patriotic," Moon, the self-proclaimed "Messiah," has repeatedly denounced "American-style democracy" and stated that his goal is "an automatic theocracy to rule the world." On other occasions he has said, "History will make the position of Rev. Moon clear," and that "his enemies, the American people and government will bow down before him."[4]

This has been a consistent message over the years. Moon told his followers in 1974 for example: "You must feel you are most privileged to be included in this congregation," and "Christians, no matter how hard they try, can get spiritual salvation at the best. In [the] Unification Church we are working towards total salvation…The entire world is our goal." He continued, "Absolute obedience to the Father—that one thing will bring certain victory…People here in America have to recognize the ability and power of Reverend Moon," he said, speaking of himself. "Whatever Reverend Moon wants to do, he will do!"[5] In any case, the theocratic goals of the church are reflected in the internal totalitarianism of the church itself. To achieve its ends, the church frequently aligns itself with far-right factions all over the world—from neo-fascist political parties, to the American Christian Right.

Particularly disturbing is the Unification Church's long-time involvement with the World Anti-Communist League (WACL), an international alliance of conservative, fascist and Nazi groups, governments, and individuals. The WACL was prominent throughout the 1980s as a co-belligerent in the aggressive anti-communist foreign policy of Ronald Reagan. The head of the Unification Church in Japan was a member of the WACL board of directors for many years. Indeed, the church's political operatives have been close to neo-fascist movements all over the world: from the neo-fascist National Front of Jean Marie Le Pen in France to the military dictatorships in the southern cone nations of Chile, Argentina, Bolivia, Uruguay and Paraguay in the 1970s and 1980s, and the Central American civil wars of the 1980s.

The Japanese section of WACL, Shokyo Rengo, was founded in 1968 as an alliance between top Unification Church officials and leaders of the Yakuza (Japanese organized crime), notably Yoshio

Kodama. Kodama and another Moon patron, Ryoichi Sasakawa, were leading Japanese "blackshirts" in pre-World War II Japan, and jailed briefly as Class-A War criminals after the war. In 1970, Shokyo Rengo hosted the annual WACL conference in Tokyo. Among the conference speakers was U.S. Senator Strom Thurmond (R-SC), who later intervened to help Moon overcome immigration difficulties to get into the U.S.[6]

Under the leadership of retired U.S. Army General John K. Singlaub, WACL helped to provide arms and financing to the Nicaraguan Contras, particularly after Congress cut off CIA-channeled funding to the Contras in 1984. Among the first groups on the scene with "private" humanitarian aid for the Contras was Moon's political front, CAUSA.[7] One writer reported seeing Contras dressed in red CAUSA T-shirts. Nevertheless, congressional investigators shied away from the role of the Unification Church and the government of Korea in the World Anti-Communist League. While the UC had its own network that was part of WACL, it also clearly had other functions. Former WACL youth leader Allen Tate Wood wrote that prior to the Koreagate scandal, Moon instructed him to "win the power centers" of the U.S. for him, beginning with academia.[8] Moon also told him that "part of our strategy in the U.S. must be to make friends in the FBI, the CIA and police forces, the military and business community…as a means of entering the political arena, influencing foreign policy, and ultimately establishing absolute dominion over the American people."[9] Religious purists in the church at first opposed political activity in the U.S. however, according to the report of the Koreagate investigative committee headed by then-U.S. Rep. Donald Fraser (D-MN), "They were told it was Master's expressed desire to begin political work in the United States. Thereafter, a member's objection to political activities was considered infidelity to Master and was like being disobedient to God."[10] Based on interviews with ex-members, Robert Boettcher, the staff director of the Fraser committee, wrote that Moon was "appalled" by American individualism and he considered relocating to Germany where people "were trained in totalism. Some former members recall Nazi films on organizing Hitler Youth were shown as examples to [church] leaders. Nothing was more important than developing a cadre of strong leaders totally subservient to his will."[11]

It is this record of support for conservative and anti-communist causes which the Christian Right and the Republican Party have embraced. And it is in this context that the church's highly paid spin doctors and law firms earn their keep. As a result, concerned citizens, attempting to take action against this controversial organization, find that there are many obstacles to gathering comprehensive and accurate information about the Unification Church.

The Unification Church permeates American politics in many surprising ways. The *Washington Times,* with a circulation of about 100,000, is the church's flagship presence in the U.S. Since its founding it has been owned, controlled, and bankrolled by church interests. Former editor Arnaud de Borchgrave once told the *Washington Post* that during a tour of Moon's Korea-based Tong-Il industries he "met the plant manager [who] said to me, 'you are seeing the logistical tail of the *Washington Times.*' They are very conscious of the fact that a certain portion of their profit comes to us to meet the subsidy."[12] The *Washington Times* is a newspaper like no other in American history— a newspaper wholly owned by foreign interests and exerting influence far disproportionate to its circulation, by virtue of its role as the number two daily in the most important city in the world. Among its house columnists have been former White House communications director Pat Buchanan and Christian Reconstructionist writer John Lofton. It was the one paper read every day by President Reagan, and has since become an institution in the nation's capital, aggressively promoting the players and agenda of the Christian Right through its pages.

Former editorial page editor, William Cheshire,[13] who resigned in protest over editorial interference from senior officials of the Unification Church, believes that the paper is operating in apparent violation of the Foreign Agents Registration Act. This law, passed in the 1930s, requires entities whose activities are controlled by foreign governments and corporations to make financial and other forms of disclosure to the Justice Department. The Act was originally passed in order to expose covert Nazi funding of German-American newspapers. Several top executives in the Moon media empire were KCIA officials during the Koreagate era, notably Sang Kook Han whose arrival at the *Times* from his previous post as Korea's ambassador to Panama precipitated the departure of founding editor and publisher, James Whelan.

Despite the questionable backgrounds of the paper's publishers, the Justice Department and most of the media have turned a blind eye to the *Washington Times*.

George Bush: Blinded by the Light?

For thirty years, a major part of the modus operandi of the Unification Church has been to gain the appearance of endorsement—if not the actual endorsement—of prominent American and world figures. This is generally accomplished by paying such individuals to speak at any of the numerous conferences hosted by church front organizations around the world. Members of Congress, senators, actors, generals, and former heads of state—somehow the church pulls them in. The biggest catch of 1995 was a twofer—former president George Bush and former first lady Barbara Bush, who spoke at a series of rallies in the U.S.[14] and Japan hosted by Mrs. Moon's Women's Federation for World Peace (WFWP). These appearances led to a minor media frenzy. The British *Daily Mail* reported that Bush received one million British pounds as payment,[15] while the *Washington Post* reported that Bush's fee was to remain secret as a matter of contract. The *Daily Mail's* figure is comparable however, to the $2 million paid to former president Ronald Reagan for appearances in Japan on behalf of Japanese corporations after he left office.[16]

At one rally Mrs. Moon declared that "It has to be Reverend Moon [who] saves the United States, which is in decline because of the destruction of the family and moral decay."[17] Unsurprisingly, these events are usually attended primarily by Unification Church members and are used to promote the views of the church. One WFWP rally in 1994 featured a two hour speech by Mrs. Moon praising her husband.

WFWP has in recent years become the church's most publicly active Moon front group. Apparently, the much younger Mrs. Moon is being groomed to succeed the seventy-six-year-old patriarch-Messiah. WFWP is also a format that conservative organizations have been using to play catch-up with the changes in gender roles, attempting to create a modern image for conservative styles of family structure. The early photos of Mrs. Moon in kimonos, standing demurely in the background, are being replaced with the image of Mrs. Moon attired in power suits, meeting with the likes of then Soviet premier Mikhail Gorbachev and sharing in the accomplishments of her husband. WFWP provides a vehicle for Hak Ja Han Moon to raise her profile and define her own image—with the well-paid Bushes as a warm-up act.

The True Family vs. The Nuclear Family

It is strange that the Unification Church plays an integral role in the "family values" movement. Stranger still that it serves as an important base of support for the Republican Party, which is publicly committed to constitutional democracy. This is one of the sustained hypocrisies of the Christian Right and the GOP and remains a source of division. With "family values," meaning support for the heterosexual nuclear family, as the centerpiece of the Christian conservative agenda, rank and file Christian conservatives are usually shocked to learn of their movement's connections to a group that urges separation from one's biological family.

When young people are recruited and indoctrinated into the church, in a few short days they abandon their previous lives and biological families to become the "True Children" of the "True Parents" (Rev. and Mrs. Moon) and thus become members of the "True Family" (the Unification Church). This phraseology is frequently prominent in, or just below the surface of, their public activities.

WFWP events, like many other Moon-backed projects are often based on a double entendre. "The Global Family Festival," for example, suggests a conference on the family in the conventional sense, but the backers also understand it to refer to the "True Family." A 1994 congressional resolution sponsored by Rep. Dan Burton (R-IN), Sen. Trent Lott (R-MS), and Sen. Orrin Hatch (R-UT)[18] supporting "Parents Day" turned out to be a Unification Church initiated effort in which the "True Parents" behind the resolution were quietly celebrated.

Perhaps the epitome of the co-optation of the Christian Right's conservative family values rhetoric was the cover of the October, 1995 issue of the *Unification News* which featured a photo of Rev. Moon, arms outstretched, under the headline "True Family Values." In this case, the message is that the "True Family" also has the true values.

As far back as 1983, Rep. Jim Leach (R-IA), then chair of the moderate Republican Ripon Society, challenged the hypocritical alliance between party conservatives and the Moon organization: "A political movement basing its appeal on old fashioned patriotism and family values simply cannot justify an alliance with a cult that preys on the disintegration of the American family and advocates allegiance to an international social order operating with cell-like secrecy."[19] The occasional scandal not withstanding, GOP and Christian Right leaders continue to headline Moon-sponsored events and quietly accept the large paychecks that usually accompany the rendering of said services.

Witting and Unwitting Collaborators

The multiple political purposes of such organizations as WFWP go back to the original Moon front group, the Korean Cultural Freedom Foundation, which was established in the early 1960s in collaboration with the Korean Central Intelligence Agency, or KCIA, and had such figureheads as former presidents Truman and Eisenhower adorning their letterhead.[20] Politicians and public figures who participate in Unification Church sponsored organizations or activities typically claim they didn't know Moon or the church was connected—or if they did know, they say that it doesn't matter, or that no one tried to convert them. The purpose behind all this is not the establishment of "legitimacy," as is often popularly reported, but the brokering of political power. Senior politicians are rarely duped as often as they are compromised, and there is no political gain in fronting for an organization as controversial as the Unification Church. Therefore, other motivations are at work.

George Bush is an outstanding example. As Director of the U.S. Central Intelligence Agency under President Gerald Ford when the Koreagate scandal broke in 1976, he handled many sensitive matters involving the highest levels of government, major politicians of both parties and relations between the U.S. and Korea. George Bush is well aware of the modus operandi and significance of the Unification Church. Unsurprisingly, his spokespersons offered up the various standard deflections when asked about his participation in WFWP events: he didn't know it was Moon,[21] and the sponsoring organization of the event was independent of the church.[22]

Mr. Bush reportedly declined all personal interviews on the subject except to Moon's own *Washington Times* (which also happens to house an office of WFWP). The apparently well-briefed former president told the *Times* that "Until I see something about the Women's Federation that troubles me, I will continue to encourage them." Bush saluted the WFWP's "great emphasis on family."[23]

Bush is just one among a legion of Moon collaborators. U.S. Sen. Jesse Helms (R-NC) addressed CAUSA-sponsored, closed-door "American Leadership Conferences" at least five times in 1988 alone.[24] The meetings brought together conservative activists and elected officials for issue briefings, strategy sessions, and indoctrination in "CAUSA ideology" or "Godism," and served as an entrée into Moon's political development events for the American Freedom Coalition. These events often became state-level scandals as state legislators and others were exposed in local papers as having participated in the Moon-sponsored conclaves.[25]Other conservative leaders who addressed the conferences included Rev. Jerry Falwell, Senators Orrin Hatch (R-UT) and Pete Wilson (R-CA), as well as former representative Jack Kemp (R-NY). For Kemp, Moon money has been a major source of income—$52,000 between January 1995 and the summer of 1996—prior to his nomination as the GOP candidate for vice-president.[26] WFWP events have attracted—in addition to the Bushes—such luminaries as TV journalist Barbara Walters, Sen. Richard Lugar (R-IN), and Marilyn Quayle, wife of the former vice president.

One Messiah, Two Ex-Presidents

The Moon organization is continually hosting big events to inaugurate international entities in media, academia, religion, world peace, and so on. Such events often cash in on the faded image of power and residual prestige implicit in the presence of former public officials and their families. Thus it came as no surprise that the July, 1996 inaugural conference of the "World Federation for Family Values," in Washington, DC, featured talks not only by Rev. and Mrs. Moon, but by former presidents George Bush and Gerald Ford, former British prime minister Edward Heath, TV preacher Robert Schuller, Ronald Reagan's daughter Maureen Reagan, former Costa Rican president Oscar Arias, the ubiquitous Jack Kemp, as well as

Boston University president John Silber, Family Research Council president Gary Bauer, and Christian Coalition executive director Ralph Reed. Entertainment was provided by Pat Boone and family,[27] and comedian Bill Cosby. Cosby later said he was duped into speaking at the event and wanted out, but the Moon organization threatened to sue.

Although the Unification Church figured prominently in the biggest scandal of the Ford administration, a flack for Ford claimed that the former President didn't know the event was Moon-connected. A Moon spokesperson said that Ford did know. Bush, on the other hand, could not plead ignorance in the wake of bad publicity surrounding his previous paid appearances at Moon events. Thus, Bush spokesman Jim McGrath claimed that Bush's "overriding concern is for the need to strengthen families...I don't think anyone is going there to endorse the Unification Church."[28]

But of course the appearance of former presidents is an implied endorsement of the Unification Church's approach to "family values" and its legitimacy as a religious, political and social factor within the GOP, the conservative movement, and society at large. There were others quoted in the press who came to these and other similar events because of the reassuring presence of Bush and Ford. The rehearsed disingenuousness of these former leaders and their spokespersons is consistent with the way that the issue is always framed to get past the inevitable one-day news coverage. The standard lies seem to work. The appearance of Ford and Bush signaled the ongoing importance of the Moon organization in the GOP, and provided cover for lesser figures whose careers might get tripped up by a Moon scandal.

Where Does the Money Come From?

Over the years one question that has fascinated journalists and the political community has been: where does the money for the Moon empire come from? There has been much speculation, but few facts. Leading theories, each of which enjoy some support and seem to have some merit, include Japanese organized crime; foreign governments and intelligence agencies; and Moon-controlled businesses around the world. While many Americans are familiar with the Unification Church's practice of requiring young members to sell flowers on the street in "mobile fundraising teams," evidence from congressional investigations, Moon's tax fraud trial, newspaper investigations and church defectors all indicate that most of the money comes from Japan. Where it originates exactly remains a matter of considerable conjecture. However, one source is becoming well documented.

The church is the subject of over 300 lawsuits in Japan which range, according to the *Washington Post*, from former members who "say they were brainwashed into slave-like devotion to the church" to those who say they were "duped into paying exorbitant prices for vases, prayer beads or other religious objects, sometimes under pressure from church members who said their relatives would 'burn in hell' unless they donated." (The church has reportedly paid out over $150 million in settlements.) The high pressure sales scam is referred to as "spiritual sales," and appears to be an important source of cash for the church's international operations.

"In the end, the only thing that mattered was how much money you could earn," reported one former member in Japan. "We were like puppets on a string, controlled by Mr. Sun Myung Moon."[29] Members sell vases, prayer beads and model pagodas for as much as $50,000 each, often targeting vulnerable older women who have assets. One former fundraising manager who oversaw the door-to-door sales program for one district in Tokyo said selling the icons at inflated prices often took in more than $1 million a month for the church. Two or three dozen such units in Tokyo reportedly raised similar sums. The church denies that it engages in high pressure sales and insists that it does not do anything unethical or illegal. However, one church spokesman said that he thought "Maybe half of these cases are legitimate."[30] In Japan, as in the United States, many people lose contact with their families, donate all their assets to the church, move into church housing and often devote their lives to the many activities of the church, including politics and fund-raising.

Much of the money raised in this way in Japan apparently ends up in the United States. Church officials say that at least $1 billion has come into the U.S. over the last twenty years, including over $800 million for the *Washington Times* alone. The *Times* has never made a profit since it was founded in 1982. Hiroshi Yamaguchi, who heads a group of lawyers who have brought most of the suits against the church, told the *Washington Post* that "Many Japanese believers are specifically told to donate money so it may be used for the *Washington Times*, the University of Bridgeport," and other church-related interests in the United States. While these entities lose money, Yamaguchi says that they lend "prestige to Reverend Moon and his church and enable him to draw people like President Bush" to church-sponsored events.[31] In fact, the university in Bridgeport is playing a growing role in the constellation of Moon interests.

Moon University: Americans for Theocratic Action

The Moon organization gained control of the University of Bridgeport (Connecticut) when the private university fell on hard economic times. Unable or unwilling to find a solution elsewhere, the trustees cut a deal in which a Moon front group, the Professors World Peace Academy, infused $50 million into the school in exchange for control of the board of trustees. The takeover bailed out local banks and other creditors who supported the plan over intense community opposition. Among the leaders of this community opposition is William Finch, a courageous Bridgeport alderman, who still leads the Coalition of Concerned Citizens in Bridgeport.[32]

After the takeover, the school's board was not only controlled by senior church officials, but the school (as critics like Finch predicted) has become a bustling hub of church activity. Church members and allies have been installed in senior staff positions. Richard L. Rubenstein, a longtime Moon apologist, was appointed president. Rubenstein acknowledged in remarks reprinted in the church's *Unification News*, that without Moon there would "certainly be no revivified University of Bridgeport" and in 1995, he presented the self-proclaimed messiah Moon with an honorary doctorate. Nevertheless, Rubenstein claims that the university is a "non-sectarian institution" and that "free expression of every religious faith is welcome on our campus."[33] The school's ten-year plan reportedly includes a thirteen-story international conference center and hotel. Moon envisions the University of Bridgeport as the flagship school of an international network.

One episode that epitomizes the university's new role in the Moon organization also underscores how the organization itself functions as a central catalyst in the conservative movement. Shortly after the takeover in June 1993, another Moon front group, the World Medical Health Foundation (WMHF) hosted a conference at UB that helped propel the Moon organization into the national politics of sex and HIV education. The event, titled the "Conference on Educational Policy and HIV Prevention," boasted a who's-who roster of activist leaders opposed to sexuality education. One featured speaker was the prominent anti-abortion leader Dr. Mildred Jefferson, a director of Massachusetts Citizens for Life and a "National Advisory Board" member of the WMHF.[34] The other conference speakers included Dr. William R. Archer II, a top official in the U.S. Department of Health and Human Services during the Bush administration; Shepherd Smith and Patricia Funderburk of Americans for a Sound AIDS/HIV Policy; Dr. Joe McIlhaney of the Medical Institute for Sexual Health; Kathleen Sullivan of Project Respect; Douglas Scott of Life Decisions International, and Richard Panzer of Free Teens.[35]

As an outgrowth of the conference, WMHF chief Dr. William Bergman, formerly a director of the Unification Church itself, produced a follow-up slide program for health educators called "The Private Plague: AIDS, Sexually Transmitted Diseases & a Strategy for Our Youth at Risk," with which he hoped to reach thousands of opinion leaders and university health staff. Consistent with the church's view that conventional sex education programs are a major underlying cause of sexually transmitted diseases and AIDS, "Private Plague" advocates abstinence from pre-marital sex as the sole effective and appropriate method of AIDS prevention.

The program cites as fact the discredited "San Marcos Miracle," as an example of the efficacy of abstinence education. In San Marcos, California, a school administrator claimed that "there was an 88 percent reduction in teen pregnancy" after a popular Christian Right "abstinence program" called "Teen Aid," was introduced. When the *San Diego Union* investigated the "miracle" in their midst, school officials had to admit that they had no evidence to support the claim.[36]

Bergman's program also proposes a political domino theory for sexually transmitted disease. The viewer of "Private Plague" learns that such diseases have their origins in the "civil rights movement" which supposedly led to "moral relativism" and "acceptance of Alcohol, Drugs & Promiscuous Sex."[37]

The church's mobilization against sex education was announced by Unification Church vice-president Tyler Hendricks in the *Unification News*, four months before the Bridgeport conference. Hendricks claimed that sex education promotes rather than solves problems such as "teen pregnancy, sexual promiscuity, and the incidence of STD's [sexually transmitted diseases]" and declared in the paper that sex education "is a front-line fight for the values in society. I encourage Unificationist Parents...who have children entering the sex-ed stage in public schools to get into it."[38]

Church member Nancy Hanna who 'got into it' in Westchester County, New York, added that Unification Church members are particularly well suited to organizations such as the Christian Coalition, Focus on the Family, and Concerned Women for America. "Because of our training by True Parents," she wrote, "we are crystal clear on issues like sex education and other traditional value issues in a way others without our theology rarely are."

Consequently, Unification Church operatives have been seeking, and sometimes gaining, access to and influence in the educational system. Bergman protégé, Richard Panzer, who spoke at the Bridgeport conference, is also an activist with a slide-show. He claims "Talking With Teens about HIV & AIDS" (AKA "Free Teens"), is being used in "public and private schools in 30 states."[39] On Long Island, Free Teens was used by such Christian Right groups as Concerned Women for America and Project Respect, as well as the Catholic Church—until they learned of the hidden Moon connection.[40] The Bronxville, New York school system dropped the program as well.[41]

Panzer graduated from the Unification Seminary in Barrytown, NY and directed the church's activities in Rhode Island in the 1980s. However, his credentials regarding teaching about sex and AIDS appear to be limited to his work with the "AIDSbusters Task Force" of Moon's American Freedom Coalition in New Jersey.[42] Nevertheless, Panzer has enjoyed some success.

Free Teens was apparently approved for use in the New York City schools as a result of a political override of the school system's own HIV/AIDS review committee. Internal school board documents show that the HIV/AIDS committee (comprised of carefully selected health educators and other professionals) repeatedly rejected the Free Teens program.

Although the committee praised some aspects of the program in January 1993, they also described the slideshow as "judgmental," "tedious," in parts, "offensive, in poor taste," and "educationally unsound." In July of that year, (just a month after the Bridgeport conference) the committee revisited and rejected the program because of its "heavy handed presentation" utilizing a "scare tactic approach" to foster its "one sided argument that sexual abstinence is the only safe option." Although the committee agreed with the general message of abstinence, the members felt that Panzer's program did "not promote the trust relationship essential to the counseling and support which we seek to establish."

All this occurred at a politically sensitive time. Schools Chancellor Joseph Fernandez had just been forced out following a nationally watched struggle over condom distribution in the schools and the presentation of sexuality issues in the proposed "rainbow curriculum." Thus when conservative school board member Irene Impellizzeri wrote to the interim chancellor, Harvey Garner, about Panzer's rejection, bureaucrats jumped.

In an August 11, 1993 internal memo, Garner finessed the issue. While he defended the integrity of the work of the HIV/AIDS committee, he simultaneously created an appeals board of three senior administrators which he assigned to review "materials disapproved" by the committee—beginning, Garner wrote, with "Mr. Panzer's material, which brought this matter to your (Impellizzeri's) attention." The World Medical Health Foundation, doing business as Free Teens, was quietly approved as a "vendor" in April 1994, which allowed local schools to hire Panzer and Bergman to put on programs. An Impellizzeri aide told the *New York Times* that she had done nothing unusual and that Panzer had not received any special favors.[43]

While it is not clear why Free Teens was able to capture the intense interest of senior school officials, the fact that it did is a fascinating example of the Moon organization moving behind the scenes and exerting considerable political muscle.

Moon Over Merrimack

Meanwhile, Rev. Sun Myung Moon himself emerged in connection with another nationally watched school board battle.[44] Moon personally presented Merrimack, New Hampshire school board member and Christian Coalition activist Shelly Uscinski with a "National Service Award" at an awards ceremony of his Washington Times Foundation in April 1996. Rev. Jerry Falwell, who has frequented Moon events over the years, was the master of ceremonies.

Merrimack had roiled with controversy since the 1994 election of stealth candidates to the school board—including Uscinski—created a conservative majority. Once on the board, they sought to implement the Christian Right agenda, and generated national attention. According to opposing school board member Ken Coleman, "One by one, the items came up for consideration—school prayer disguised as a moment of silence, creationism in the science courses, removal of psychological counseling services and opposition to Goals 2000" (the federal education reform program).[45] Although much of this was thwarted, the board did eliminate the school's health program, which included sex education.

The board also imposed an anti-gay policy—with back-stage direction from Rev. Lou Sheldon of the California-based Traditional Values Coalition which has historically emphasized anti-gay politics.[46] The policy barred the presentation of "homosexuality as a positive lifestyle alternative," and threatened disciplinary action against teachers who strayed across the line.[47]

In May 1996, just weeks after Rev. Moon's blessing, the town voted to overturn the policy, and replaced one conservative board member with a progressive by a two-to-one margin, thus ending Christian Right control. Voter turn-out was up fifty percent from the previous election[48] demonstrating, as the Christian Right feared, that the vast majority are opposed to their tactics, their allies and their agenda.

However, while the censorship lasted, fearful teachers and administrators dropped a film about poet Walt Whitman that mentioned his homosexuality, and William Shakespeare's play *The Twelfth Night*, in which one of the characters is supposedly gay. Teachers also avoided discussion of homosexuality in such works as *Moby Dick*, *Of Mice And Men*, *A Raisin in the Sun*, and *The Glass Menagerie*.[49]

Helping Sell the Gulf War

The Moon organization's role in American society runs the gamut from life and death to war and peace. In 1990 and early 1991 during the build-up to "Desert Storm" Moon's American Freedom Coalition (AFC) staged high-profile pro-war rallies in all fifty states. One such mediagenic rally of 400 people at the Statute of Liberty was organized by none other than Richard Panzer.[50] These jingoist displays, which helped serve up the appearance of grassroots popular support for the war, are typical of the Moon organization's activities whenever dubious U.S. foreign policy initiatives have been at stake during the last two decades. For example, during the Vietnam War, Moon agents collaborated with the Nixon White House to create the appearance that young people supported the war through a Moon-controlled front group "American Youth for a Just Peace."[51]

In 1990, a Moon-connected politician named Sam Zakhem emerged as the head of two organizations which sought to promote American military intervention in the Persian Gulf—the Coalition for America at Risk and the Freedom Task Force.[52] The coalition was headquartered at the Alexandria, VA public relations firm of Keene, Shirley & Associates, which also served as the PR firm for the AFC. Among the "advisors" on the Coalition for America at Risk letterhead were such stalwarts of the Moon Right as John Singlaub, Richard Viguerie, Gary Jarmin, Robert Grant, Tim LaHaye, David Keene (of Keene, Shirley) and Ralph Reed as well as California State Senator H.L. Richardson.[53]

In September of 1990, Iraq released captured documents including a letter from Kuwait's U.S. ambassador, Saud Nasser Sabah, to the Kuwaiti oil minister. The document, dated May 18, 1990 indicated that Zakhem wanted a job at one of Kuwait's many U.S. businesses in order to ensure a "legal income" through 1992 "enabling him to be totally dedicated to his next electoral campaign." Sabah recommended him.[54] Zakhem (who ran unsuccessfully for the GOP Senate nomination from Colorado in 1992), later told the *New York Times* that the letter was Iraqi propaganda. Still, less than three months after the purported letter was written, Zakhem was ensconced as co-chairman and main spokesman for the Kuwaiti media campaign.[55]

Zakhem's groups waged a propaganda campaign of TV spots

(notably on ABC News *Nightline*), and full-page *Washington Times* newspaper ads targeting Washington opinion leaders and the constituents of anti-war liberals. This was the media equivalent of carpet bombing the opposition before crucial congressional votes. Significantly, WJLA, the ABC affiliate in Washington, DC, which ran Zakhem's ads on *Nightline*, refused to run ads opposed to the Gulf War which had been produced by the Military Families Support Network.[56]

Although Zakhem and his associates claimed these activities were funded entirely by private citizens,[57] it later turned out that the government of Kuwait and the Kuwaiti royal family provided most of the funds—$7.7 million according to a federal indictment.[58] Zakhem was personally indicted on charges of violating the Foreign Agent Registration Act for receiving $1.5 million from Kuwait for his activities—the charges were later dropped, and he was acquitted on related federal tax charges.[59]

Zakhem is a native of Lebanon and a former Colorado state senator, who participated in the formation of the U.S. branch of CAUSA in 1983. He was a featured speaker at CAUSA's American Leadership Conferences and served on the organization's advisory board. President Reagan appointed him U.S. Ambassador to Bahrain, (the small Gulf state which neighbors Kuwait) in 1986. Zakhem distinguished himself by granting an interview at the U.S. Embassy with the publisher of a Moon-owned newspaper, the *Middle East Times*.[60] In a bizarre explanation of U.S.-Arab relations, Zakhem invoked (the Moon doctrine of) "Godism" as something that the U.S. and the Arab world have in common.

The role of "Godism" in politics was explained by a Unification Church official in 1983: "Democracy arose out of the lack of absolute values, absolute power, and absolute being. When there are no absolutes, the majority opinion is considered the best idea. Godism, however has not been the majority idea. God's teaching has not been the majority teaching. Therefore through democratic elections, people have not selected God's will, goodness, True Parents, or the messiah. Our goal and purpose is to follow Godism."

In that same interview with the *Middle East Times*, Zakhem also weirdly claimed that the nation of Israel had a "communist system" that was more communist than "communist China." He later claimed, in a letter to the editor, that these faux pas were a "miscommunication of my true views" and said he understood that Israel is a "representative democracy."[61] Although this interview appeared in an English-language weekly distributed all over the Middle East, Zakhem was kept on for two years. His tenure as ambassador ended in 1989; he was not reappointed after the story broke in the U.S.

Moon's Mail Man: Fronts Within Fronts

The American Freedom Coalition is but the latest in a series of Moon political fronts. One of the linchpins in Moon's political operations over the years has been Richard Viguerie, best known as the direct mail entrepreneur who is credited with producing the critical cash for the New Right in the 1970s and 1980s. Lore has it that Viguerie got his start by hand copying the donor lists of the 1964 Barry Goldwater for President campaign. Less well known is that one of his first clients—in 1965—was the Korean Cultural Freedom Foundation (KCFF)—a front for the UC and the KCIA. The group's ostensible purpose was to promote anti-communism. However, the day-to-day activities of the KCFF were handled by the military attaché at the Korean embassy, Lt. Colonel Bo Hi Pak, who was also Moon's top operative in Washington. The founder of the KCIA, Kim Jong Pil, was the group's "honorary chairman." The KCIA chief, according to congressional investigators, explained to church members that he was using the church for political purposes.

Viguerie handled one of KCFF's most sensitive projects, Radio of Free Asia,[62] an explicitly KCIA operation that broadcast propaganda programs from studios in South Korea into North Korea, China and North Vietnam. According to Koreagate investigator Robert Boettcher, "Moon and Pak conducted mass mailings to Americans, asking them to pay for the broadcast facilities in Korea, but arranged for free use of transmitters and studios through the KCIA. The money could be pumped into the Unification Church or other Moon activities, as needed...."[63].

This was not Viguerie's only Koreagate connection. He was also an original investor and director of the Washington, DC-based Diplomat National Bank, which investigators for the Securities and Exchange Commission discovered was secretly and illegally controlled by the KCIA and the Unification Church. Although Viguerie was not implicated in any wrong-doing, ultimately, church leaders were forced to divest control of the bank.[64]

Over the years, Viguerie's client list has been a who's who of the New Right—including the Moon connected Christian Voice and the NCIA (which was later folded into the AFC) and the *Washington Times*. In 1987, Viguerie's business, reportedly $1.5 million in debt, was saved when Bo Hi Pak purchased a building owned by Viguerie for $10 million.[65] Viguerie subsequently became an officer of the AFC, and handled its direct mail account.

Convicted Felon Sun Myung Moon

One of the precursors to the Christian Right's effective use of the theme of religious bigotry and persecution was the felony conviction of Sun Myung Moon on a series of tax related charges which originated with the Koreagate investigation. Moon served an eighteen-month sentence beginning in 1984 for conspiring to file false tax returns, to obstruct justice, and to commit perjury.[66] Moon's defenders claimed that he and his co-defendant Takeru Kamiyama were unfairly and selectively prosecuted due to racial and religious intolerance. It later turned out that the Moon organization skillfully manufactured and exploited these sentiments with the assistance of public relations firms including the Washington-based Gray & Co. The campaign for "religious freedom" was integral to the multi-faceted Moon agenda. In 1984, Moon's top aide Col. Bo Hi Pak explained that "freedom of religion has become a major issue in America, and Reverend Moon is the rallying point."[67]

There was significant evidence of willful violation of the law, making what might have been a relatively minor civil action, a matter of criminal prosecution. Tax lawyers told Moon's representatives to keep his assets separate from those of the church. This advice was ignored, and when the IRS came calling, ledgers were forged and backdated to hide Moon's assets within those of the church. The prosecution proved, among other things, that the paper used to falsify the 1973 records was not even manufactured until 1974. Moon's defense on appeal is consistent with his theocratic ambitions. Moon claimed that because some of his followers believed he is "potentially the new Messiah," the "embodiment" of the Church, that he is thus exempt from personal income taxes. The court held, however, that even Messiahs are not exempt from taxes, and have a status distinct from the church. Freedom of religion is "subordinate to the criminal laws of the country...to allow otherwise would be to permit church leaders to stand above the law."[68]

The catalyst for the issue was the Coalition for Religious Freedom (funded with at least $500,000 of Moon money[69]), which became a pivotal organization at the time of Moon's conviction, framing and promoting the issue of supposed religious persecution at the hands of the secular state. The board was at various times populated with such leading evangelical and Christian Right figures as Rev. Tim LaHaye who chaired the Executive Committee,[70] Rev. Jerry Falwell, Rev. James Robison, Rev. Rex Humbard, Rev. Jimmy Draper, Rev. D. James Kennedy, Marlin Maddoux, Rev. Everett Sileven, Rev. Jimmy Swaggart, Rev. Don Wildmon and former Indiana Moral Majority leader Rev. Greg Dixon.[71] The Coalition for Religious Freedom blamed Moon's prosecution on "the ungodly secular humanist philosophy that has contaminated our schools, the media, and the various levels of government."[72] It was odd indeed, for such stalwarts of evangelical Christianity to denounce "humanism" in unison with the proponents of Moonism, which asserts that Jesus "failed" and that Moon is the "true messiah." Eventually, most of them dropped out as the Moon connection was revealed in evangelical circles.

Part of Moon's strategy has been to seek alliances with, and even help create the religious right. However the relationship has always been highly controversial within the movement. Rumors ran rampant in conservative circles as to who was receiving funds from the Moon organization. One effort to document the money trail found $1,550,000 in 1984-85.[73]

However this is nothing compared to the billions of dollars that have poured into the *Washington Times,* and related publications since its founding in 1984.

Attack Ads for Freedom

Typical of the Moon organization's appropriation of the theme of religious freedom and racial justice was a campaign in April of 1989, accusing the national news weekly *U.S. News & World Report* of inaccuracy, racism, and religious bigotry in a report on the political activities of the Unification Church and the American Freedom Coalition.[74] A Moon front group, called the "National Committee Against Religious Bigotry and Racism," was created for the occasion and quietly bankrolled with $200,000 from CAUSA. The committee ran an ad campaign in major publications including the *New York Times*, *USA Today*, *Editor & Publisher*, and Moon's own *Washington Times*. The unsupported accusations were evidently a diversionary tactic, intended to stifle further reporting on the Moon organization's forty-year record of anti-democratic statements and actions.

The ads, which appeared to be independent of the Moon organization, were signed by "Committee" spokesperson Dr. Jakie Roberts of Chicago, who charged that the *U.S. News & World Report* article was "riddled with racially and religiously bigoted slurs." After "Moonies," Roberts wondered, "What epithets will you use next… Will it be 'gooks,' 'kikes,' 'niggers,' 'papists' or 'holy rollers'?" The term "Moonie" appears once in the 2,500 word article, the tone of which is sober and uninfected with bigotry. The context of its use was to accurately report that Moon's followers have commonly been called "Moonies."

The campaign was doubly disingenuous because church leaders at the time often referred to themselves as Moonies. Moon himself fondly called his followers "Moonies" several times in a 1987 sermon—which was translated by none other than then-CAUSA chief Bo Hi Pak, and printed in the *Unification News*. An Associated Press photo shows a church member wearing a T-shirt in the "I Love New York" genre which declared: "I'm a Moonie and I Love It!"[75]

Like other minorities, Unification Church members are sometimes victims of racial and religious intolerance, and the term "Moonie" has sometimes been used as an epithet directed against them. Steve Hassan, a former church member who now counsels former cult members and their families, opposes "discrimination toward anyone who merely has different religious beliefs…I remember how I felt being spit upon, kicked, punched and verbally abused because I was a Moonie. Such treatment is always uncalled for, and only served to reinforce my feeling that I was being persecuted for my faith in God."[76] However, the cynical media blitz against *U.S. News & World*

Report, was not due to outrage over racial or religious bigotry in reporting, but an effort to intimidate the news media from probing more deeply into the dark side of the Moon organization.

Covert Theocratic Action

But the dark side has a way of leaking out anyway. A Christian Right activist named David Racer who worked for the Orwellianly named American Freedom Coalition during its start-up phase in 1987, later wrote a small book detailing the duplicitous Moon role in the AFC, which is essentially an organizational marriage between Christian Voice and CAUSA. Racer (who went on to manage Alan Keyes's unsuccessful campaign for the 1996 GOP presidential nomination) recognized that the AFC's ultimate purpose was to seek "totalitarian rule" under Sun Myung Moon, using the pseudo-patriotism of a crusade to "save America."[77]

In the course of this crusade, important experimentation in the political techniques that built what we now call the Christian Right were carried out by Moon-financed political operatives. Mass distribution of voter guides through churches and political networks was a technique largely developed by Christian Voice, which was founded by Rev. Bob Grant, Colonel V. Doner, and former Unification Church leader Gary Jarmin in 1976 in Pasadena, California. Their version of voter guides, called Biblical Scoreboards or "moral report cards," were credited with helping defeat a number of prominent incumbent Democratic senators and congressmen in 1978 and 1980. David Racer alleged that the Moon organization helped bankroll Christian Voice in the mid-1980s by purchasing "millions of these report cards over the years," and that these sales "amounted to millions of dollars" for Christian Voice. In 1988, following George Bush's defeat of Pat Robertson in the presidential primaries, AFC distributed millions of "presidential scoreboards" tilted to favor George Bush over Democrat Michael Dukakis.[78]

But Racer[79] and others note that Moon underwriting of Christian Right efforts often cannot stand the light of day. One major Christian Right/Republican initiative fell apart largely because the Moon organization's role was exposed by *Mother Jones* magazine.

The American Coalition for Traditional Values (ACTV)—originally created as a GOP front to mobilize white evangelicals on behalf of Ronald Reagan's 1984 election campaign—received a portion (along with Christian Voice and the Moral Majority) of $1 million from GOP fundraiser Joe Rogers and other Republican sources.[80] Colonel V. Doner, who chaired the Reagan/Bush re-election campaign's Christian "mobilization task force" was responsible, he later wrote, for "funding and co-publishing five million Presidential Biblical Scoreboard magazines,"[81] which were partly distributed by Christian Voice.

The White House had wanted to mobilize white southern evangelical voters in order to off-set the gains Rev. Jesse Jackson had made in his drive to register tens of thousands of southern blacks who would probably vote for Democratic presidential candidate Walter Mondale.[82] The Reagan White House was concerned that Reagan could lose some southern states. Headed by Rev. Tim LaHaye, ACTV included such Christian Right luminaries as Rev. Jerry Falwell, James Dobson, Rev. Don Wildmon, and Bill Bright of Campus Crusade for Christ, and appeared to have a solid future. But the revelation that top Moon aide Bo Hi Pak had apparently made a large contribution, and had been featured as a speaker at a major ACTV event in Washington[83], exacerbated other schisms and ACTV was disbanded in 1986.[84] LaHaye was damaged by the Moon connection and distanced himself from the Moon organization by resigning from the board of Christian Voice, and from the chairmanship of the Moon's Coalition for Religious Freedom. Rev. Robert Grant took over when LaHaye could no longer take the heat. It was an incestuous tangle. One of LaHaye's top field directors for ACTV had been Gary Jarmin, a "former" church member who remained deeply involved in Moon political work. (Jarmin and Grant later assumed the leadership of the AFC.)

ACTV was largely, and probably not coincidentally, comprised of the same group of television preachers and political operatives as Moon's Coalition for Religious Freedom,[85] Moon however, did not appear nearly as noble a victim to the constituents of the Christian Right as to their opportunistic leaders.

Although the AFC played a pivotal organizing role in helping build popular support for George Bush's war on Iraq in 1990, by 1992, the AFC had faded, and the Christian Coalition had emerged as the leading electoral entity of the Christian Right. In retrospect it appears that the AFC was an interim Christian Right political organization. Its predecessors, the Moral Majority, the ACTV, and Pat Robertson's Freedom Council all fell by the wayside. Christian Voice was never a mass-based organization. The Christian Coalition was not formed until 1989. For a brief moment, the central religious right organization in the United States was a front for the Unification Church of Sun Myung Moon.

The conservative movement has assisted in the legitimation and promotion of the Unification Church which in turn has served as a conveyor belt of conservative movement ideas through its organizations and its publications from the *Unification News* to the *Washington Times*. The efficacy of the strategy of mobilizing religious conservatives on behalf of the GOP as articulated by Colonel V. Doner, and developed by various religious right agencies since, is suggested in a major study by the Pew Research Center for the People & Press, which found that the percentage of white evangelical Protestants, among registered voters, rose from nineteen percent to twenty-five percent between 1987 and 1996. Over the same time span, the percentage identifying themselves as Republicans jumped from thirty-five to forty-one percent. Only thirty percent of all respondents in the 1996 study identified themselves as Republicans.[86] What is generally unremarked upon is the pivotal role of the Moon organization in the development and implementation of this strategy.

Free to Go In, Free to Go Out

Political alliances with the likes of George Bush, and the prominence of the *Washington Times* not withstanding, the "cult issue" remains the indelible image of the Moon organization for many Americans. The cult issue is also complicated and controversial in ways that conveniently divert attention from the business and political operations of the Moon organization.

Much has been written about the violation of the religious freedom of "new" or minority religions through "deprogramming," but curiously little has appeared about the violation of the religious rights of cult recruits and members by the cultic groups themselves. The individual rights of "conscience," are enshrined in constitutional law, and in the philosophies of the enlightenment that undergird modern understanding of religious rights.

Steve Hassan was Jewish when he was approached by recruiters for the Unification Church. He believes that his religious rights as a Jew were violated when Unification Church recruiters lied to him about their intentions. Hassan says that when he specifically asked if they represented a religious group, and if they were recruiting, they said that they were not. He says that the nutrition and sleep deprivation, the social isolation and other techniques of rendering individuals into states of vulnerability for purposes of indoctrination are an outrage. Hassan believes that people should be thoroughly informed regarding the process of recruitment, and that before one makes a lifetime commitment the organization has an obligation to "reveal all doctrines and goals." In the case of the Unification Church, for example, he believes prospective recruits should know that church leaders will select who they will marry, that he or she may be a perfect stranger, that the church will decide when the couple will be allowed to have sex, and that they may be separated by order of the church for years at a time.

Hassan says that the recruiting and indoctrination practices, or "heavenly deception" that made the church notorious in the 1970s continue today. One example, the story of how Cynthia Lilley's daughter Cathryn was induced into the church through its campus recruiting arm, CARP (Collegiate Association for the Research of Principles), was exposed on NBC's *Today Show*. Lilley subsequently wrote that Cathryn was made to "raise funds for long hours for the church," and that her daughter was "systemically trained to perceive me and the rest of her family as controlled by Satan, and she was kept from contacting us for months at a time."[87] After the *Today Show* piece focused national attention on the Lilley case, the church allowed Cathryn to visit her family, and she eventually decided to leave the church. Of course the church denies Lilley's version of events. Unfortunately, few families victimized by the tactics of the Unification Church have the *Today Show* or other powerful national media to serve as their personal consumer advocate.

Although they would certainly support the right to believe in the theocratic doctrine of the Unification Church and the right to join the church itself, the framers of the Constitution would have deplored the recruiting and indoctrination tactics used on Steve Hassan in the 1970s and Cathryn Lilley in the 1990s and many others in the short history of the church. What would be more problematic in the eyes of at least Madison and Jefferson, however, would be how the church and its apologists have hijacked the issue of religious freedom, and used it to serve their own totalitarian ends.

The framers might also take a dim view of the bogus history served up in their name. The *Unification News* for example, in October 1995, printed a piece by columnist Bradford Haven Gow, who claimed that Thomas Jefferson's phrase "separation of church and state" has been "terribly misused" by "groups like the American Civil Liberties Union, Americans United for Separation of Church and State, and the American Jewish Congress to grossly mislead the American people regarding the thinking of the Founding Fathers concerning the proper role of religion in public life." Gow claimed that Jefferson's phrase is "taken out of context" because "Jefferson quickly added that 'the wall is one directional. It keeps the government from running the church, but it makes sure that Christian principles will never be separated from the government."[88] Although this canard has circulated in the Christian Right for years, Jefferson's letter says nothing about a one directional wall, nor does it say anything about "Christian principles" in government.[89]

Invasive Procedures

Early in his career, James Madison wrote a political essay, *Memorial and Remonstrance against Religious Assessments*, a 1774 text which historians generally agree, was a key source of the First Amendment's establishment clause which bars the adoption of official religions. Although the essay was written to argue against a proposed tax to fund clergy in Virginia, it served as an opportunity to propound a broader philosophy of proper relationship between church and state. Madison also discussed a theme that is increasingly relevant to modern society—protection of the religious rights of individuals against "invasion" by other sects. Madison's conclusion was simple: the role of government should be "protecting every Citizen in the enjoyment of his Religion with the same equal hand which protects his person and his property; by neither invading the equal rights of any Sect, nor suffering any Sect to invade those of another."[90]

Towards the end of his life, Madison reaffirmed this view in a discussion of the proper relation between church and state observing that "The tendency to a usurpation on one side or the other, or to a corrupting coalition or alliance between them, will be best guarded against by an entire abstinence of the Government from interference in any way whatever, beyond the necessity of preserving public order, and protecting each sect against trespass on its legal rights by others."[91]

Although discussions such as these usually focus on how church and state ought not impede on the prerogatives of the other, Madison also clearly stressed that government should help to preserve religious rights not only against government interference but against other religious groups.

Steve Hassan has years of experience in assisting the victims of predatory recruiting and indoctrination practices of cultic groups like the Unification Church. He agrees with Madison that government ought to find a way to help protect the religious freedom of its citizens, although he is unsure how this should work and urges caution that any such policy not interfere with anyone's religious rights. Part of the problem of addressing the recruiting and indoctrination practices of "cults," according to Hassan, is that there are no generally agreed upon ethical standards for what constitutes fair recruitment. There are also no laws which attempt to distinguish the difference between evangelization and fraud. And nervous government officials are reluctant to be seen as persecuting religious groups of any sort.

This is particularly relevant because the advocates and defenders of "new religions" often ignore predatory recruiting and indoctrination practices that con people out of their own beliefs, and induce them to abandon their families without what, under other circumstances, would be described as informed consent. Small and misunderstood groups are sometimes subjected to religious bigotry, but this is not a justification for engaging in activities that are unethical, illegal, or in violation of the constitutional rights of adherents to other faiths. Americans should not ignore the anti-democratic views and activities of the Unification Church and its affiliates just because they enjoy some political cover from blinkered apologists for "new religions." Nor should we be impressed or distracted by the Moon organization's capacity to purchase the implied endorsement of opportunistic or corrupt politicians. Politicians who lend (or more accurately, rent) their prestige to the cultic and theocratic Unification Church should be held accountable.

Although this is not the place to discuss every aspect of the "cult" issue, it should be noted here that there are also many terminological issues around this word. This results in the kind of terminological gridlock, discussed in Chapter 1, that hobbles public discourse on this theocratic organization. There are many people who oppose use of the word "cult" as an unfair label on minority religions. While the term "cult" can be used in a way that is unfairly disparaging, it arguably also has legitimate descriptive meanings. Anti-cult experts define a cult not in terms of what it believes, but in terms of what it does in the area of deceptive recruitment and manipulative indoctrination practices such as food and sleep deprivation, and inducing people to secluded locations in which contact with family, friends and the outside world is impossible. In this sense, the Unification Church is a classic cult.

The Unification Church of Sun Myung Moon has been one of the principal beneficiaries of the "new religions" fan club due to the high profile of academic and legal disapproval of the practice of "deprogramming"—the involuntary dissuasion from one's beliefs, or involvement with a group. Although opposition to deprogramming has been largely framed in terms of violation of religious liberties, in fact people have also been deprogrammed or counseled out of political, business, and psychotherapy cults.

One does not have to endorse "deprogramming" to be concerned about the predatory recruiting and indoctrination practices of cultic groups. The problem does not necessarily define the solution. Thanks to the attorneys and spin doctors representing the Unification Church and others, the problem has been denied through conflation with this one uncommon and controversial solution. In fact, involuntary "deprogrammings" are rare, and deprogrammers are few. Yet the issue of deprogramming, like disapproval of the word "cult," has been used to obscure serious issues related to the Unification Church itself.

Steve Hassan, for five years a recruiter and supervisor of recruiters, says that he was taught that whenever doubt crept into his mind, it was actually Satan trying to get in, and he was taught "thought stopping techniques" to erase any doubts.

The deceitful and predatory practices of the Unification Church which result in young people turning their lives over to the church in as little as a weekend seminar, stand in contrast to the long-standing practices of monastic Catholic orders. The latter seek to fully educate would-be recruits in the nature of the life, *before* they enter into lives of total commitment.

Thomas Jefferson wrote that a church is a "voluntary society" of which a person "should be as free to go out as he was to come in."[92] However inducing people to secluded locations and willfully impairing critical faculties of recruits and members for purposes of indoctrination and continuation in membership, is a far cry from a Jeffersonian—or any other—definition of voluntary association.

Respect for religious freedom means respect for the integrity of the conscience of the individual. Groups that use deception and coercive forms of persuasion to induce people to abandon their own conscience and adopt the beliefs of another, certainly violate the the religious freedom of individuals, even if governments and cult apologists turn a blind eye to such abuses and the slow corrosion of this area of constitutional rights.

According to cult watchers, and former members, the Unification Church is just as deceptive and manipulative in its recruiting and indoctrination practices as ever. Religious freedom is not merely a doctrine for protection of minority religious groups against majority religions, but is the basis for respect and protection for the rights of the conscience of the individual against fraud and coercion from all sources.

The recruiting and indoctrination tactics of the Unification Church have more in common with the methods of professional confidence men than honest evangelists of any persuasion. If these methods were used to fleece people of their personal belongings, it would be a job for the fraud division of the police force. In fact, the church seems to be actively a part of just such schemes in Japan, where most of the money for its U.S. operations comes from.

It is not possible in this short essay to sort out all the complicated questions (that are far from settled) regarding cults. For example, what is the difference between a legitimate convert and one who has been victimized by deception and "mind control?" How does one distinguish between fraud, undue influence and evangelization techniques? And who is to judge?

The point here is that the internal totalitarianism of the Unification Church generally reflects its theocratic political ambitions. In order to begin to understand the Unification Church, it is necessary to appreciate its predatory recruiting practices, and its totalist culture as well as its theocratic political agenda. These issues are also essential to appreciating the breathtaking scale of the hypocrisy of the Christian Right and the Republican party in their long standing alliance with the Moon organization.

CHAPTER 4

Laying Down the (Biblical) Law

Reconstructionism by the Book

While Pat Robertson's Christian Coalition has received most of the credit for the strategic successes of the Christian Right to date, largely overlooked is a theological shift over the past three decades that has provided the ideological basis for this growing political movement. The catalyst for this shift is Christian Reconstructionism, arguably the driving ideology of the Christian Right today.[1]

The significance of the Reconstructionist movement is not in its numbers but in the power of its ideas and their surprisingly rapid acceptance. Many on the Christian Right are unaware that they hold Reconstructionist ideas. Many who are consciously influenced by Reconstructionism avoid the label because it is controversial, even in the evangelical community. This furtiveness masks a potent ideology.

Generally, Reconstructionism seeks to replace democracy with a theocracy that would govern by imposing their version of "Biblical Law." As incredible as it seems (and as will be detailed in the coming pages), democratic institutions such as labor unions, civil rights laws, and public schools would be on the short list for elimination. Women would be generally relegated to hearth and home. Men deemed insufficiently Christian would be denied citizenship, perhaps executed. So severe is this theocracy that capital punishment would extend beyond such crimes as kidnapping, rape, and murder to include, among other things, blasphemy, heresy, adultery and homosexuality. Who are these people and where did they come from?

Reconstructionism as a movement has grown out of the works of a small group of scholars working in the 1960s and 1970s to inform a wide swath of conservative Christian thought and action. One conservative Christian scholar notes that "The Reconstructionist movement has had substantial influence among... fundamentalists and evangelical Christians, especially among independent Baptist congregations and within smaller Reformed denominations...." He also notes the Reconstructionist influence among "charismatic Christians around the world" as well as "home schoolers, libertarians and the Religious Right."[2] While many Reconstructionist political positions are commonly held conservative views, what is significant is that Reconstructionists have created a comprehensive program, with biblical justifications for far-right political programs. Many post-WWII conservative and anti-communist activists were also conservative Christians. However the Reconstructionist movement calls on conservatives to be Christians first, and to build a church-based political movement from there.

For much of Reconstructionism's short history it has been an ideology in search of a constituency. But in recent years, its influence has grown far beyond the founders' expectations. As Reconstructionist author Gary North observes, "We once were shepherds without sheep. No longer."[3] In this chapter, the extraordinary goals of this movement will be detailed. Its influence will be traced in Chapter 5.

"Biblical Theocratic Republics"

Reconstructionism is a theology that arose out of conservative Presbyterianism, which asserts that contemporary application of the laws of Old Testament Israel is the basis for reconstructing society towards the Kingdom of God on earth.

Reconstructionism argues that the Bible is to be the governing text for all areas of life—such as government, education, and law—not merely for "social" or "moral" issues like pornography, homosexuality, and abortion. Reconstructionists have formulated a "Biblical worldview" and "Biblical principles" to govern and inform their lives and their politics.

Reconstructionist theologian David Chilton succinctly describes this view: "The Christian goal for the world is the universal development of Biblical theocratic republics, in which every area of life is redeemed and placed under the Lordship of Jesus Christ and the rule of God's Law." [4]

Reconstructionists believe that there are three main areas of governance: family, the church, and civil government. Under God's covenant, the nuclear family is the basic unit. The husband is the head of the family, and the wife and children are "in submission" to him. In turn, the husband "submits" to Jesus and to God's laws as detailed in the Old Testament. The church has its own ecclesiastical structure and governance. Civil government exists to implement God's laws. All three institutions are under Biblical law, the implementation of which is called "theonomy."

The original and defining text of Reconstructionism is *The Institutes of Biblical Law*, published in 1973 by Rousas John Rushdoony—an 800 page explanation of the Ten Commandments, the Biblical "case law" that derives from them, and their application today. "The only true order," writes Rushdoony, "is founded on Biblical Law. All law is religious in nature, and every non-Biblical law-order represents an anti-Christian religion."[5] In brief, he continues, "every law-order is a state of war against the enemies of that order, and all law is a form of warfare."[6] Gary North, Rushdoony's son-in-law, wrote an appendix to the *Institutes* on the subject of "Christian economics." It is a polemic which serves as a model for the application of "Biblical Principles" in society.

Rushdoony, and a younger theologian, Rev. Greg Bahnsen, were both students of theologian Cornelius Van Til, who taught at Westminster Theological Seminary in Philadelphia. Reconstructionists claim him as the father of their movement, although Van Til never became a Reconstructionist himself. According to Gary North, Van Til argued that "There is no philosophical strategy that has ever worked, except this one; to challenge the lost in terms of the revelation of God in His Bible... by what standard can man know anything truly? By the Bible and *only* by the Bible."[7] This idea that the only way to view reality is through the lens of a Biblical worldview is known as presuppositionalism. "He rejected neutrality in every area of life," writes North. "Van Til launched a revolution. It is this and *only* this that is the clearly new element in the Christian Reconstruction movement." North further says that Protestants of other traditions are adopting this kind of Bibliocentric world view, "and when they really do believe it," he notes, "they become the chief targets of Christian Reconstruction's recruiting program."[8]

North says that Van Til stopped short of proposing what a biblical society might look like or how to get there. That is where Reconstructionism begins. While Van Til states that man is not autonomous and that all rationality is inseparable from faith in God and the Bible, the Reconstructionists go further and set a course of world conquest or "dominion," claiming a biblically prophesied "inevitable victory."

Reconstructionists also believe that "the Christians" are the "new chosen people of God," commanded to do what "Adam in Eden and Israel in Canaan failed to do... create the society that God requires."[9] Jews, once the "chosen people," failed to live up to God's covenant and therefore are no longer God's chosen. Christians, of the correct sort, now are.

Rushdoony's *Institutes of Biblical Law* consciously echoes a major work of the Protestant Reformation, John Calvin's *Institutes of the Christian Religion*. In fact, Reconstructionists see themselves as the theological and political heirs of Calvin. The theocracy Calvin created in Geneva, Switzerland in the 1500s is one of the political models Reconstructionists look to, along with Old Testament Israel and the Calvinist Puritans of the Massachusetts Bay Colony.

The leading Reconstructionists include:

- R.J. Rushdoony, the patriarch of the clan at 80 years of age, has published over 30 books and is a longtime conservative movement leader serving on the Council for National Policy, as well as on the advisory board (with fellow Reconstructionist Gary North) of Howard Phillips' Conservative Caucus. He established the Chalcedon Foundation in 1965, in Vallecito, California, after having served as an Orthodox Presbyterian pastor and missionary. He is also an ideological guiding light of the far-right U.S. Taxpayers Party.

- Dr. Gary North heads the Institute for Christian Economics in Tyler, Texas. He is a prolific and gleefully acerbic writer and publisher known for his take-no-prisoners radical rhetoric. He once wrote that "Rushdoony is the Karl Marx of our movement. I am trying very hard to be the Engels."

- The late Dr. Greg Bahnsen was an ordained Orthodox Presbyterian minister and a leading Reconstructionist theologian. His major work, *Theonomy in Christian Ethics*, was a "bombshell in the evangelical theological community" because it argued that the Old Testament penal code—"every jot and tittle" should be applied today.

• Dr. Gary DeMar, who studied with Bahnsen at Reformed Theological Seminary in Jackson, Mississippi, is president of the Atlanta-based American Vision, an influential Reconstructionist publishing enterprise which publishes books primarily for Christian schools and home schools.

Happiness is a (Cheap) Execution

Epitomizing the Reconstructionist idea of biblical "warfare" is the centrality of capital punishment. Doctrinal leaders (notably Rushdoony, North, and Bahnsen) call for the death penalty for a wide range of crimes in addition to such contemporary capital crimes as rape, kidnapping and murder. Death is also the punishment for apostasy (abandonment of the faith), heresy, blasphemy, witchcraft, astrology, adultery, "sodomy or homosexuality," incest, striking a parent, incorrigible juvenile delinquency, and in the case of women, "unchastity before marriage."[10]

Rushdoony insists that Biblical law requires "death without mercy" for "idolatry." He notes, however, that the death penalty is not required for privately held beliefs (a policy which might be characterized as, if asked, don't tell). Death is intended for "attempts to subvert others and to subvert the social order by enticing others to idolatry." He calls idolatry "treason" against "the one true God."[11]

Gary North suggests that women who have had abortions should be publicly executed, "along with those who advised them to abort their children."[12] Rushdoony concludes: "God's government prevails, and His alternatives are clear-cut: either men and nations obey His laws, or God invokes the death penalty against them."[13]

Some Reconstructionists insist that "the death penalty is the maximum, not necessarily the mandatory penalty."[14] However, such judgments may depend less on biblical principles than on which factions gain power in the "Biblical republics." The potential for bloodthirsty episodes on the order of the Salem witch trials or the Inquisition is inadvertently revealed by Reconstructionist writer Rev. Ray Sutton of Tyler, Texas, who claims that biblical theocracies would be "happy" places to which people would flock because "capital punishment is one of the best evangelistic tools of a society."[15]

Just as Reconstructionists would adhere to biblical justifications for capital punishment, so would they adhere to biblically approved methods of execution—including burning (at the stake for example), stoning, hanging, and "the sword."[16] Gary North, the self-described economist of Reconstructionism, prefers stoning because, among other things, stones are cheap, plentiful, and convenient.[17] Punishments for non-capital crimes generally involve whipping, restitution in the form of indentured servitude, or slavery. Prisons would likely be only holding tanks, prior to the imposition of the actual sentence.

Reconstructionist sympathizers often flee the label because of the severe and unpopular nature of these views. Even those who would gladly assume the mantle of authority in the Christian Nation often waffle on the particulars, like the death penalty for sinners and unbelievers. Unflinching advocates, however insist upon consistency. Rev. Greg Bahnsen, in his book *By This Standard*, writes: "We... endorse the justice of God's penal code, if the Bible is to be the foundation of our Christian ethic."[18]

Gary DeMar, however, waffled to the *Atlanta Journal-Constitution*. "There is no push," he said, "to put laws on the books to put practicing homosexuals to death."[19] However in his book *Ruler of the Nations* he wrote that "The law that requires the death penalty for homosexual acts effectually drives the perversion of homosexuality underground, back into the closet..."[20] "The long term goal," he adds, should also be "the execution of abortionists and parents who hire them. If we argue that abortion is murder, then we must call for the death penalty."[21] DeMar claims that Christians "are not to impose a top-down tyranny to ram the Bible down people's throats." However, he insists, "we must elect public officials who say they will vote for Biblical laws."[22]

Another key doctrine is "covenantalism," the idea that biblical "covenants" exist between God and man, God and nations, God and families, and that they make up the binding, incorporating doctrine that makes sense of the world. Specifically, Reconstructionists identify a series of covenant structures that make a biblical blueprint for society's institutions. They further believe that God "judges" a whole society according to how it keeps covenantal laws. This is the theological origin behind the claim by some that AIDS is a "sign of God's judgment," to cite one example.

Some take this idea farther than others. Rev. Ray Sutton writes that "there is no such thing as a natural disaster. Nature is not neutral. Nothing takes place in nature by chance... Although we may not know the exact sin being judged," he declares, "what occurs results from God."[23]

The U.S. Constitution:
"A Legal Barrier to Christian Theocracy"

An essential component of the Reconstructionist worldview is a revisionist view of history called "Christian history," which holds that history is predestined from "creation" through the inevitable arrival of the Kingdom of God. Christian history is written by means of retroactively discerning "God's providence."

Most Reconstructionists, for example, argue that the U.S. is a "Christian Nation," and that they are the champions and heirs of the "original intentions of the Founding Fathers." While the notion of a "Christian Nation" is not unique to the Reconstructionists, this dual justification for their views, one religious, the other somehow constitutional, is the result of a form of historical revisionism that Rushdoony frankly calls "Christian revisionism."[24]

Christian revisionism is integral to the Christian Right's approach to politics and public policy. If one's political righteousness and sense of historical continuity are matters of faith, what appears as fact to everyone else becomes fiction before the compelling evidence of faith. Whatever does not fall neatly into a "Biblical worldview" becomes problematic, perhaps a delusion sent by Satan.

The invocation of the Bible and the Founding Fathers is a powerful ingredient in religious-nationalist demagoguery. However, among the stark flaws of Reconstructionist history is the way Christian revisionism distorts historical fact.

For example, by interpreting the framing of the Constitution as if it were a document inspired by and adhering to a Reconstructed version of Christianity, Reconstructionists avoid such inconvenient facts as Article VI of the Constitution. Most historians agree that Article VI, which states that public officials shall be "bound by oath or affirmation to support this Constitution; but no religious test shall ever be required as a qualification to any office or public trust under the United States," was a move toward the disestablishment of churches as official power brokers, and the establishment of the principles of religious pluralism and separation of church and state.

Rushdoony writes however, that "The Constitution was designed to perpetuate a Christian order," then asks rhetorically: "Why then is there, in the main, an absence of any reference to Christianity in the Constitution?" He argues that the purpose was to protect religion from the federal government, and to preserve "states rights."[25]

Such a view requires ignoring Article VI. Before 1787, most of the colonies and early states had required pledges of allegiance to Christianity, if not a particular sect, and that one be a member of the correct sect to vote or hold public office. Part of the struggle toward democracy at the time was the "disestablishment" of the state churches—the power structures of the local colonial theocracies. Thus the "religious test" was a significant philosophical matter. There was little debate over Article VI, which passed unanimously at the Constitutional Convention.[26] Most of the states soon followed the federal lead in bringing their legal codes into the constitutional framework. Delaware was the first, in 1792, to bring its laws into conformity with this constitutional provision.[27]

Gary DeMar, in his 1993 book *America's Christian History: The Untold Story,* also trips over Article VI. He quotes from colonial and state constitutions to prove they were "Christian" states. And of course, generally they were, until the framers of the Constitution set disestablishment irrevocably in motion. Yet DeMar tries to explain this away, claiming that Article VI merely banned "government mandated religious tests"—as if there were any other kind at issue. He later asserts that they did not intend disestablishment.[28]

By contrast, historian Garry Wills sees no mistake. The framers of the Constitution, he concludes, stitched together ideas from "constitutional monarchies, ancient republics, and modern leagues… but we (the U.S.) invented nothing, except disestablishment… No other government in the history of the world had launched itself without the help of officially recognized gods and their state connected ministers."[29] Similarly, historian Robert Rutland, of the University of Virginia, writes that the United States was founded "on purpose in the bright light of history. The mere existence of the nation," he observed, "was itself a kind of Declaration of Independence from the folk gods and religious and semi-religious myths that had always and everywhere surrounded governments and their rulers."[30]

Disestablishment was the clear and unambiguous choice of the framers of the Constitution, most of whom were serious Christians. They were also well aware of the history of religious persecution carried out in the name of Christianity. The Protestant Reformation had a horrific record of persecution and religious warfare long before it provided the basis for religious liberty. Rutland notes that one tenth of the population of Germany was killed during the Thirty Years War between 1616 and 1648, "the very time that the New England Puritans were settling in the New World in quest of their own religious liberty, and incidentally, their freedom to persecute in their own way."[31] Similarly, neo-conservative scholar Michael Novak observes that the authors of the Constitution "had learned from the bitter experience of the religious wars that they had to treat well the matter of religion. They had to do so in a practical way that would work."[32]

Even Gary North (who holds a Ph.D. in History) sees the connection between Article VI and disestablishment, and attacks Rushdoony's version of the "Christian" Constitution. North writes that "In his desire to make the case for Christian America, he (Rushdoony) closed his eyes to the judicial break from Christian America: the ratification of the Constitution." North says Rushdoony "pretends" that Article VI "does not say what it says, and does not mean what it has always meant: a legal barrier to Christian theocracy," leading "directly to the rise of religious pluralism."[33] "The long-term national goal," he concludes, "has to be the substitution of a Trinitarian national oath for the present prohibition against religious test oaths."[34]

Meanwhile, North believes that, as a matter of strategy, it may be worthwhile to temporarily advocate pluralism while plotting for the takeover.[35] North predicts that *"pluralism will be shot to pieces in an ideological (and perhaps even literal) crossfire,"* as "Christians" and "humanists" sharpen and harden their positions in "an escalating religious war"[36] (emphasis in the original). He notes that since it is legally possible for voters to amend the Constitution, it would be possible to limit citizenship to members of the correct sects— just as the Twenty-first Amendment ended prohibition, which had been enacted by the Eighteenth Amendment.

The "dilemma of democratic pluralism," North explains, is that the same constitutional doctrines that protect political and religious expressions also protect those who oppose pluralist, constitutional government, including "those who say that no one holding a rival view will be allowed to vote," once the Constitution is amended. North notes that convicted felons are denied the right to vote and that this should be done to "those who hold religious or ideological views that would threaten the very foundations of Christian Civilization."[37] North and his colleagues of course, do everything they can to exploit this "dilemma."

North's view that the Constitution was not intended to be a Christian document or to promote Christianity is, however, the exception on the Christian Right. The falsely nostalgic view of a Christian Constitution, somehow subverted by modernism and the Supreme Court, generally holds sway. Christian historical revisionism is the premise of much Christian Right political and historical literature. Revisionist works by Gary DeMar, among others, are being widely taught in Christian schools and home schools, which in turn inform the political understanding of the broader Christian Right and serve as a dangerously polarizing factor in contemporary politics.

Born-Again Birchers

As a movement primarily of ideas, Reconstructionism has no single denominational or institutional home. Nor is it totally defined by a single charismatic leader, nor even a single text. Rather, it is defined by a small group of scholars who are usually identified with Reformed or Orthodox Presbyterianism. The movement networks primarily through magazines, conferences, publishing houses, think tanks and bookstores. As a matter of strategy, it is self-consciously decentralized and publicity-shy.

Reconstructionist leaders seem to have two consistent characteristics: a background in conservative Presbyterianism, and connections to the John Birch Society (JBS).

In 1973, R.J. Rushdoony compared the structure of the JBS to the "early church." He wrote in *Institutes*: "The key to the John Birch Society's effectiveness has been a plan of operation which has a strong resemblance to the early church; have meetings, local 'lay' leaders, area supervisors or 'bishops.'"[38]

The JBS connection does not stop there. Reconstructionist literature can be found in JBS affiliated American Opinion bookstores. Indeed, the conspiracist views of Reconstructionist writers (focusing on the United Nations and the Council on Foreign Relations, among others) are consistent with those of the John Birch Society. A classic statement of the JBS worldview, *Call It Conspiracy*, by Larry Abraham, features a prologue and an epilogue by Gary North.[39] Former JBS chairman, the late Larry McDonald, may himself have been a Reconstructionist. Rev. Joseph Morecraft, (who presided at McDonald's funeral) has written that "Larry understood that when the authors of the U.S. Constitution spoke of law, they meant the law of God as revealed in the Bible. I have heard him say many times that we must refute humanistic, relativistic law with Biblical Law."[40] McDonald sent his children to the Fairfax Christian School, headed by Reconstructionist Robert Thoburn.[41]

As distinct from JBS beliefs, however, Reconstructionists emphasize the primacy of Christianity over politics. Gary North, for example, insists that it is the institution of the church to which loyalty and energy are owed, ahead of all else. (Rushdoony emphasizes the family.) In any case, Christians are called to Christianity first and foremost, and that Christianization should extend to all areas of life. Among the political implications of this 'Christianity first' position is that in the 1990s the JBS worldview is more persuasive to more people when packaged as a *Biblical* worldview. Jerry Sloan, author of a study of the Christian Right in California, has observed that the "John Birch Society didn't die, they were just born again."

"Only the Right Have Rights"

Reconstructionism's decentralist ideas have led to the creation of a network of churches across a number of denominations, all building for the Kingdom. One Reconstructionist pastor writes that "the leadership of the movement is now passing to hundreds of small local churches that are starting to grow, both numerically and theologically. Their people are being trained in the Reconstruction army. And at least in Presbyterian circles… we're Baptizing a whole generation of Gary Norths, R.J. Rushdoonys and David Chiltons."[42]

Part of the reason for this decentralism is that Reconstructionism cloaks its identity, as well as its activities, understanding the degree of opposition it provokes. For example, Gary North was caught donating Reconstructionist books (mostly his own) to university libraries under the pretense of being an anonymous alumnus.[43] What might seem like a small matter of shameless self-promotion—getting one's books into libraries, by hook or by crook—is actually part of the larger strategy of covert influence and legitimation.

Similarly, while claiming to be reformers, not revolutionaries, Reconstructionists recognize that the harsh theocracy they advocate is revolutionary indeed. Gary North warns against a "premature revolutionary situation," saying that the public must begin to accept "the judicially biding case laws of the Old Testament before we attempt to tear down institutions that still rely on natural law or public virtue. (I have in mind the U.S. Constitution.)"[44] Reconstructionists are aware that such ideas must be discreetly infused into their target constituency. The vague claim that God and Jesus want Christians to govern society is certainly more appealing than the bloodthirsty notion of "vengeance," or the overthrow of constitutional government.

The claim that they do not seek to impose a theocracy from the top down—waiting for a time when a majority will have converted and thus want to live under Biblical law—is consistent with Reconstructionists' decentralist and anti-state populism, which they often pass off as a form of libertarianism. Even so, there is an inevitable point when the "majority" would impose its will. North bluntly states that one of his first actions would be to "remove legal access to the franchise and to civil offices from those who refuse to become communicant members of Trinitarian churches."[45] Quick to condemn democracy as the idea that the law is whatever the majority says it is, North et al. would be quick to cynically utilize a similar "majority" for a permanent theocratic solution. In a claim that could change forever the meaning of "politically correct," Rushdoony envisions a society in which only "the right have rights."[46]

Epitomizing the way that Rushdoony's views are the measure by which many Christian Right leaders determine their own stances, Herb Titus, founding (and former) dean of Pat Robertson's Regent University Law School, says that he differs with Rushdoony over the "jurisdiction of the civil ruler" in capital cases. Titus says that God's covenant with all nations calls for the death penalty for kidnapping, rape and murder. But "with regard to other forms of death penalty there are differences of opinion among Christians. I do not happen to subscribe to Dr. Rushdoony's view with regard to the authority of the state with regard to say, adultery or committing homosexual behavior."[47] The "differences of opinion" to which Titus refers go to the heart of the matter. If the leading scholars of the Christian Right cannot agree among themselves as to what God's laws require, the nature of law and government depends entirely on who gains power, and is thus not "absolute," as leading demagogues of the Christian Right are fond of claiming.

The Long and Winding War for Control

No movement is monolithic, of course. One of the important variations within Reconstructionism is the matter of the timing of the Kingdom, as defined by when the Christians take power. For example, Rev. Everette Sileven of Houston, Missouri, thinks the Kingdom is long overdue. In 1987, Sileven predicted the crumbling of the economy, democracy, the judicial system and the IRS before 1992.[48] From this crisis, he believed the Kingdom would emerge. Rev. Sileven is best known for his battle with the state of Nebraska in the mid-1980s, when he refused to certify the teachers in his private Christian school as required by state law. His brand of Reconstructionism seems to have since drifted into the racist theology of "Christian Identity." Sileven gave a classic explanation of his Identity ideology to sociologist Sara Diamond in 1995. Diamond reported that, "He explained to me that the ten lost tribes of Israel… migrated and became the Anglo-Saxon people. That does not mean that the Anglo-Saxons are saved. But he said that 'in the Kingdom'—code for the theocracy his brand of Christians plans to establish one day—only people of the white race will hold leadership positions. He assured me that other races won't be killed but will be allowed to live 'in the Kingdom,' if they obey 'the Law.'"[49] This view is similar to a common Reconstructionist expression of how they would deal with people of other religions—anyone can live in the Kingdom as along as they follow its laws. Sileven's table at the "Christian patriot" conference, where Diamond heard him speak, was "stocked with tapes and pamphlets on the evils of 'race mixing.'"[50]

There is an important theological link between Reconstructionism and Christian Identity, a theology which informs much of the white supremacist movement in the U. S.—from the Aryan Nations to the Posse Comitatus. This link is embodied in a book published by Rushdoony titled *The Church Is Israel Now* by Charles D. Provan. This book is an argument that the Jews, the people of Old Testament Israel, engaged in "centuries of rebellion against God, culminating in their rejection of Jesus the Messiah." As a consequence, the special status of "Israel" is a matter of faith, and thus the "titles, attributes and blessings of Israel were transferred to all those who accept Jesus Christ as Lord and Savior, and to no one else, regardless of Abrahamic descent."[51] This is also a core notion of Christian Identity, that "the church" is Israel, and that certain select Christians are the "true Jews" or God's chosen people, hence their "identity." Although Identity believers share many of the same social views as the Christian Right—on abortion, homosexuality, and public education for example—they generally shun the fundamentalists, who in turn, view Identity as heresy.

David Chilton has a longer term vision than Sileven. He believes the Kingdom may not begin for 36,000 years.[52] Most Reconstructionists, however, would argue for the Kingdom breaking out in the next few generations, possibly even the next.

Rev. Charles McIlhenny, an anti-gay crusader and friend of Rushdoony, wrote in his book, *When the Wicked Seize a City*, that we are engaged in "a very long war for control of our culture," a war between "secular humanism, the religion of our dominant American culture, and orthodox Christianity." He believes that "Christianity will eventually win the world for Christ, and I don't believe there is any compromise possible in this war."[53]

McIlhenny, a Reconstructionist-oriented pastor of an Orthodox Presbyterian Church in San Francisco, believes not only that "the homosexual rights movement is God's judgment upon a fearful and ineffective Church which has not taken an active role in society," but that homosexuality is actually a "religion" that "clashes squarely and directly with the Scriptures of the Old and New Testament."[54] He further argues that "faith is totalitarian" in so far as it "encompasses a whole worldview and life view," and that "[t]he gay rights movement is as totalitarian in its belief as is Christianity."[55]

Of course homosexuality is not a religion, let alone "totalitarian." To most readers, it may seem to be stating the obvious to say that there are gay men and lesbians of all faiths and of all political persuasions—but in the "totalitarian" worldview of Rev. Charles McIlhenny, there is no room for such a possibility.

Reconstructionist educator Robert Thoburn also sees a totalitarian threat, but he sees the source as Unitarianism. "Unitarian theology results in totalitarian politics," he claims, because Unitarians do not believe in the Trinity, and emphasize "oneness and unity."[56]

A general outline of what the reconstructed "Kingdom," or confederation of biblical theocracies, would look like emerges from the large body of Reconstructionist literature. This society would feature a minimal national government whose main function would be defense by the armed forces. No social services would be provided outside the church which would be responsible for "health, education, and welfare." A radically unfettered capitalism (except in so far as it clashed with Biblical law) would prevail. Society would return to the gold or silver standard or abolish paper money altogether. The public schools would be abolished. Government functions, including taxation, would be primarily at the county level.

Women would be relegated to the home and home schools, and would be banned from government. Indeed, Joseph Morecraft states that the existence of women civil magistrates "is a sign of God's judgment on a culture."[57] Those qualified to vote or hold office would be limited to males from biblically correct churches.

Democratic values would be replaced by intolerance of many things. Rushdoony writes that "In the name of toleration, (in contemporary society) the believer is asked to associate on a common level of total acceptance with the atheist, the pervert, the criminal, and the adherents of other religions."[58] He also advocates various forms of discrimination in the service of anti-unionism: "an employer," he writes, "has a property right to prefer whom he will in terms of color, creed, race or national origin."[59]

Unsurprisingly, some critics discern coded forms of racism in Rusdoony's works. The Anti-Defamation League, for one, has documented Rushdoony's flirtation with Holocaust Revisionism.[60] However, as detailed by Project Tocsin in Sacramento, California, the code can be traced through the examples he uses to illustrate his points. For example, in his discussion of idolatry as a treasonous capital offense, he cites the efforts of world religious leaders to intervene on behalf of captured opponents of the white supremacist government of Rhodesia (now known as Zimbabwe). Rushdoony writes that they were seeking to "persuade Rhodesian authorities to set aside the death penalty for some murders on the claim that these were 'freedom fighters.'" Rushdoony believes that in doing so, these leaders, including Pope Paul and the Queen of England, "were defying and despising the law of God."[61]

Gary North and his colleague David Chilton zeroed in on an additional dimension of the psychology of Reconstructionism and its role in the Christian Right. They argue that "Power flows from faith in the inevitability of a cause" and in the "Christian world today, only the Calvinists possess this faith in the inevitability of Christ's cause." They cite, for example, Muslim beliefs in predestination in the 7th and 8th centuries as a crucial component in their ability to conquer "Northern Africa and even parts of Europe by means of the motivation which this doctrine provided." They also cite Marxists who have "relied on 'the inevitability of history' to undergird their arguments."[62] It is this transcendent notion of the inevitability of their *political* cause, that animates much of the contemporary Christian Right.

The Emerging "Nightmare Scenario"

The leaders of Reconstructionism see themselves as playing a critical role in the history of the church (and of the world)—salvaging Christianity from modern fundamentalism as well as theological liberalism. Because they are political activists, as well as orthodox Christians seeking to pick up where the Puritans left off, they have constructed a theology that provides the ideological direction for a new kind of conservatism. It is a formidable theology designed to take on all comers. In order to wage a battle for God's dominion over all aspects of society, they needed a comprehensive analysis, game plan, and justification. That is exactly what Reconstructionism provides to a wide range of evangelical and other would-be conservative Christians.

Howard Phillips, the founder of the U.S. Taxpayers Party, believes that Reconstructionism, as expressed by Rushdoony and

North, "provided [evangelical Christian] leaders with the intellectual self-confidence"[63] to become politically active. Additionally, many conservatives apparently felt that they had no positive program and had been left in the role of reactionaries—just saying no to modernism and liberalism. As Gary North likes to put it, "you can't fight something with nothing." Reconstructionism offers a platform that integrates the religious and the political.

Many other Christian Right thinkers and activists have also been significantly influenced by Reconstructionism: the late Francis Schaeffer,[64] whose book *A Christian Manifesto* was an influential call to evangelical political action that sold two million copies; John Whitehead, president of the Rutherford Institute, a Christian Right legal group; and Michael Farris, 1993 GOP candidate for Lt. Governor of Virginia, among others.

Francis Schaeffer is widely credited with providing the impetus for Protestant evangelical political action against abortion. Randall Terry has said, for example, that "You have to read Schaeffer's *Christian Manifesto* if you want to understand Operation Rescue."[65] Schaeffer, a longtime leader in Rev. Carl McIntire's splinter denomination, the Bible Presbyterian Church, was a reader of Reconstructionist literature but was reluctant to acknowledge its influence and rejected the modern application of Old Testament laws. [66] Schaeffer eventually split with McIntire and ended up in the Presbyterian Church in America (PCA).[67]

John Whitehead was a student and protégé of both Schaeffer and Rushdoony and credits them as the major influences on his thought.[68] The Rutherford Institute, named for 17th century Scottish minister Samuel Rutherford, is an influential Christian Right legal group with chapters throughout the U.S., and offices in a number of countries. Rutherford, whose book *Lex Rex* is *de rigueur* in theocratic circles, defied the King of England by proclaiming that God's laws were higher than those of the King and were to be followed if they conflicted with the King's laws. As he has grown in prominence, Whitehead has sought to disassociate himself from Reconstructionism. However, perhaps he doth protest too much. Whitehead's roots are certainly in Reconstructionism, even if his present beliefs are not. Rushdoony, who wrote the outline for Whitehead's first book (which Whitehead researched in Rushdoony's library),[69] introduced Whitehead at a May 1983 conference, calling him a man "chosen by God," and that consequently, "there is something very important in the ministry of John Whitehead." Rushdoony then spoke of *"our* plans, through Rutherford," which was founded the year before, in 1982, "to fight the battle against statism and the freedom of Christ's Kingdom."[70] Rushdoony and fellow Chalcedon director and funder Howard Ahmanson were among the seven founding directors of the Rutherford Institute.[71]

Prior to the founding of Rutherford, Rushdoony steered cases to Whitehead—including the 1979 case of Rev. Charles McIlhenny who was sued for firing his church organist because the organist was gay. McIlhenny reports not only that "our theological compatibility made for a good working relationship" but that Whitehead's courtroom victory "helped to nudge him closer to founding the Rutherford Institute."[72]

Whitehead also has a long trail of dominion-oriented political statements. He says, "The challenge of the Christian attorney…is to be a vocal, dynamic spokesman for the true legal profession—the one with Christ at its center—and to stop at nothing less than reclaiming the whole system." He also said that the public education system, including universities, "must be reinstilled with Christian theism." If there is no hope of such reforms, he says, "then Christians must remove their financial support from the system."[73] Whitehead also wrote a strong, favorable forward to Gary DeMar's 1987 book *Ruler of the Nations* (published as part of Gary North's Biblical Blueprints Series), in which Whitehead endorses the Reconstructionist view of "three types of government established by God—the family, the church, and civil government… under the ultimate authority of God."[74]

Nevertheless, Rutherford attorney Alexis I. Crow insisted to Skipp Porteous of the Institute for First Amendment Studies that "John Whitehead is not a Reconstructionist and he never has been."[75]

Michael Farris, as head of the Home School Legal Defense Association, former general counsel to Concerned Women for America, and Christian Coalition-backed but unsuccessful candidate for Lt. Governor of Virginia in 1993, is one of the most prominent Christian Right politicians in the U.S. Farris raises the matter of Reconstructionism, albeit somewhat obliquely in his 1992 book *Where Do I Draw the Line?*[76]

"[T]here are those," he writes, "who advocate the idea that America should enact the Old Testament law right down to the rules for conducting trials."

"I am not one of those people," he declares, "but I do believe the moral principles of God apply to every age. The principles of the Ten Commandments, for example, will forever be valid and should be honored in modern America."[77] However, epitomizing the stealth nature of the theological underpinnings of the Christian Right agenda, Farris also writes that "as a matter of strategy," it's good to conceal the biblical root of one's views and frame the issues in terms of "right and wrong."[78]

Farris also waxes nostalgic for the pre-Constitutional Protestant theocracies and invests them with the authority of the signers of the Constitution—even though religious tests for state and federal offices were banned by Article VI of the Constitution. "[T]he founders of this country believed that the principles of God's word should be used in our nation," according to Farris, an ordained Baptist minister and "constitutional lawyer."

"The laws of Massachusetts," he explains, "once proclaimed that 'The ordinances of Jesus Christ shall be enforced by the magistrate in every community.'"[79] Farris also wistfully notes that, "In order to hold office in Delaware, the state constitution of 1776 required the following oath: 'I_____ do profess faith in God the Father, and in Jesus Christ His only Son, and in the Holy Ghost, of God, blessed for evermore; and I do acknowledge the Holy Scripture in the Old and New Testament to be given by divine inspiration.' The founding fathers," he concludes approvingly, "employed the Word of God in the public arena."[80]

Although Farris glibly invokes the "founding fathers" as a kind of ancestral anchor for his contemporary views, he conveniently ignores the founders who unanimously passed the Constitutional proscription on religious tests, not to mention the state legislatures that ratified the Constitution.

Farris narrowly lost the lt. governorship, apparently due to controversy over his role in the Christian Right, while his running mate George Allen won the governor's office. Allen is a conservative, but not explicitly Christian Right. Nevertheless, Allen owed his nomination to the Farris forces, which controlled the Virginia GOP convention in 1993.[81] (This was reflected in his administration, which was populated with Christian Right activists, notably Kay Cole James, an anti-abortion leader, and former vice-president for public policy of the Family Research Council, who served as his Secretary of Health and Human Services and has since been appointed Dean of the Pat Robertson School of Government at Regent University.) Farris served as a co-chair (along with Larry Pratt and Don Wildmon) of Pat Buchanan's campaign for the 1996 Republican presidential nomination. Farris, who enjoys the support of the Virginia Beach-based Robertson empire, is likely to remain a force in Virginia politics.

Harvey Cox, a professor of Divinity at Harvard, acknowledged the centrality of Reconstructionism and dominion theology to the Christian Right in an important article in the November 1995 issue of the *Atlantic Monthly*: "The thought of Rushdoony's disciples gaining governmental power," Cox concluded, "qualifies as the real nightmare scenario presented by the religious right."[82]

CHAPTER 5

Theocrats in Action

From Theory to Practice

However alarming Reconstructionist ideology is, to what extent are its leaders succeeding in advancing their cause? One key step in a movement's development is healing the rifts that keep it splintered. The story of how those differences have been healed or papered over, and the complex strategy and multi-faceted fronts on which Reconstructionists are waging their battles contains important lessons for those who want to further defend and advance American democracy.

The theocratic movement, now advanced far beyond its early stages, is still evolving and growing in power. While the Christian Coalition has gotten most of the attention, the growth of Christian Reconstructionism and related movements has played a pivotal role in the emergence of the Christian Right as a political force. Reconstructionism has generally managed to fly under the radar of the mainstream media and the political community and thus its role is vastly under-appreciated.

The role of Reconstructionism is epitomized by the 1982 formation of the Coalition on Revival (COR), which has brokered a series of theological compromises among differing, competing factions and evangelical leaders. Founded and headed by Dr. Jay Grimstead, COR has sought in this way to forge a trans-denominational theology—a process that has included the creation of 17 "Worldview" documents, a Manifesto of the Christian Church, and a set of theological tenets called the 25 Articles. COR claimed that "112 national theologians and leaders working with 500 experts in those 17 different fields worked together in 17 committees."[1]

The leadership has included such Christian Right leaders as John Whitehead, Michael Farris, Randall Terry, Francis Schaeffer's son Franky, Don Wildmon of the American Family Association, Beverly LaHaye of Concerned Women for America, Connaught Marshner of the Free Congress Foundation, Houston GOP leader Dr.

Stephen Hotze, lobbyist Robert Dugan of the National Association of Evangelicals, former U.S. Representatives Bill Dannemeyer (R-CA) and Mark Siljander (R-MI), televangelists Tim LaHaye, Ron Haus, and D. James Kennedy. It has also included leading Reconstructionists R.J. Rushdoony, Gary North, Joseph Morecraft, David Chilton, Gary DeMar, Rus Walton of the Plymouth Rock Foundation, and Rev. Raymond Joseph of Southfield, Michigan.

A major focus has been to reconcile the two main evangelical eschatologies (end-times theologies). Most evangelicals in this century have been pre-millenialists, that is, Christians who believe it is not possible to reform this world until Jesus returns (the Second Coming), which will be followed by a 1000-year rule of Jesus and the Christians. The otherworldly orientation of pre-millennialism has tended to keep the majority of evangelicals on the political sidelines. The key episode in pre-millennial theology is an event called "the rapture" in which all the saved Christians, dead and alive, are brought up into the clouds with Jesus prior, during or after (depending on the school of theology) a period called "the tribulation." The rapture is ridiculed by Gary North as "God's great helicopter evacuation."

The minority post-millenialist/Reconstructionist camp generally believes it is necessary to build the Kingdom of God here and now, before the return of Jesus. Thus for post-millenialists, Jesus will return when the world has become perfectly Christian, the return crowning 1000 years of Christian rule. This eschatology urges political involvement towards Christian theocracy.

COR has sought to deter quarreling on matters of eschatology which once deeply divided the evangelical community. Instead, COR emphasizes building the Kingdom of God *in so far as it is possible* until Jesus returns. This neatly urges political involvement and action without anyone having to say how much can actually be accomplished. It reconciles the difference over eschatology that has divided evangelicals and opens the door to political involvement and action without requiring either of the two sides to abandon its eschatology. One critic astutely observed that COR avoids defining both the means and the ends of establishing the Kingdom and that COR's activities "seem to be devised to obtain if not the cooperation of the (pre-millenialist) dispensationalists, at least their neutrality."[2]

Grimstead is clear about the reason for setting aside theological differences in the interests of political unity. He seeks unity with "fundamentalist, evangelical, charismatic and Catholic Christians whose foundation is the Bible and the Lordship of Christ. We're going to bring America back to its biblical foundations."

Nevertheless, when journalists exposed the role of Reconstructionism in COR, Grimstead was compelled to explain to the members, many of whom were on the spot because of the controversies surrounding Reconstructionism in the evangelical community. "COR's goals, leadership and documents overlap so much with those of Christian Reconstruction that in the eyes of our enemies we... are a monolithic Reconstructionist movement," he wrote. "The fine technical distinctions we make between ourselves," he explained, "are meaningless to these enemies of Christ. To them, anyone who wants to rebuild our society upon Biblical Principles... is a Reconstructionist. So we must simply live with the Reconstructionist label, and be grateful to be in the company of brilliant scholars like Greg Bahnsen, Gary North and R.J. Rushdoony."

Grimstead can't help but acknowledge their significance to the Christian Right: "These men were rethinking the church's mission to the world and how to apply a Christian worldview to every area of life and thought 10 to 20 years before most of the rest of us had yet awakened from our slumbers. We owe them a great debt of gratitude for pioneering the way into Biblical world changing, even if we can't accept everything that they teach."[3]

Theological Mop-Up?

Grimstead's fig leafs not withstanding, a number of COR Steering Committee members have had to drop out because even mere association with Reconstructionism was too hotly controversial.[4] Among these were Don Wildmon, Robert Dugan, and Tim LaHaye. In an interview in January 1991, LaHaye explained that COR "is just too infiltrated by the Reconstructionists and the Kingdom Now people."[5]

One evangelical critic of COR was skeptical of the authenticity of such gestures. He observed that those who signed the COR documents had to be "willing to die in the attempt to establish a theonomic political state. This statement makes the COR

Manifesto-Covenant more than just a covenant; it is a blood covenant, sworn on the life of the signers."[6]

A key, if not exclusively Reconstructionist, doctrine uniting many evangelicals is the "dominion mandate," also called the "cultural mandate." This concept derives from the Book of Genesis and God's direction to "subdue" the earth and exercise "dominion" over it. While much of Reconstructionism, as one observer put it, "dies the death of a thousand qualifications,"[7] the commitment to dominion serves as a unifying principle while people debate the particulars.

Although this debate has raged in the evangelical community, it has been barely noticed elsewhere. The failure of mainline Christianity, the major political parties, the media, and progressive and mainstream interest groups to pay serious attention to important trends in the Christian Right has helped pave the way for their successes. It wasn't until 1995 that Reconstructionism finally emerged as a defining part of the discussion of the Christian Right in major articles in the *Atlantic Monthly* and *Mother Jones*.[8] By 1996, even Ralph Reed, executive director of the Christian Coalition, was compelled to discuss Reconstructionism in his book *Active Faith*—if only to try to distance the Republican wing of the Christian Right from the charge of being theocrats.[9] But Reed's public relations problem was closer to home than one would think from just reading his book. The Christian Coalition itself has direct links into Reconstructionism. The Coalition's membership tabloid, the *Christian American*, promoted and sold a book co-authored by Reconstructionist George Grant which advocated capital punishment for homosexuality.[10]

Characteristically, Gary North thinks it's too late for anyone to do anything to stop or slow down the Reconstructionist movement, and has declared victory. "Our ideas are now in wide circulation," he writes. "They no longer depend on the skills or integrity of any one person... We are a decentralized movement. We cannot be taken out by a successful attack on any one of our institutional strongholds or any one of our spokesmen. Our authors may come and go (and have), but our basic worldview is now complete. We have laid down the foundations of a paradigm shift."

"The main theological battle is already over," he declares. We are now in the 'mopping up' phase."[11]

Nevertheless, even North is on guard. For example, in a book designed to reply to evangelical critics of Reconstructionism, he and Gary DeMar felt compelled to hide their advocacy of capital punishments for religious and sexual crimes. This is a weak point, and they know it. They know that Reconstructionism will, as Ronald Reagan might have put it, be consigned to the dust bin of history if and when pluralist America comes to appreciate what the Reconstructionist and Christian Nationalist agenda will mean for them. Indeed, even Ronald and Nancy Reagan, who regularly consulted an astrologer while in the White House, would have been in big trouble in the little biblical tyrannies envisioned by the likes of Rushdoony, Gary North, and Randall Terry.

Healing the Rifts and Moving to Action

In the late 1970s the Christian Right had broken onto the national scene in the form of the Moral Majority and the high profile televangelists. However, they were generally unable to push through many of their public policy views.

Colonel V. Doner (his name, not his rank), a former top Christian Right strategist, described a two part solution to the early "failures of the Christian Right." The first, he said, is that "the Christian Right better be able to command complete and total loyalty and selfless dedication and sacrifice to its objectives on the part of its supporters." Second, Doner (a COR Steering Committee member) insisted on "an orthodox... Christian doctrine that clearly demands that all Christians be active...."[12]

Doner's "doctrine" was clearly Reconstructionism or some variant. The "total loyalty" he would require is expressed by a disturbing movement known as the "shepherding/discipleship" model of church growth and church organization. Shepherding is a highly authoritarian system of personal supervision by a hierarchy of elders or "shepherds." Over the years, this system has been fraught with abuses. Shepherds often control all one's important decisions, from choice of marriage partner and career to personal finances and, of course, politics. In an apparent slap at the shepherding controversy, Gary North wrote that: "Cults are marked by continual top-down monitoring; churches are marked by self-governance under God's law."[13]

In September 1987, COR chief Jay Grimstead and his pastor,

Mike Kiley, organized a meeting of evangelical pastors in Santa Clara county—the area around San Jose—in order to set up a "pastors committee" for long-range social and political takeover. Grimstead proposed a program to ground pastors in COR-approved theology and shepherding techniques over 18 months. They would then select six to twelve "elders, deacons, (or) staff" to become their personal disciples. When ready, they in turn would disciple other church members. Grimstead enthused that with 25 churches in a community so discipled, "we would create an army... of people who are ready to die for Jesus. And to die for your vision as a pastor."

Rev. Kiley described a discipleship program in which dissenters would be brought into obedience or expelled. He also said that when a city gathers enough disciples, "This is when Jay [Grimstead] comes in, because once we raise up people, many of them are called to areas of government... And we are able to filter them right into the right type of places because they've been well trained."

Grimstead explained that "several national groups of strategists are looking at 60 major cities" for long-term influence. This would include: "Replace[ment] of anti-biblical elected officials with biblically oriented candidates." "So," he concluded, "we are launching today... an experimental effort to get a model for how that is to be done."[14]

A part of this effort turned out to be running stealth candidates for office in Santa Clara county. One Grimstead-backed candidate won a city council seat in Gilroy, California in 1989.[15] By 1992, the Christian Right had successfully taken over the county Republican Central Committee.

One COR activist is Rev. Billy Falling, whose Christian Voters League in Escondido, California published a book in 1990 called *The Political Mission of the Church*. Thousands of copies of this popularization of Reconstructionist ideas were distributed in California, and nationally, through Citizens for Excellence in Education headed by Robert Simonds. Falling argues that "according to the Bible, legitimate civil government is the police department within the Kingdom of God on earth," and one of its functions is to impose "God's vengeance upon those who abandon God's laws of justice."

"Both Church and State" Falling continues, "are to be under subjection to the Word of God. This requires a political mission of the

Church."[16] Then-U.S. Rep. Bill Dannemeyer (R-CA), who wrote the introduction, ran unsuccessfully for the GOP nomination for the U.S. Senate, while Falling became a member of the California GOP State Committee.

Guns for Christ

In 1990, COR also created a political program and action arm called the National Coordinating Council (NCC) which advocated[17] abolition of the public schools, the IRS, and the Federal Reserve by the year 2000, and sought to Christianize all aspects of life from the arts and sciences to banking and the news media. The COR/NCC hoped to establish a "kingdom" counterculture of sorts, including a "Christian" court system. The NCC plan called for a grassroots effort to elect Christians of the correct sort to county boards of supervisors and sheriff's offices and, once in power, to establish county militias. In an interview Grimstead said that these militias were needed because the federal government cannot be trusted to defend the U.S. against an invasion from a future "Communist Mexico," which will "march across the Rio Grande."[18] He described a "Red Dawn scenario" (referring to the preposterous Reagan-era movie which depicted a Nicaraguan/Mexican invasion of the U.S.) in which the U.S. armed forces would refuse to defend the nation. Such a view does not suggest a civilian adjunct to the local sheriff (as some militia apologists say) but heavily armed military units. Among those listed as members of the NCC at the time were Falling, Dr. Robert Simonds, Gary DeMar, Joseph Morecraft, and Dr. Stephen Hotze. Grimstead identified Larry Pratt as the architect of the NCC's notion of the role of citizen militias.[19] Little noticed, Pratt has been the chief theoretician of the militia movement. In1983, he wrote that militias were necessary because "Anti-Christian governments such as we have in the United States cannot be counted on to keep the peace."[20]

Pratt is an important figure who is able to connect the Christian Right with the gun advocates and with the white supremacist movement.[21] He is an elder in the Harvester Presbyterian Church, a PCA church in Virginia,[22] and heads several related organizations including Gun Owners of America, its PAC, the GOA Political Victory Fund, and the Committee to Protect the Family Foundation.[23] The latter served as a fundraising arm and conduit for Operation Rescue at a time when Randall Terry was taking the group's finances "underground" to avoid court ordered fines and judgments.[24] Pratt plays a pivotal role in American politics. According to Leonard Zeskind, a prominent expert on white supremacist groups, "[He] has one foot in the political mainstream and the other in the fringe."[25] As previously noted, Pratt was propelled into national prominence during the 1996 GOP presidential primaries, when he was compelled to step aside as a national co-chair of Pat Buchanan's campaign because it was revealed that he had repeatedly spoken to gatherings of white supremacists.[26]

Pratt's notion of the significance of county level government is consistent with the views of R.J. Rushdoony, who claims that the Constitution made counties "the basic and determinative unit of American civil government" with the power to enforce local "religious laws" as well as "the two other great arms of civil power... the power to tax property, and second, criminal law."[27] The notion of county governments enforcing religious, civil and criminal law with county militias is a vision embraced by many in the far right.

Time to Party

There is a growing political expression of Reconstructionism in the U.S. Taxpayers Party, headed by longtime conservative activist Howard Phillips. The party also epitomizes a growing split in the Christian Right between the "pragmatists," such as Ralph Reed of the Christian Coalition, and the purists, as represented by Randall Terry and the USTP.

Founded in 1992, the party ran Phillips for president in 21 states. During the campaign he attacked the idea of public education because "inevitably government conveys anti-Christian premises about the nature of God and man." He therefore believes that this violates the establishment clause of the First Amendment to the Constitution. "Congress shall make no law respecting the establishment of a religion or prohibiting the free exercise thereof."[28] Much of Phillips' campaign in Iowa was devoted to gory anti-abortion ads on cable television. These ads included photos, names and addresses of doctors who perform abortions.

Although Phillips got few votes, the party successfully fused elements of the historic racist right (such as elements of the American Party of George Wallace and the former Populist Party of David Duke and Green Beret veteran Bo Gritz)[29] with the Reconstructionist movement and Operation Rescue. Rushdoony himself spoke at the party's founding convention in 1992, as well as at the 1996 presidential nominating convention. Phillips calls Rushdoony "my wise counselor."[30] Other Reconstructionists who figure prominently in the young party are Rus Walton, who chairs the party in New Hampshire; Joseph Morecraft, who chairs the party in Georgia; anti-abortion activist George Grant;[31] businessman Philip Elder of Kansas, who is a board member of American Vision; and Samuel Blumenfield, a homeschooling advocate, who is a staff writer for Rushdoony's *Chalcedon Report*. Randall Terry, who has worked hard to build the party over the past few years, actively campaigned for USTP-backed candidate for U.S. Senate Joe Slovenec in 1994. Slovenec, a former Operation Rescue leader, ran for the open seat of retiring U.S. Sen. Howard Metzenbaum, and received 15% of the vote.

Phillips himself appears to have flirted with, if not converted to, Reconstructionism many years before coming out in 1995. In the late 1970s, Phillips told author Alan Crawford that the only answer for America was "to resort to Biblical law."[32]

Phillips arranged for Gary North to speak at the first National Affairs Briefing in 1980, sponsored by The Religious Roundtable.[33] This event, a political watershed in the development of the Christian Right, was held in tandem with the 1980 GOP convention and was addressed by candidate Ronald Reagan and the major televangelists. North was struck by the theological significance of this event. He wrote: "Here was a startling sight to see: thousands of Christians, including pastors, who had believed all their lives in the imminent return of Christ, the rise of Satan's forces, and the inevitable failure of the church to convert the world, now standing up to cheer other pastors, who had also believed in this doctrine of earthly defeat all their lives, but who were proclaiming victory, in time and on earth."[34]

In 1989, Phillips authored a fundraising letter soliciting $1,000 donors for the Chalcedon Foundation in which he wrote "Each of us who has read the *The Institutes of Biblical Law*... has been uniquely privileged. God has blessed us with the opportunity for exposure to the insights and teachings of a great theologian and servant... I have no doubt that he will be ever after regarded as one of the most significant figures in the history of Christian thought and advocacy."[35]

In 1996, The Religious Roundtable once again hosted a National Affairs Briefing at which leading Christian Right figures and GOP presidential candidates spoke. Keynote speaker Howard Phillips declared, "Our goal shall be unequivocally to restore this once great nation of ours to its biblical premises."[36] Reconstructionists dominated the 1996 presidential nominating convention of USTP, which was held in the elite Hotel Del Coronado in San Diego. Party leaders had hoped to persuade GOP presidential aspirant Pat Buchanan to defect to USTP following the GOP convention in San Diego. But Buchanan stuck with the Grand Old Party, and USTP once again nominated Phillips for president, and former Regent University Law School dean, Herb Titus for vice president. The USTP was on the ballot in over 40 states in 1996, a quantum leap from 21 states only 4 years before.[37]

Shock Troops for Jesus

While the radical Reconstructionists are slowly emerging, their ideas continue to percolate in less obvious forms. Nowhere has the impact of Reconstructionism been more extensive than in Pentecostal and charismatic churches.

Pentecostals, best known for speaking in tongues and practicing faith healing and prophesy—known as "gifts of the spirit"—include televangelists Jimmy Swaggart and Oral Roberts. Charismatics are those who have been members of mainline Protestant or Catholic churches and have experienced the "gifts of the spirit" like Pentecostals. Among the well-known charismatics are Pat Robertson and Supreme Court Justice Clarence Thomas. Historically, Pentecostals have been generally apolitical, being classic pre-millenialists. However, since about 1980, dominion theology has slowly come to dominate the Pentecostal and charismatic communities. This is not an accident.

Reconstructionists have sought to graft their theology onto the experientially oriented, and often theologically amorphous, Pentecostal and charismatic traditions. Following a 1987 Reconstructionist/Pentecostal theological meeting, Joseph Morecraft exclaimed:

"God is blending Presbyterian theology with Charismatic zeal into a force that cannot be stopped!"[38] Gary North adds that this growing alliance has disturbed major elements of both pre-millenialism and Reformed Presbyterianism, and that "The critics worry about the fact that the Pentecostalism's infantry is being armed with Reconstructionism's field artillery."[39] North says the three major legs of the movement are "the Presbyterian oriented educators, the Baptist school headmasters and pastors, and the charismatic telecommunications system."[40]

The influence of Reconstructionism is far wider than is generally thought. Joseph Morecraft told journalist Bill Moyers in 1987, that "the groups we've touched" go far beyond anyone who would call themselves Reconstructionists—including Baptists, Methodists, Episcopalians and Catholics. "Denominational affiliation means very little in this whole movement today…our influence goes into many of the leading conservative organizations of the New right today…[and] it has become one of the most influential and one of the fastest growing movements in American Christendom."[41] Robert Billings, one of the founders of the Moral Majority and later a director of the Free Congress Foundation, has said that "if it weren't for [Rushdoony's] books, none of us would be here."[42]

The result has been that hundreds of thousands of Pentecostals and charismatic Christians, as well as many fundamentalist Baptists, have moved out of the apolitical camp. Many have thrown themselves into political work—not merely as voters, but as ideologically-driven activists, bringing a reconstructed "Biblical worldview" to bear on their area of activism. This has been one of the most significant changes in modern American politics and is epitomized by the role of Pat Robertson—mobilizing Pentecostals and charismatics into politics through his books, TV programs, Regent University, the 1988 presidential campaign, and his political organizations—first in The Freedom Council in the 1980s and now in the Christian Coalition.

One of the key events in the politicization of Pentecostalism was a massive rally on the mall in Washington, DC, called Washington for Jesus and organized by a Pentecostal pastor John Giminez of Virginia Beach, Virginia.[43] Billed as a "prayer rally" (primarily for Pentecostals and charismatics), controversy erupted when a political declaration which was to be released at the supposedly apolitical event leaked to the press. Drafted by rally leaders, including Pat Robertson, Bill Bright of Campus Crusade for Christ, and Demos Shakarian of the Full Gospel Businessmen's Fellowship International, the declaration claimed that "unbridled sexuality, humanism, and Satanism are taught [in the schools] at public expense" and "our currency has been debased... and our armed forces weakened." They called for "laws, statues, and ordinances that are in harmony with God's word." Some, seeking prayer, not politics, dropped out. In the name of unity, the declaration was dropped as well.

Nevertheless, Bill Bright called the event "the single most important day in the history of America since the signing of the Declaration of Independence." Rally coordinator Ted Pantaleo said "I think President Reagan was elected as a result of what happened up there." Hyperbole aside, the belief in the direct consequence of prayer as action is an important element of the psychology of the Christian Right.

"Man of God" in the White House?

Soon after the WFJ rally for "Godly government," the non-profit Freedom Council was organized.[44] Pantaleo, the founding director of The Freedom Council said in 1982 that they were organizing in every congressional district toward "a Christian president, and a Christian government." Robertson, provider of the "original vision" for the Freedom Council, also supplied the group with office space at his Christian Broadcasting Network (CBN), mailing lists and money.

U.S. News and World Report reported that "Robertson's Christian Broadcasting Network communications empire funneled $8.5 million in donations to his Freedom Council, a tax-exempt organization set up before the campaign to promote political education and participation by Christians. In fact, the Council concentrated its 'educational' work in key early voting states like Michigan and Iowa—where Robertson's campaign has subsequently done so well."

By the fall of 1987, the Internal Revenue Service and the press were probing for links between the Freedom Council and Robertson's undeclared candidacy. (Tax-exempt funds cannot be used to fund political campaigns.) That October, the Freedom Council shut down. (The results of the IRS investigation were never made public.)

Four months later, Giminez announced Washington For Jesus 1988 with Pantaleo as coordinator. Former Freedom Council officials later admitted that they fronted for the Robertson campaign. "The entire process was to create a launching pad for Pat Robertson's bid for the presidency," former Council executive director Dick Minard told NBC News.[45]

Still, Rev. Giminez insisted to a reporter that WFJ 1988 was not political—an earlier press release notwithstanding, in which Giminez had declared that WFJ was needed because "AIDS... abortion, the prayer ban in the public schools and a swing towards liberalism devoid of moral standards must be submitted to prayer and repentance to avoid Divine Judgment."

On July 6, 1986, the guest speaker at Rev. Giminez's church was top Robertson aide Jerry Curry. Following Curry's talk, the flamboyant Giminez leaped up and gave a fervent rendering of a vision he said God had given him of "the president of the United States, looking into the cameras and prophesying the Word of the Lord over the country and over the world."

"I believe with all my heart in this generation we are going to see the Man of God sitting in the White House," Giminez continued.

"We who are God's anointed," he concluded, "are beginning to realize that... you and I and the Church are the ones who are supposed to be in the positions of rulership."

Political Brush Fires

Reconstructionist strategists see opportunities to build influence through an activist response to crises in established institutions, from the public schools to democracy itself. This "decentralist" activism is not necessarily "independent" or "grassroots." Political brush fires can be set and are, in fact, "a fundamental tool of resistance" according to Gary North, " but it takes a combination of a centralized strategy, and local mobilization and execution."[46]

This is precisely what is being carried out by the Christian Right. From the lawsuits, brought by the Rutherford Institute and the American Center for Law and Justice, to stealth—and open—takeovers of school boards, the effort is to subvert the normal functioning of society in order to make room for the growth of theocratic evangelicalism.

The Christian Broadcasting Network (CBN) has an extraordinary capacity to magnify local battles and communicate them to a national audience. CBN and other politically oriented television ministries are a key component in increasing the impact of decentralized "brush fire wars," in which battles over abortion, pornography, zoning for Christian schools, etc., happen in many places at once to strain the system. "Without a means of publicizing a crisis," writes North, "few pastors would take a stand."

Unsurprisingly, Reconstructionism plays an important behind-the-scenes role in the multifaceted Christian Right empire of Pat Robertson. Although the Robertson organization denies a Reconstructionist orientation, it is doing exactly what Gary North describes. The Christian Coalition, for instance, follows a clearly decentralist political plan, directed and encouraged by highly centralized media, educational and political units.

The Christian Coalition, forged from Robertson's mailing lists and his 1988 presidential campaign, in a few years became the largest and most politically significant formation of the Christian Right. Its comprehensive, locally-focused efforts to take over the Republican party "from the bottom up" and to run "stealth" as well as open "Christian" candidates for public office have become a fixture of American political life.

Robertson himself seems to lack the long-term vision of Reconstructionist thinkers, but he is clearly driven by a short-term, militant "dominion" mandate. Historian Garry Wills found the dominionist doctrine clearly present in Pat Robertson's book, *The Secret Kingdom.*[47] Gary DeMar describes Robertson as an "operational Reconstructionist."[48]

Reconstructionist influences are evident at Robertson's Regent University. For example, texts by Rushdoony and North have been used in courses at the law school,[49] as well as in the Pat Robertson School of Government, where Reconstructionist Joseph Kickasola teaches.[50] The library has extensive holdings of Reconstructionist books and tapes.

According to the Regent University catalog, "The mission of the Robertson School of Government is to help restore a biblical foundation and renew the Christian witness in public affairs in the United States, and among the nations of the world."

The Holy Bankrollers

Meanwhile, the Reconstructionist movement has forged an ideology (and an accompanying political strategy) by which the Christian Right will continue to measure itself. Some embrace it completely; others reject it. As recently as a few years ago, most evangelicals viewed Reconstructionists as a band of theological misfits without a following. But Reconstructionism has come of age, along with the Christian Right political movement it engendered. Neither evangelicalism nor American politics will ever be the same.

Among those Reconstructionists who have achieved significant power and influence are two directors of R.J. Rushdoony's Chalcedon Foundation; philanthropist Howard Ahmanson (who has contributed over $700,000 to Chalcedon)[51] and political consultant Wayne C. Johnson, who epitomizes the current political strategy of the new Christian Right.

Heir to a large fortune, Howard Ahmanson, 46, is an important California power broker who has said, "My purpose is total integration of Biblical law into our lives."[52] He bankrolls Christian Right groups and political campaigns, largely through an unincorporated entity called the Fieldstead Company which has, for example, been a major contributor to Paul Weyrich's Free Congress Foundation.[53] Fieldstead has also co-published, with Crossway Press, a series of Reconstructionist-oriented books called *Turning Point: Christian Worldview Series*, which are widely available in Christian bookstores.

Ahmanson and his wife Roberta have spent millions of dollars supporting California political candidates, as well as supporting school voucher initiatives in Colorado and California.[54] He also teamed up with a small group of California businessmen, notably Rob Hurtt of Container Supply Corporation of Garden Grove, to form a series of political action committees. The direct donations from these PACs and the personal contributions of Ahmanson and Hurtt, coupled with those of other PACs to which the same group of businessmen substantially contributed, amounted to nearly $3 million to 19 right-wing candidates for the California State Senate and other conservative causes in 1992.[55] A dozen Christian Right-backed candidates won. Ahmanson himself is a member of the GOP state Central Committee, along with many other Christian Rightists, who have gained power by systematically taking over California GOP county committees.

The San Diego surprise of 1990 in many respects had its origins with Howard Ahmanson and his colleagues who, at the time, called themselves the Capitol Commonwealth Group (CCG), an unincorporated entity which served as a strategy group and a "conduit of funds for various candidates and causes."[56] In 1988, Ahmanson and company set out to recruit "like-minded" candidates for local offices and state offices in what has become a surge towards control of the California legislature

The CCG helped to bankroll the first big wave of conservative takeovers of county level GOP Central Committees in 1990. Included in this was the right-wing takeover of the San Diego County GOP Central Committee in June of 1990, which was the precursor to the November victory of 60 of the 90 Christian Right "stealth candidates" for local offices, in what has become known as the 1990 San Diego Surprise. The distribution of voter guides by the CCG-backed California Pro-Life PAC on the Sunday before the Tuesday election is generally credited as one of the decisive factors. The same tactic was used in the sleepy June 1990 GOP primary in which Christian Right stealth candidates for the county central committee were swept into office.

The GOP, which is contending for control of the State Senate, elected Rob Hurtt as minority leader in 1995, after only two years in office. Hurtt had picked up his seat in a 1993 special election. Soon thereafter he became chairman of the Republican campaign committee for the state legislature. Ahmanson and his colleagues had at that point helped elect one fourth of the 120 members of the Senate and Assembly. Rob Hurtt epitomizes the still emerging power of the Christian Right; according to the *Los Angeles Times* he "pumped more than $3 million in donations and loans into California politics since 1992, an unprecedented sum for one person in state races" ($1.2 million in 1994 alone).

Although Hurtt himself claims not to be a member of the Christian Right, he is certainly one of its political leaders and financial godfathers. In 1987, Hurtt and Ahmanson co-founded and co-funded the Capital Resource Institute (CRI), a Christian Right legislative think tank based in Sacramento, the state capital. Together they have funneled at least $1.5 million into CRI through 1995.[57] This represented 71% of the organization's annual budget. And since 1990, the pair have spent a combined $7.1 million on political campaigns in California, helping elect 26 of 41 Republicans to the assembly, and seven of 16 Republicans to the state senate.[58] Thus a longtime Reconstructionist leader and his ideological partner have become two of the most powerful power brokers in California politics.

Hurtt, who generally avoids public identification with the Christian Right, has contributed $1 million to CRI since it opened 1987.[59] Ahmanson has also been a major contributor.[60] CRI is one of over 30 state level public policy think tanks associated with James Dobson's Focus on the Family—to which Hurtt and Ahmanson contributed $250,000 and $279,000 respectively in the late 1980s. [61] Ahmanson and Hurtt have both also been major contributors to the Traditional Values Coalition—Lou Sheldon of the TVC calls Hurtt "our Daddy Warbucks,"[62] and $35,000 from Ahmanson financed the mailing of TVC voter guides to 8,000 churches in California in 1990 and 1992.[63]

The CRI also functions as a grassroots lobbying agency, helping establish Community Impact Committees in churches. As Jerry Sloan and Tracey Jefferys-Renault wrote in their ground-breaking 1994 study of the California Christian Right, "The CIC is a lay-led group working under the supervision of a pastor. Its goal is to keep informed about current issues and engage in grassroots lobbying… CRI's goal is to have one such committee in each Evangelical church." One seminar held at a Baptist church near Sacramento drew over 600 people.

CIC's stated goal, reported Sloan and Jefferys-Renault, "was for Christians to become what Focus on the Family calls 'The Gatekeepers.' Gatekeepers are described as the people who control politics, education, media, law, entertainment and so on. Whether you call it Biblical law or Gatekeepers," they concluded, "the idea is the same—this is Reconstructionist, theopolitical thought."[64]

Hurtt, formerly an apolitical but pro-choice businessman who took over his family's business, Container Supply Company, in 1982, was led into politics by none other than James Dobson.

Although Hurtt generally stays above the legislative fray, one of his legislative leaders is Sen. Ray Haynes, who received $512,000 for his 1994 campaign from Hurtt and a PAC led by Hurtt and Ahmanson.[65] Haynes led the (unsuccessful) 1995 fight to end state funding for abortion. Uncoincidentally, Hurtt believes that "abortion is murder," and like many other Christian Right leaders compares abortion as a constitutional and moral issue to slavery, only worse. "We were not killing people," declared Hurtt, "We were keeping them in bondage, and we fought [the Civil War] over that. Now," he continued, "we're not even willing to fight a war over life, the beginning of life."[66] During his first campaign he said that although Christianity isn't for everyone, he wishes that Biblical creationism were taught in the schools alongside evolution. "Evolution is a theory and there's some pretty big gaps, and it takes as much or more imagination to say that's the way we came about as with creationism," he told the *Los Angeles Times*.[67]

Meanwhile, Sen. Haynes has become a director of the conservative American Legislative Exchange Council, (ALEC) which generates model legislation for conservative state legislators. Ahmanson contributed $80,000 to ALEC in 1996. Some 35 bills designed by ALEC were introduced in the California legislature in 1996, many by Sen. Haynes himself. Thus, there is at least one other series of legislative proposals emanating from an Ahmanson-funded think tank and sponsored by politicians who owe their seats to Ahmanson and Hurtt.

One of the key operatives in the Reconstructionist march on the California state legislature has been Wayne C. Johnson—an architect of California's 1990 term limits initiative who has also managed campaigns of Ahmanson and Hurtt backed candidates.[68] The practical impact of term limits has been to remove the advantage of incumbency (both Democratic and Republican), a situation which the Christian Right is prepared to exploit, having created a disciplined voting bloc and having the resources to finance candidates.

At a Reconstructionist conference in 1983, Johnson outlined an early version of the strategy we see operating in California today. According to Johnson, the principal factor in determining victory in California state legislative races was incumbency, by a ratio of 35 to 1. The legislature at the time was dominated by Democrats and insufficiently conservative Republicans. The key for the Christian

Right was to be able to: 1) remove or minimize the advantage of incumbency, and 2) create a disciplined voting bloc from which to run candidates in Republican primaries—where voter turnout was low and scarce resources could be put to maximum effect. In the past few years, Christian Rightists have been able to do both. Thanks to Ahmanson and Hurtt and others, they now also have the financing to be competitive.

Since the mid-1970s, the Christian Right, under the tutelage of former John Birch Society organizer and then-State Senator H.L. Richardson,[69] has targeted open seats and would only finance challengers, not incumbents. By the early 1980s, Johnson had joined Richardson's staff, recommended by Rushdoony.[70] By 1983, they were able to increase the number of what Johnson called "reasonably decent guys" in the legislature from four to twenty-seven. At the Third Annual Northwest Conference for Reconstruction in 1983, Johnson stated that he believed they may achieve "political hegemony…in this generation."[71] In 1995 they were not far from that goal with virtual ties between the Republicans and the Democrats in both chambers and the Christian Right the dominant faction in the GOP. Although the Democrats regained both chambers in the wake of the Clinton landslide in in 1996, the struggle continues.

How to Create a Constitutional Crisis

If the Christian Right ever came to power it's anyone's guess what would actually occur, but an instructive example of what happens as theocratically-informed factions advance is Cobb County, Georgia where the powerful Cobb County Commission came under the control of the Christian Right. In the summer of 1993, homosexuality was denounced, arts funding cut off, and abortion services through the county public employee health plan banned, making national news.[72] The Commission's anti-gay stance led to a national boycott of Cobb, which among other things led to the elimination of Cobb from siting of Olympic events during the 1996 Summer Olympic Games in Atlanta.

Rev. Joseph Morecraft, whose politically active Reconstructionist Chalcedon Presbyterian Church is located near Marietta, Georgia, the Cobb County seat, was asked at the time where he saw Biblical law advancing, he cited "the county where I live," where "they passed a law... that homosexuals are not welcome in that county, because homosexuality was against the community standards. The next week," he continued, "they voted on whether or not they should use tax money of the county to support art—immoral, pornographic art, so they make the announcement, not only are we not going to use tax monies in this county to sponsor pornographic art, we're not going to use tax money to sponsor any art, because that's not the role of civil government. And last week," he concluded, "that no tax money in Cobb County will be spent on abortions."[73]

These are, however, but incremental steps towards Morecraft's vision of a society under Biblical law. Morecraft discussed with relish the police power of the state to persecute non-believers and the insufficiently orthodox. He described democracy as "mob rule," and stated that "the purpose of civil government" is to "terrorize evil doers... to be an avenger!" he shouted, "To bring down the wrath of God to bear on all those who practice evil!"

"And how do you terrorize an evil doer?" he asked. "You enforce Biblical law!...The purpose of government is to protect the church of Jesus Christ," and, "Nobody has the right to worship on this planet any other God than Jehovah. And therefore the state does not have the responsibility to defend anybody's pseudo right to worship an idol!"

"There ain't no such thing," as religious pluralism, he declared. Further, "There has never been such a condition in the history of mankind. There is no such place now. There never will be."[74]

Behind the headlines and the issue-specific activism and news coverage was a group of prominent Reconstructionists, according to a local civil rights research group, The Neighbors Network. Reconstructionists Ralph Barker and Gary DeMar of American Vision, had "been both active and influential in this dispute since the Resolution's inception...They have accomplished this while concealing the radical and extremist character of their broad agenda."[75] Media coverage of the controversy spotlighted Reconstructionism as a major issue for the first time in a major political battle.[76]

Gordon Wysong, the leader of the rightist faction on the Cobb County Commission—who says he's not religious himself—was a featured speaker at the annual fundraising banquet of American Vision in 1994. In his banquet speech, Wysong blasted homosexuals, exclaiming, "We should blame them for every social failure in America." He received a standing ovation. American Vision President Gary DeMar called him a "statesman."[77]

The keynote speaker was board member Dr. Stephen Hotze, who has written that to "solve our nation's social and moral problems, our government must enforce biblical law."[78] Hotze was, at the time, chairman of the Harris County (Houston) GOP, and remains prominent in Texas Republican politics.

In his speech, he called for destabilization of the federal government. "What we need in America today," Hotze declared, "is judges, we need mayors, we need governors who are willing to stand up to our Supreme Court, to our president and [apparently referring to abortion] say 'Not in our city.'" Hotze continued, "I am convinced if men of courage in positions of leadership... would stand, they would bring about a significant constitutional crisis." Hotze concluded, in the presence of a number of candidates for state, local and federal office, "We need to get men elected to do that."[79]

Accompanying American Vision's growth and significance is an escalation of its attacks on religious freedom. The fundraising banquet speaker for 1996 was televangelist D. James Kennedy. Just prior to Kennedy's appearance, DeMar declared that "God does not tolerate rival religions, and neither should we."[80]

The Party of Armed Resistance?

Meanwhile, Hotze is not alone in his ideas. Howard Phillips and Herb Titus, who both acknowledge the influence of Rushdoony,[81] sounded similar themes on the occasion of their nomination for the 1996 USTP ticket.

Phillips and Titus argued that *Roe v. Wade* and other Supreme Court decisions are unconstitutional and should be neither enforced nor obeyed. These decisions included overturning the "male only" admissions policy at the state sponsored Virginia Military Institute, and declaring unconstitutional Colorado's Amendment 2, which would have barred localities from enacting civil rights protections for gays and lesbians.

Titus said that if he and Phillips were elected they would appoint federal district attorneys who would prosecute abortion providers on murder charges. Although a candidate for president espousing such views may never be elected, similar opinions are beginning to enter higher levels of public discourse. Titus urged action against *Roe v. Wade* under a Calvinist notion called the doctrine of the lower civil magistrate.

Here is part of a colloquy between Titus and the author at the news conference following the acceptance speeches by Phillips and Titus:

Clarkson: Mr. Titus, in your presentation…(on the prosecution of abortion providers) you also invoked the doctrine of the lower magistrate, which, as I understand it, is also a justification and authority for rising up in armed insurrection against tyrannical states and unjust laws. Do you see any potential for use of the doctrine in that regard if there was federal resistance from various elements to refuse to disregard *Roe v. Wade* or perhaps other decisions?

Titus: What we are saying is that to deny to the people of America the right to bear arms, as established under the Second Amendment is to deny our heritage. It is to turn our backs on those who risked their lives, their fortunes and their honor, who signed the Declaration of Independence. You can read the Declaration of Independence and you will find the doctrine of the lower magistrate. That's the very foundation, it's the very legitimacy of this nation… The United States Supreme Court is running roughshod over the people's rights and over the Constitution and it needs to be checked constitutionally, by the president who has the authority under Article Two to do so.

Clarkson: And by lower magistrates?

Titus: Yes, and by lower magistrates because if an opinion is contrary to law, it does not deserve to be obeyed.

Although Phillips and Titus were careful not to directly invoke the militia, the role of the citizen militias movement was implicit in their views of the Second Amendment and its relevance to the party platform's notion that *Roe v. Wade* must be "resisted."[82] It was also present in the person of militia theorist Larry Pratt, who attended the entire convention, made several speeches, and sold his book from a table near the convention floor. On the first page he argues that county sheriffs and other state and local officials need armed militias "to resist any tyrannical act on the part of the federal government."[83] Pratt's book is co-published with the publishing house of anti-abortion and Tennessee USTP leader George Grant.

Public School:
Satan's Choice That Must Be Destroyed

Although the Reconstructionists are becoming bolder in their public pronouncements, it is in the next generation that most Reconstructionists hope to seize the future. "All long-term social change" declares Gary North, "comes from the successful efforts of one or another struggling organization to the minds of a hard core of future leaders, as well as the respect of a wider population."[84] The key to this, they believe, lies with the Christian school and the home schooling movement, both deeply influenced by Reconstructionism.

Unsurprisingly, Reconstructionists seek to abolish the public schools, which they see as a critical component in the promotion of a secular world view. It is this secular world view with which they declare themselves to be at war. "Until the vast majority of Christians pull their children out of the public schools," writes Gary North, "there will be no possibility of creating a theocratic republic."[85]

Across the country, parents and others are struggling to save school budgets from deep cuts. Often those arguing for the cuts cite the desire to eliminate waste as a key motivation. But behind the fiscal concerns voiced by some is the entirely different and unmentioned agenda of the Reconstructionists—an agenda which, if not dealt with directly by those fighting for schools, may continue to succeed through stealth. Among the top Reconstructionists in education politics is Robert Thoburn of Fairfax Christian School in Fairfax, Virginia, whose stated goal "is not to make the [public] schools better." Rather it is to "hamper them" and ultimately "to shut down the public schools."[86] His book, *The Children Trap*, published as part of Gary North's "Biblical Blueprints" series, is a widely-used sourcebook for Christian Right attacks on public education.[87] Thoburn urges Christians to pull their children out of public schools, run for school board, and seek to "cut off funding for public schools."[88] "Your goal" (once on the board) he declares, "must be to sink the ship." While not every conservative who runs for school board shares this goal, those who do will, as Thoburn advises, probably keep it to themselves.[89] Such disruptive tactics are consistent with North's notion of the "brushfire" strategy of destabilizing the normal functioning of society.

Thoburn's influence extends beyond his writings. He is also an activist who has helped establish hundreds of Christian schools, and the headmaster of Fairfax Christian School outside Washington, DC. His students have included the children of such top conservative leaders as Howard Phillips, Richard Viguerie, political strategist Morton Blackwell of The Leadership Institute, the late Rep. Larry McDonald (R-GA) and Rep. Phillip Crane (R-IL).[90]

Characteristic of the conspiracist/siege mentality that often characterizes Reconstructionist views on education, Larry Pratt, who has been a close ally of Thoburn in Virginia politics, wrote that "We are on the threshold of overt prohibitions against teaching Christianity. Already in the name of the non-Constitutional doctrine of 'separation of church and state' and 'academic freedom,' Christianity cannot be taught in public institutions."[91]

Joseph Morecraft, who also runs a school, said in 1987: "I believe the children in the Christian schools of America are the army that is going to take the future. Right now... the Christian Reconstructionist movement is made up of a few preachers, teachers, writers, scholars, publishing houses, editors of magazines, and it's growing quickly. But I expect a massive acceleration of this movement in about 25 or 30 years, when those kids who are now in Christian schools have graduated and taken their places in American society, and moved into places of influence and power."[92] Reflecting a similar outlook, Gary North explained how it is necessary to exploit "the doctrine of religious liberty to gain independence for Christian schools until we train up a generation of people who know that there is no religious neutrality... Then they will get busy in constructing a Bible-based social, political and religious order which finally denies the religious liberty of the enemies of God."[93]

The Christian "home schooling" movement is part of this longer-term revolutionary strategy of Reconstructionism. Home schooling advocate Christopher Klicka writes: "Sending our children to public school violates nearly every Biblical principle... It is tantamount to sending out children to be trained by the enemy." He claims that the public schools are Satan's choice.[94]

In the forward to Klicka's book, televangelist D. James Kennedy waxed nostalgic, in the fashion of many Christian Right leaders, for more theocratic times, noting that"from 1620 when the Pilgrims landed until 1837, virtually all education in this country was private and Christian."[95]

Klicka advocates religious self-segregation and advises Christians not to affiliate with non-Christian home schoolers in any way. "The differences I am talking about" he declares, "have resulted in wars and martyrdom in the not too distant past."[96] Klicka, who is an attorney with the Home School Legal Defense Association (headed by unsuccessful 1993 Virginia lt. gubernatorial candidate, Michael Farris), writes that "as an organization, and as individuals, we are committed to the cause of Christ and His Kingdom."[97]

One of the main home schooling curriculums is produced by Reconstructionist Paul Lindstrom, president of Christian Liberty Academy (CLA) in Arlington Heights, Illinois. CLA claims that it serves about 20,000 families. Lindstrom hosted a campaign rally for Howard Phillips at CLA in September, 1996. Phillips saw parents who homeschool their children as an important base for his campaign and for the longterm growth of the party.

Estimates of the number of home schooling families vary enormously. The U.S. Department of Education estimates that there are about 500,000, while home schooling advocates claim as many as 1.2 million.[98] Klicka estimates that 85-90% are doing so "based on their religious convictions." "In effect," he concludes, "these families are operating religious schools in their homes." Because of this, he argues that "home visitation" by public officials to assure that education is actually taking place is a violation of the establishment clause of the First Amendment.[99]

A fringe movement no longer, Christian home-schoolers are increasingly accepted at major colleges and universities, and are actively recruited by the arch-conservative Hillsdale College. Reflecting the role of the Christian Right at the GOP 1992 convention, the right to home school was enshrined in the Republican Party platform.

Thou Shalt Lie:
The Rationale for Stealth Theology and Politics

The stealth theology of Reconstructionism is also manifested in the politics of the Christian Right. Although much has been made of the "stealth tactics" of the Christian Coalition, many contemporary Christian Rightists have lowered their religious profile or gone undercover. In fact, these practices have been refined for years as Robert Thoburn's education strategy suggests. Gary North proposed stealth tactics more than a decade ago, urging "infiltration" of government to help "smooth the transition to Christian political leadership... Christians must begin to organize politically within the present party structure, and they must begin to infiltrate the existing institutional order."[100]

While stealth tactics may not be surprising in political life, it may seem strange coming from people who present themselves as adhering to a higher standard. However, R.J. Rushdoony provided the rationale in a 1959 discussion of the Biblical story of Rahab, who lied for and hid two Israelite spies and thus saved their lives. Rushdoony rationalizes the lies as having saved the lives of "godly men." He further argues that the Christian requirement to tell the truth under normal circumstances "does not apply to acts of war. Spying is legitimate, as are deceptive tactics in warfare."[101]

Rushdoony advocates the gradual conversion and replacement of existing laws with Biblical law, and generally advocates civil obedience and that truth be told in the normal functioning of society.[102] However, the story of Rahab becomes significant in light of others' belief in a contemporary religious war and the frequent uses of military metaphors to describe the activities of normal political contests. Rushdoony himself repeatedly says that other religions are by definition at war with Christianity. Gary North refers to Rahab as a "righteous revolutionary" against "Satan's kingdom."[103] Rushdoony's preference not withstanding, many others appear to have taken the notion of "warfare" literally and seriously (as we will see in Chapter 7), and are prepared to lie in many circumstances in order to accomplish "Godly," and revolutionary ends. Interestingly, Michael Farris invoked the Rahab rationale in defense of Oliver North, who was convicted of lying to Congress in connection with his Iran/Contra activities. (North's convictions were later overturned on a technicality.) "I don't want to be too glib about sin," declared Farris. "But motives count too." Farris explained that some Republicans felt that "what Ollie North did was basically the moral equivalent of what the spies and Rahab did in Jericho. Rahab lied to protect lives."[104]

Similar stealth tactics have epitomized the recent resurgence of the Christian Right as groups like Citizens for Excellence in Education and the Christian Coalition have quietly backed candidates who avoided running as overtly "Christian" candidates. The Christian Coalition actually proposed something similar to Gary North's notion of "infiltration" when its 1992 "County Action Plan" for Pennsylvania advised that "You should never mention the name Christian Coalition in Republican circles." "This way" continues the manual, " you get a copy of the local committee rules and a feel for who is in the current Republican Committee." The next step is to recruit conservative Christians to occupy vacant party posts or to run against moderates who "put the Republican party ahead of principle."[105]

Antonio Rivera, a New York Christian Coalition political advisor, suggested similar ideas in 1992. While urging that Christian Coalition members seek to place themselves in influential positions, he advised that "You keep your personal views to yourself until the Christian community is ready to rise up, and then wow! They're gonna be devastated."[106]

CHAPTER 6

The Devil in the Details

How the Christian Right's Vision of Political and Religious Opponents as Satanic May Lead to Religious Warfare

There has been much public discussion and scholarly hand-wringing about the mutual demonization by opposing sides in the so-called culture war. The loaded language, name calling, and "labeling" that drives the direct mail fundraising business and the "sound bites" on television greatly contribute to the corrosion of civil discourse. However, there is a dimension of the problem of demonization that is far more corrosive than direct mail hyperbole. Elements of the Christian Right believe that their opponents are often literally demonic. The worldview of many Christian Right leaders and their followers is, in fact, infused with demons and satanic agents.

Contending with a political movement that sees demons where others see citizens—a movement that characterizes religious, political and sexual diversity as demonic activity—is profoundly different than confronting mere political differences of opinion. If opponents are demons, then shooting people working in abortion clinics—or gays and lesbians—is not a matter of killing people, but ridding the world of evil. Moreover, it is likely that the trend towards seeing people as demons, not just different, fosters the growing view among the Christian Right that religious warfare is on the horizon, if not already underway.

The Gay Movement as the "Lie of Satan"

Rev. Charles McIlhenny of San Francisco, for example, is a leading anti-gay crusader, a friend of R.J. Rushdoony, and a pastor of an Orthodox Presbyterian Church. In his book, *When the Wicked Seize a City,* he tells of his life as an anti-gay activist in the most openly gay city in the world. McIlhenny concludes that "it is the law of God that must, and ultimately will prevail" against this "demonic trend."[1] He regards as "the lie of Satan" the claims of "the gay movement" that it only seeks "freedom of expression" and that they don't seek "to force themselves on anybody."[2] McIlhenny, who has suffered violent backlash for his views and activities, further writes, "As we see this kind of venomous hatred from gays, lesbians and witches, it becomes more and more obvious that this is not just a political issue, but a religious war. It is a clash between the forces of light and darkness."[3]

A similarly demagogic example is Baptist minister Rick Scarborough, who has mobilized his Pearland, Texas congregation into an electoral force that has taken many of the top offices in this Houston suburb. Scarborough believes that homosexuality is explicitly derived from "Satan," and that "[h]e is not going to stop until he is forced to stop." Satan is also "the father of the lie" of separation of church and state, according to Scarborough.

To battle these "lies", Scarborough has organized a Reconstructionist-oriented political organization called Vision America, whose vision is framed by a violent metaphor: to "cut off the head of the wicked giant" of secular humanism. In this regard, he denounces the "wicked secular humanist lie of feminism." Emblematic of his growing political influence, in 1995 Scarborough administered a "Christian oath of office" to freshman Member of Congress Steve Stockman (R-TX)—who later joined Scarborough's church.[4]

Many believe, like Rev. McIlhenny, that there is no compromise in the "religious war" with the forces of Satan, but that victory is inevitable, if only they persevere. This eternal work ethic of totalitarian Calvinism fuels the war of aggression against democracy and pluralism. Stopping abortion or returning gays and lesbians to the closet is not now, nor has it ever been the primary issue. Waging spiritual warfare against Satan's agents, while preparing for a larger physical showdown, is the actual backdrop to much of the culture war.

The Evil of Halloween

On one side of this "warfare" is Rev. Dick Bernal of Jubilee Christian Center—a megachurch in San Jose, California. Bernal, an activist in the theocratic Coalition on Revival, wages weirdly colorful "spiritual warfare" campaigns against Halloween because he believes it promotes "actual worship of the devil." In Bernal's war on the demons, "prayer warriors" have been dispatched to abortion clinics, New Age organizations, and even the offices of the *San Jose Mercury News*. Bernal was joined in 1990 in his crusade against the "demons" of Halloween by then up-and-coming televangelist Larry Lea, a protégé of faith healer Rev. Oral Roberts, who sometimes wore military fatigues while conducting "spiritual warfare." The *San Francisco Chronicle* reported that "According to Bernal, San Francisco is ruled by the Spirit of Perversion. Oakland is controlled by the Spirit of Murder. San Jose by the Spirit of Greed, Watsonville by the Spirit of Poverty, and Marin County by the New Age Spirit." Peter Wagner, a professor at the evangelical Fuller Theological Seminary in Pasadena, California, coordinates a "spiritual warfare network," which promotes ideas like Bernal's that "territorial spirits" rule certain places. "Satan can't be omnipresent," Wagner claims, "so he has to delegate this to a hierarchy of demons."[5]

Steve Baldwin, a Christian Right politician from El Cajon, California, epitomizes how the contemporary politics of demons plays out. In a demagogic speech during his campaign for the state legislature in 1991, Baldwin raised the specter of satanic forces in public life. "We now have official state witches in certain states," Baldwin claimed. "In Massachusetts we have an official state witch." He further claimed that "in the Air Force, there is an official Air Force witch," and that there are "classes taught in our state schools on witchcraft."[6] Baldwin was widely ridiculed when these claims were reported. He lost that race. However, he made it on the second try, and a combination of the GOP takeover of the state Assembly and the implementation of term limits led to his appointment to the chairmanship of the Education Committee.

Dupes of Satan

Meanwhile, Pat Robertson has long been a general on the front lines of political combat with the demons. At the first national strategy conference of his Christian Coalition in November 1991, Robertson warned his followers that they were arrayed against "satanic forces" and declared: "We are not just coming up against just human beings to beat them in elections. We're going to be coming up against spiritual warfare. And if we're not aware of what we're fighting, we'll lose."[7]

Similarly, Gary North and a colleague stressed in 1983 that in order to "conquer the whole world for Jesus Christ… Christians need an understanding of their God, His law, and their satanic opponents."[8]

Robertson and most others in the Christian Right believe that a Biblically prophesied end-times scenario is being played out, although people disagree about the details and the time frame. As the year 2000 draws near, the numerical and semantic coincidence of the "millennium," and the massive egos and opportunism of aging leaders like Pat Robertson (who has claimed that he will be alive to broadcast the Second Coming of Christ from the Mount of Olives) should combine into an extraordinary political environment. The stakes will not be limited to which social philosophies will prevail, but will include visions of the eternal history of God's Kingdom.

For his part, Robertson foresees a violent struggle with a satanic-backed "New World Order." During a prayer service at the head-quarters of his Christian Broadcasting Network, Robertson advised his followers not to fear the coming bloody battle, which will be simultaneously physical and supernatural. "God is going to give us tremendous protection," Robertson predicted. "He is not going to let us get hurt. If somebody's got a machine gun pointing at you, you can just walk right up to it, and it won't hurt you. If there's a fire burning right beside you, you can walk right through it. It's not going to burn you. We shouldn't fear for ourselves, for our lives. We shouldn't fear anything."[9]

In Pat Robertson's book, political opposition is by definition anti-Christian. In fact, in his book *The New World Order*, Robertson describes former presidents Jimmy Carter (a devout Baptist) and George Bush (Episcopal) as unwitting agents of Satan because they support the United Nations: "Indeed, it may well be that… Jimmy Carter, and George Bush, who sincerely want a larger community of nations living at peace in our world, are in reality unknowingly and unwittingly carrying out the mission and mouthing the phrases of a tightly knit cabal whose goal is nothing less than a new order for the human race under the domination of Lucifer and his followers."[10]

Similarly, Robertson sees academics who disagree with him politically as dupes of Satan, although he is less polite about it than when he spoke of the former presidents of the United States. Robertson predicts that his opponents will pay. "The silly so-called intellectuals of academia who are spouting their politically correct foolishness will find themselves considered first irrelevant and then expendable when the real power begins to operate."[11]

Such language is common among the most militant elements of the Christian Right. Randall Terry, the founder of Operation Rescue, has written regarding "Planned Parenthood, Queer Nation and their cohorts from hell," that "[w]e will not put the flawless, eternal Word of God on the same par with godless laws, or the ungodly lies of men and demons."[12] Fr. Paul Marx, the founder of Human Life International (a far-right Catholic group) has written that "After Satan, the principal author of the moral morass in our society today is Margaret Sanger."[13] Sanger, the founder of Planned Parenthood, was long dead when Marx wrote this. Fr. Marx's successor as president of HLI, Fr. Matthew Habiger, found similar evil in a contemporary series of United Nations conferences on Population and Development. Habiger denounced the "hellish forces that are trying to destroy the family" at a conference in Cairo, Egypt. "You don't have to be a prophet to discern the dark forces now at work in the world," he declared.[14]

Operation Rescue co-founder Rev. Joseph Foreman, a pastor in the PCA, denounces as "the doctrines of demons" anything short of all-out opposition to abortion. "Rescue," he writes, "is nothing more than orthodox Christianity transforming Christians in the arena of legalized child murder."[15] Foreman's explanation is a typical example of the integrated theocratic idea in which abortion is seen as a symptom and not the problem itself, and that deviations from Christian political as well as religious orthodoxies are demonic. "Power, when divorced from godly authority, becomes progressively demonic," Rushdoony wrote in *The Institutes of Biblical Law*.[16] Christian Right theorist Gary North sees a permanent religious war in which there is no possible reconciliation, and that "there can never be more than a truce or temporary cease fire...." "*This is a war for the hearts and minds of men,*" he concludes. "*It is also inevitably a war for the lawful control over all of mankind's institutions*" (emphases in the original).[17] Those who oppose the "legitimacy" of the biblical theocracy, according to North, "are affirming the validity of... some variation on the society of Satan."[18] This "political-theological war," he says, has been "going on throughout history."[19]

Religious Cleansing and Fumigation

The cultural base of the politics of demons pervades the charismatic evangelical community, as well as some Catholic congregations. While not all of this culture is explicitly theocratic in orientation, it is slowly being molded to conform to the long-range public policy objectives of the theocrats, which is to institute a Christian Nation, in which other religions are banned, and dissidents from the prevailing orthodoxy are prosecuted and possibly executed.

Since adherents of other religions are often considered by Christian Right leaders to be demonic, there would be many candidates for stoning or forms of mass execution. Pat Robertson complains, for example, that "[I]n Third World countries that practice idolatry, the idols are representatives of demonic power, and their worship often involves actual demon possession."[20] He also identifies the "satanic background of the New Age" religions and "the Buddha."[21]

As discussed in Chapter 2, Robertson has often said that everyone but Christians and Jews are not really qualified for public office. "If anybody understood what Hindus really believe," Robertson ominously declares, "there would be no doubt that they have no business administering government policies in a country that favors freedom and equality."[22] He also insists that "there is absolutely no way that government can operate successfully unless led by godly men and women operating under the laws of the God of Jacob."[23] He claims that Christians built the great institutions of the U.S., but that "the termites are in charge now," and that "the time has arrived for a godly fumigation."[24] The Anti-Defamation League (ADL) has denounced Robertson's profound religious bigotry: "Robertson's repeated references to America as a 'Christian nation' and to American governance as a 'Christian order' insults not merely Jews but all who value religious freedom."[25]

Robertson is not alone in his claims of the demon infestation of the world in the form of other religions. Dr. Lester Sumrall, a prominent author, educator and Pentecostal evangelist based in Indiana, devotes a whole textbook to the problems of demons. In *Demonology & Deliverance: Principalities & Powers,* Sumrall, like Robertson, claims that adherents of other religions are demons or demon influenced. [26] He complains for example, about people who have "curios from foreign lands" such as "idols of Buddha and Confucius" in their homes. "I don't believe they should be there," he explains. "They may not have hurt you yet, but I believe we should clean them out in Jesus' name." [27] What is disturbing about Dr. Sumrall, who epitomizes the pre-millennialist camp, is that his theology, like Pat Robertson's, is moving in a dominionist direction, and is focused on manifestations of demons. Sumrall, like Robertson, believes that the fast-approaching end times will include a "tribulation period of incalculable proportions," a "world of woe masterminded by Satan and his hosts." [28]

Sumrall specifically names contemporary manifestations of demons and evil spirits: Hinduism, Mormonism, Christian Science, Buddhism, Jehovah's Witnesses, Father Divine, Jeanne Dixon, drug pushers, horoscopes, good luck charms, and homosexuals.

Like Dick Bernal, Sumrall believes that certain cities are governed by evil spirits. He names Hollywood and New York City as dominated by evil spirits because "much of the filth on television comes from these two great centers." [29] He also cites the Biblical cities of Sodom and Gomorrah, where "the devil commanded supreme power," and "caused men to make love with men rather than with women," and that because "Sodomy became so dominant,... God was obliged to wipe that sinful city off the face of the earth." [30]

Sumrall believes Christians must take "dominion" over the world. "Dominion" he writes however, "implies action." [31] He specifically urges anyone who has a Ouija board at home "to take it out and burn it." If Ouija boards should be burned, what should be done about Mormons and homosexuals, which are of at least comparable concern to Dr. Sumrall? He does not specifically say, but his larger vision is ominously vague. "Demon power is a driving force" behind the "assault of Satan on the human family," he claims. And because time is short on the Biblical time clock, "Satan has unleashed his demon forces to do violence and to take peace from the earth." [32] In preparation for the coming battles, Sumrall urges resistance to evil sprits and satanic manifestations of all kinds. Chillingly he adds, however, that resistance to the devil "is a military action."[33]

Reflecting the widespread nature of such concerns, and the sense of urgency about it, evangelical Christian bookstores are loaded with books on "spiritual warfare"—including lots of fiction. Such books are marketing a philosophy which encourages the Christian Right constituency to see symptoms of demonic activity as opposed to simple religious or political differences among their fellow citizens, or just fellow human beings.

Satanic Conspiracy Nuts or Serious Threat to Democracy?

Significantly, conspiracy theory is integral to the demonology of the Christian Right. Reconstructionism plays a major role in packaging and promoting conspiracy as a matter of doctrine by providing a unifying framework for the many conspiracy theories that drive elements of the right. Gary North explains that, "There is one conspiracy, Satan's, and ultimately it must fail. Satan's supernatural conspiracy is *the* conspiracy; all other visible conspiracies are merely outworkings of this supernatural conspiracy."[34] Robertson makes a similar argument in *The New World Order.*

This conspiracist component of Reconstructionist thought is heavily populated with demonic agents. Rev. Charles McIlhenny explains, for example, that the gay rights movement "is simply one late 20th century event in a long history of little conspiracies down through the ages. We do believe in the grand overall conspiracy of Satan's attempt to destroy the people of God and His Church... but we believe in a much greater conspiracy and that is the triumph of the Kingdom of Jesus Christ, which has been placed over all the world now and forever."[35] Such views are utterly normal, according to Rushdoony. "The view of history as conspiracy..." he explains, "is a basic aspect of the perspective of orthodox Christianity."[36]

A conspiratorial view of history is also a consistent aspect of Christian Right ideology, and is often used to explain the failure of conservative Christian denominations with millennial ambitions to achieve or sustain political power. The blame for this is most often assigned to the Masons, particularly an 18th century Masonic group called the Illuminati, and ultimately to Satan.

Panicked Congregationalist clergy faced with disestablishment of state churches (and thus their political power) in the 18th and 19th centuries fanned the flames of anti-Masonic hatred with conspiracy theory.[37] One of the inheritors of this tradition is Gary North, who declared in 1991 that among the first steps that prospective theocratic churches should take is to "excommunicate anyone who remains a Mason... Churches must publicly break with this covenant with evil." "Bible-believing churches got us into this mess by refusing to cast out Freemasons beginning 250 years ago, [and this] ...led to the secularization of the republic." North adds that public schools "are based on the same theology that Masonry promotes: common ground ethics and government. Parents must break with the public schools as surely as churches must excommunicate Freemasons."[38] Meanwhile, an anti-Mason campaign in the 15-million-member Southern Baptist convention has been brewing for several years, led by Dr. James L. Holly of Beaumont, Texas, who casts himself as David fighting the Masonic Goliath. "I believe the philosophy and theology that underlies the Masonic Lodge is Luciferian. That is, satanic," Holly says. Holly wants to oust the million or more Masons from the largest Baptist denomination.[39] Similarly, throughout *The New World Order* Robertson refers to Freemasonry as a satanic conspiracy out to destroy Christianity and thwart Christian rule.

Robertson's conspiracism was well exemplified in one widely publicized episode. In 1992, there was a proposal on the ballot in Iowa to include an Equal Rights Amendment to the state constitution. In a fundraising letter, Robertson claimed that "radical feminists" have a "secret agenda" which "is nothing less than open war on the American family." Then came one of his most famous outbursts of religio-political hyperbole. "The feminist agenda is not about equal rights for women. It is about a socialist, anti-family political movement that encourages women to leave their husbands, kill their children, practice witchcraft, destroy capitalism, and become lesbians."[40] While fundraising letters are not always as representational of the thinking of the leaders of political organizations under whose signature they go out, this letter stands out as one which, in fact, is very much in character.

Exemplifying the political reach of conspiracism is Dr. Stanley Montieth, a member of the Christian Coalition, Coalition on Revival, and a star of the anti-gay propaganda film *The Gay Agenda*.[41] In his book *AIDS, The Unnecessary Epidemic: America Under Siege*, Montieth argues that AIDS is the result of a conspiracy of gays, humanists and other "sinister forces which work behind the scenes attempting to destroy our society."[42] Montieth and others in his movement often work side by side with parallel conspiracy theories. At a 1994 conference of Human Life International, he shared a book table with a book distributor who displayed books claiming to expose the Masonic conspiracy and crude works of anti-Semitism.[43] Dr. Montieth, who insists that he is not anti-Semitic, also chairs the health and human services committee of the California Republican Party.

One of the more disturbing elements is the degree of anti-Semitism present in conspiracy theories driving the millennial ideologies of the Christian Right. In a major, if belated review of *The New World Order* in the *New York Review of Books*, former conservative activist Michael Lind explained the links between Pat Robertson's satanic conspiracy theories, and the "underground literature of far-right populism that purports to interpret world history as dominated by Jews, Freemasons, and 'international bankers.'"

"Not since Father Coughlin or Henry Ford," Lind concludes, "has a prominent white American so boldly and unapologetically blamed the disasters of modern world history on the machinations of international high finance in general and on a few influential Jews in particular."[44]

The ADL concludes that *The New World Order* could be dismissed as largely "harmless kookery," except that Robertson "leads a major movement," and the book has appeared on the *New York Times* best seller list with a half million copies in print. "Robertson's philosophy, in this light, is not merely troubling—it's a national issue."[45]

When they are being particularly frank, Christian Right theorists tend to describe everything they oppose, or all who opposes them, as satanic. For example, R.J. Rushdoony writes of those who he sees as disconnected from Biblical law: "*all* sides of the humanistic spectrum are now, in principle, demonic; communists and conservatives, anarchists and socialists, fascists and republicans...."[46] (emphasis in the original). Of course, there are few beyond Rushdoony who are frank—or impolitic—enough to declare that biblically incorrect conservatives and Republicans may find themselves on the chopping block, or in the stoning circle, come the Biblical republic.

Moon's Demons

The theocratic Unification Church of Sun Myung Moon is also propelled by the politics of demons. In its indoctrination practices, new members are taught that Satan may be working through their own biological parents. Evil lurks everywhere outside the church.[47] In an interview, former church leader Steve Hassan explained that once in the church, recruits are taught that doubts or questions about faith in Moon are understood as satanic attacks, or evil spirits trying to get in. As discussed in chapter 3, he learned "thought stopping techniques" to keep out demonic presences. This had the effect of self-imposed totalitarian thought control. As a new member, he was taken to see the film *The Exorcist* (in which a girl is possessed by an evil spirit) and was told that this is what would happen to him if he ever left the church. Later, he was "repeatedly told horror stories" about deprogrammers, who were described as "Satan's elite soldiers committed to breaking people down and destroying their faith in God."[48]

In his book, *Combatting Cult Mind Control*, Hassan tells the horrifying story of how he considered killing his own father while being "deprogrammed." Hassan was a church leader who had gone home in a cast to recuperate after falling asleep at the wheel of a van full of church fundraisers in the 1970s. Hassan's father arranged for a group of people to talk with his son about his involvement in the church. He writes that he "knew" that the "deprogramming team had been sent directly by Satan. In my terror," he wrote, "their faces looked like images of demons. It was very surprising to me then, when they turned out to be warm and friendly." The discussions lasted the better part of a week. On the second day, Hassan writes that while driving down the Long Island Expressway, "my first impulse was to escape by reaching over and snapping my father's neck. I actually thought it was better to die or to kill than to leave the church."

On the fourth day, writes Hassan, the deprogrammers "discussed Hitler and the Nazi movement, comparing Moon and his philosophy of world theocracy to Hitler's global goals for German national socialism. At one point I remember saying, 'I don't care if Moon is like Hitler! I've chosen to follow him and I'll follow him 'til the very end!' When I heard myself say that, an eerie chill went down my spine. I quickly suppressed it." Eventually Hassan decided that he had been had, and left the church.[49]

The conditions that led Steve Hassan to see his parents as demons sent by Satan, are unfortunately not unique to the Unification Church.

From Guatemala to Lebanon: "Religious War" Is Not a Metaphor

One place where the politics of demons was played out in a particularly horrific fashion should serve as a warning. Guatemalan Gen. Efrain Rios Montt seized power in a 1982 military coup that was hailed at the time by U.S. evangelicals who were excited that one of their own (Rios Montt is a member of a U.S.-based Pentecostal sect) was now a head of state. What Pat Robertson refers to as the "enlightened leadership" of the Rios Montt regime,[50] lasted into 1983 when it fell to another military coup. Robertson was and remains a Rios Montt booster, despite, or perhaps because of Rios Montt's scorched earth counter-insurgency campaign that killed as many as 10,000 civilians. This genocidal campaign, ostensibly against a guerrilla insurgency, was often framed in religious terms, according to author Sara Diamond. This episode epitomizes the logical outcome of the politics of demons—what happens when religious intolerance is conflated with the political/military aims of state power. One pastor from Rios Montt's group, the U.S.-based Gospel Outreach, explained: "The Army does not massacre the Indians. It massacres demons, and the Indians are demon possessed; they are communists. We hold Brother Efrain Rios Montt like King David of the Old Testament. He is the King of the New Testament."[51] Gospel Outreach members also reportedly participated in the Montt regime's "espionage and torture-interrogation operations."

Since then Robertson has urged continual preparation for violence in a demon-infested world. The televangelist and power broker fears "the emergence of a New Age world religion," derived from the human potential movement, which he sees as "part of a continuum" which "leads straight to demonic power" and "in turn to a single source of evil identified by the Bible as Satan."[52]

Robertson has repeatedly predicted that the struggle, in which he sees himself engaged, for political control of the world will be violent. On one occasion he lumped together the ACLU, the National Council of Churches and the Communist Party, and declared that the "strategy against the American radical left should be the same as General Douglas MacArthur employed against the Japanese in the Pacific: Bypass their strongholds, then isolate them, bombard them, then blast the individuals out of their power bunkers with hand to hand combat... The battle to regain the soul of America won't be pleasant, but we will win it."[53] In 1992 Robertson wrote that he expected "physically bloody" confrontations in the efforts of "Christians" to win political power.[54]

"Violence is inevitable," he predicts, "it is going to be like Lebanon."[55] Robertson further predicts a "world horror" propelled by "demonic spirits" in which two billion people will die.[56] He is surprisingly frank in his writings, even while the Christian Coalition and Regent University are seeking a more mainstream face.

Meanwhile, the whipping up of fear and hatred of people because of their religious, sexual, or political orientation remains the stock-in-trade of many elements of the Christian Right. This powerful mix of belief in supernatural evil, and ascribing such evil in the form of demons to those with whom they disagree, almost inevitably leads to the kind of violence predicted by Robertson. The *Army of God Manual*, the underground handbook of anti-abortion violence, is a good example. The anonymously written text explains that "This is a manual for those who have come to understand that the battle against abortion is a battle not against flesh and blood, but against the devil and all the evil he can muster among flesh and blood to fight at his side. It is a How-To Manual of means to disrupt and ultimately destroy Satan's power to kill our children, God's children." The manual goes on to describe the U.S. as "a nation under the power of Evil—Satan, who prowls about the world seeking the ruin of the souls of mankind... a nation ruled by a godless civil authority that is dominated by humanism, moral nihilism, and new-age perversion of the high standards upon which a Godly society must be founded, if it is to endure."[57]

That violence would result from such views is unsurprising, and will be discussed in more detail in Chapter 7. Whether this violence emanates only from small bands of anti-abortion guerrilla warriors and militias, and sporadic hate crimes against gays and lesbians, or grows into full blown civil war will depend on whether those who are dedicated to a democratic, pluralist, and just society recognize the growing danger of the contemporary theocratic political movements in time.

CHAPTER 7

Bombings, Assassinations, and Theocratic Revolution

Vigilantes Enforce "God's Law"

Simply because some members of religious sects espouse violence doesn't mean that they will act upon it. Of course, it also doesn't mean that they won't. Similarly, a handful of violent incidents does not necessarily presage a wider "religious war." However, since there are people who not only espouse violence, but have been convicted of violent acts and are writing books and articles on the justifications for religious war, it is something to be taken seriously, even if skeptically, in light of the ongoing political violence in the U.S.

How big is this problem? There have been over 160 arsons and bombings at women's health centers in the U.S. over the past dozen years. (The phrase "abortion clinics," which is often used in this context, is inaccurate because many of the targeted clinics did not provide abortions.) Dramatic examples of this violence against clinics were the assassination of abortion provider Dr. John Britton and his unarmed escort James Barrett in Pensacola, Florida, and the arson which burned a Planned Parenthood family planning clinic to the ground in central Minnesota less than two weeks later. For 23 years, the clinic in Brainerd, a town of 12,000, served about 2,000 mostly low- and middle-income women every year and had never performed abortions. The clinic had been picketed occasionally, but had never before been the target of violence. In contrast, the Planned Parenthood clinic in St. Paul, the only one of 27 Planned Parenthood facilities in the state to provide abortions had, according to Executive Director Tom Webber, been hit by arson or bombings 13 times since 1977.[1]

Violence like this comes about not because of lone nuts or "extremists" but because of cold calculations arising from the theology of vigilantism; the justification for taking violent action is the enforcement of "God's laws." Such views cross denominations, and are adopted by both Protestants and Catholics. Some of them are rooted in Christian Reconstructionism.

The simplest expression of the theology of vigilantism is a slogan Operation Rescue has used from its earliest days: "If you believe that abortion is murder, then you must act like it's murder." The effort of religious leaders to get their followers to *believe* abortion is murder, then to call upon them to *act* like it's murder, is a transparent mobilization for vigilante action. Additionally, because abortion is not murder, but a legal medical procedure with specific constitutional protections, this appeal to religious zeal left the kinds of action required open-ended. They did not say that "If you believe abortion is murder, you must protest non-violently, and respect the civil and constitutional rights of doctors and patients."

Although the advocacy and practice of violence has created rifts in the Christian Right, there is a great deal of disingenuousness among some of the recently righteous opponents of violence. Most have turned a blind eye to nearly two decades of domestic terrorism, and some have tacitly encouraged it. Among the many proponents and practitioners of violence against women's health centers there are a few key theorists worthy of special attention, notably Michael Bray, Paul Hill and Michael Hirsh.

Murder, Militias. What's Next?

The first public proponent of the theology of vigilantism was Rev. Paul Hill, who would later act on his beliefs with the shotgun murder of a doctor and his escort, and the serious wounding of another escort. These acts, for which he now sits on death row, were preceded by over a year of media celebrity, beginning with the *Phil Donahue Show* in 1993, following the murder of abortion provider Dr. David Gunn in Pensacola, Florida by Michael Griffin. Hill argued that the act was a "justifiable" use of "lethal force" to protect unborn children. National anti-abortion leaders, such as Rev. Phillip "Flip" Benham of Operation Rescue, immediately claimed they had never heard of him, and blamed the media for giving him a platform. The pro-choice community was outraged that Hill was allowed to propound violence on national television, with the debate often framed between anti-abortion leaders who favored violence and those who didn't. But media critics Jeff Cohen and Norman Solomon argued that people with views like Hill's should not be banned from the airwaves. Instead, "their extremism ought to be exposed rather than indulged when they do speak on the air."[2]

It seems likely that Hill's emergence from obscurity was no accident. Hill was well known along the Gulf Coast as a public militant years before he emerged as the proponent of the notion of "defensive action." Hill attended Reformed Theological Seminary (RTS) in Jackson, Mississippi from which he was awarded a masters degree in 1983. Jackson anti-abortion activist Roy McMillan said that while Hill was in seminary, "What he did was to go to abortion clinics [to protest] which was a novel thing here then."[3]

In March 1993, Michael Griffin, a Pensacola, Florida anti-abortion activist, shot and killed Dr. David Gunn, an abortion provider who had been the subject of a "wanted poster" campaign throughout the South. The posters identified his usual weekly itinerary and other personal information. In the wake of the assassination, which made national news, Hill released a lengthy statement explaining why he felt Griffin's action was justifiable. This idea was clearly not novel to Hill, and he had obviously given it a great deal of thought. He called it "defensive action" on behalf of the unborn. Whatever one thinks of Hill, it is clear that he embodies the ideology of a growing movement.

Although this document was widely circulated, and Hill's shocking views justifying the murder of doctors were widely publicized, little noticed was his discussion of the possible need for theocratic revolution. He discussed (as do other Reconstructionists)[4] that one option for combatting abortion "is to take up arms in a defensive war under a lower magistrate." He advocates this in part because he believes God may punish the U.S. for its abortion policies, and therefore "Government leaders… have the God-given responsibility to resist our civil government that we may escape the wrath of God due to our country." Citing the "urgency of our cause, and the lack of any other justifiable course of action," he explained that it is "our duty to pursue a defensive war if possible." Such a "just war" would be "unwise" he wrote, "until there are enough men and resources available to offer a reasonable hope that the effort to overthrow the existing government will be successful."

It is in this context that Hill quotes from the Second Amendment to the U.S. Constitution, which he believes upholds not only the right to keep and bear arms, but the right to form militia groups to "defend the defenseless." He further explains that "One of the reasons we have the responsibility to keep and bear arms is so we may individually and corporately take all just action necessary to protect innocent life." In a chilling comparison, Hill explains that "thousands died" during the Civil War, "for a lesser cause"—the cause being the abolition of slavery.[5]

Hill's past was a prologue to his revolutionary views. He became a theonomist while attending RTS, and in less than a decade had become first an advocate, and then a vigilante enforcer of his view of God's laws. The late Reconstructionist theologian Greg Bahnsen had been a controversial figure at RTS just prior to Hill's arrival. Bahnsen's "bombshell" book *Theonomy in Christian Ethics* was published in 1977, and the theological controversy which ultimately led to his dismissal was still hot when Hill arrived on campus. According to Gary North, after three years Bahnsen left RTS "just as he came: fired with enthusiasm!"[6]

Hill pastored churches affiliated with the Presbyterian Church in America (PCA) and later an Orthodox Presbyterian Church (OPC) from 1984 through 1990. He reportedly gave up his ministerial credentials in the OPC in 1992. After leaving the pastorate, Hill became a car painter, and his wife, a certified public accountant, stayed home to home school their children. In the wake of the killing of Dr. Gunn, and Hill's assuming the mantle of spokesman for assassins, the PCA church he attended excommunicated him for his vigilante views.[7] Hill wrote that the Trinity Presbyterian Church directed him to cease his advocacy of violence, and that he was "formally tried and excommunicated for... non-compliance with their directive on May 10, 1993."[8] That summer, he participated in ten days of Operation Rescue demonstrations in Jackson, Mississippi.[9]

Greg Bahnsen, writing in 1990, rejected the idea that Reconstructionists "would condone vigilante justice or *ex post facto* enforcement of God's laws." Bahnsen also understood the risk of people doing just these things—although he was willing to gamble on his ideas of a Godly society. "I prefer imperfect efforts in society to use *God's righteous commandments* to the destructive... use of *fallen man's unrighteous ones*" (emphases in the original). He concludes that, "Even as an extreme an example as the Salem witch trials (where, once, twenty people died) would not be worthy to be compared to the one and a half million babies which are slaughtered by American humanism every year...."[10] Bahnsen's notion that "humanism" is somehow the prevailing religion or power in the United States is also advocated by much of the Christian Right. It is also the major straw man the Christian Right uses to attack society. R.J. Rushdoony wrote that "The real issue is not between church and state, but it is simply this: the state as a religious establishment has progressively disestablished Christianity as its law and foundation, and while professing neutrality, has in fact established humanism as the religion of the state."[11] What to do about the supposed religion of humanism is one of the major questions addressed by different factions of the Christian Right.[12]

Hill subsequently gathered about 35 signatories to a "Defensive Action" statement which was initiated in September 1993: "We the undersigned, declare the justice of taking all Godly action necessary to defend innocent human life, including the use of force. We proclaim that whatever force is legitimate to defend the life of a born child is legitimate to defend the life of an unborn child.

"We assert that if Michael Griffin did in fact kill David Gunn, his use of lethal force was justifiable provided it was carried out for the purpose of defending the lives of unborn children. Therefore he ought to be acquitted of the charges against him."[13]

Among those who signed at various times were Rev. Joe Foreman, a co-founder of Operation Rescue and Rev. Michael Bray, who rose to prominence through his association with Paul Hill, Rev. Matthew Trewhella of Missionaries to the Preborn (MPB), and Fr. David Trosch, a former Catholic priest from Mobile, Alabama.

Gary McCullough, a "media consultant" to Defensive Action during the Griffin trial, helped to found and is currently the director of Prisoners of Christ, a fundraising support group for people (and their families) convicted of anti-abortion related crimes, including arson, kidnapping and murder. Prisoners of Christ is a project of Missionaries to the Preborn, an Operation Rescue spin-off founded by Rev. Matthew Trewhella and Rev. Joe Foreman.[14]

The Vigilante's Lawyer
(A Proud Graduate of Regent University Law School)

Michael Hirsh was a rising star in the Robertson organization as a young lawyer working for the American Center for Law and Justice (ACLJ) when Paul Hill murdered two people, Dr. John Britton and his unarmed escort, and wounded another escort. Hirsh had been the Director of Operation Rescue in Atlanta, during the mass protests at the Democratic National Convention in Atlanta in 1988. During his tenure directing OR in Atlanta, he incurred a permanent injunction against blockading clinics and harassing patients. Reacting to the injunction at the time, Hirsh said "We are not bargaining with children's lives. I will comply with this judge's order only in so far as it is in compliance with the judge's [God's] order."[15]

Hirsh subsequently attended law school at Regent University in Virginia Beach, Virginia, from which he graduated in 1993. Regent U. is a graduate school whose founder and self-appointed "chancellor" is televangelist Pat Robertson. Originally the school was called CBN University, because of its affiliation with Robertson's Christian Broadcasting Network. In explaining the name change, Robertson implied that he is attempting to set up an interim government. A "regent" he explained, is one who "governs a kingdom in the absence of a sovereign." And Regent University trains students to rule until Jesus, the absent sovereign, returns. "One day, if we read the Bible correctly," he predicted, "we will rule and reign along with our sovereign Jesus Christ."[16]

The 1994-1996 Regent University catalog explains that the "law school curriculum rests upon an historical and biblical foundation which presupposes that God, the Creator of the universe, impressed upon His creation an objective legal order that man is bound to obey. The study of law, therefore, involves the discovery of the principles of law, the communication of those principles, and the application of them to all areas of life."[17]

Regent had a "provisional" accreditation with the American Bar Association for most of its existence, but did not achieve full accreditation until 1996.

Herb Titus, the dean of the law school at the time Hirsh attended, used the works of Rushdoony and North in his classes. While in law school, Michael Hirsh also worked for American Vision, a Reconstructionist think tank headed by Gary DeMar, and based in Atlanta. Like Reformed Theological Seminary, there was a range of views represented at Regent University among the faculty and student body—and Hirsh's were well known at the school.

At the time of the double murder, Hirsh and the ACLJ were representing Hill on charges of trespassing and violation of a noise ordinance (shouting at patients and staff at another clinic) two weeks before the murders took place.[18] Interestingly, John Whitehead of the Christian Right's Rutherford Institute, who insists that he "condemns violence," initially offered to represent Hill. "It surprises me a little bit," Whitehead observed, "how the pro-life movement runs for the hills on these things… He's a pro-lifer until he's been proven otherwise."[19] However, as events would demonstrate, public relations takes precedence over the presumption of innocence at Regent Law.

The Robertson organization, epitomizing the rest of the anti-abortion movement and the Christian Right generally, had tolerated, if not encouraged, violent views in their midst, while publicly advocating non-violent solutions.

Cover-up at Robertson Headquarters

The murders and Hill's arrest occurred on a Friday. On the following Monday the Robertson organization broke into full-scale PR retreat. First the ACLJ sought to terminate their representation of Hill on the misdemeanor charges (the judge later refused to allow the ACLJ to withdraw). Regent University did succeed in withdrawing 500 already printed copies of the *Regent University Law Review* from circulation (except for the ones that leaked to the press). The reason for the withdrawal was that the journal contained a now inconvenient 60 page article by Hirsh, based on his 1993 Regent University thesis,[20] arguing that the murder of Dr. Gunn was "consistent with Biblical Truth" and, under Florida law, justifiable if one "reasonably believes that such force is necessary to prevent the imminent death or great bodily harm to himself or another."[21] Hirsh wrote that the "presuppositions" he brings to any discussion "come from the Bible… it is impossible to fully consider this hypothetical defense of Michael Griffin without Scriptural support for the argument."[22]

At the time, the review's faculty advisor, Douglas H. Cook, said that Hirsh initiated the suppression of the piece because he was concerned that it might hurt his career.[23] However, Hirsh, and the *Law Review*'s editor Barbara J. Weiler, later gave a somewhat different account. They said that Hirsh's boss, ACLJ director Keith Fournier had threatened to fire him unless he got the article pulled. Hirsh told the *Virginian-Pilot* newspaper that he "decided to pull the article to try and protect Keith from charges of censorship." A few weeks later, Hirsh, under similar duress, was exiled to the ACLJ office in New Hope, Kentucky. He was eventually fired in October 1994, according to Fournier for "philosophical differences." When CBN spokesperson Gene Kapp was asked what the philosophical differences might have been, he said, "I think if you look at the content of the article, that's an indication."[24]

Apparently the usual disclaimer printed inside the *Review* was insufficient to distance the Robertson organization from responsibility for Hirsh's views: "Opinions expressed in any part of the *Regent University Law Review* are those of the individual contributors and do not necessarily reflect the policies and opinions of its editors or staff, Regent University School of Law, its administration and faculty, or Regent University."

Once on his own, Hirsh unsuccessfully sought to represent convicted clinic arsonist John Brockhoeft in negotiating the terms of his parole.[25] Most recently, Hirsh joined Hill's defense team, making arguments in the Florida Supreme Court that Hill's murder of Dr. Britton and his escort was "justifiable homicide"—a version of the "necessity defense." This was the first time such an argument was made in an American courtroom.[26]

Fournier's Red Herring

Fournier would later enter into another controversy about censorship in which his lack of commitment to the First Amendment was further exposed, along with his apparent disingenuousness on the subject of anti-abortion violence.

The May 1995 premier issue of *Culture Wars*, a conservative Catholic magazine published "in cooperation with the American Center for Law and Justice," featured an editorial by Fournier. Fournier had come to the ACLJ from the Franciscan University of Steubenville, Ohio, a center of the Catholic charismatic movement and anti-abortion activism. It is reportedly the only college in the country that offers a minor in "Human Life Studies." The far-right Human Life International (HLI)[27] helps bankroll a "Human Life International Chair" to teach pro-life and pro-family issues.[28]

Fournier's article, "Is Planned Parenthood Killing Abortionists?"[29] expressed his displeasure with an ad in the *New York Times* run by Planned Parenthood of New York City following the murders of clinic staff in Brookline, Massachusetts by John Salvi. The ad had criticized religious leaders who incite "terrorism and death." For this, Fournier accused Planned Parenthood of "censorship."

"I have frequently and consistently," wrote Fournier, "joined my voice to the majority of pro-life voices condemning the use of violence in the name of the prolife cause...These kinds of crimes are a threat to the civil order. Intentional killing is simply not prolife." Fournier insists, however, that the "unchangeable" teaching of his church is "crystal clear: 'a Human life must be respected and protected absolutely from the moment of conception.'"

He wrote that he has a right to the "free exercise" of his Catholicism "in spite of Planned Parenthood's opposition." Of course Planned Parenthood did not oppose Fournier's right to exercise his religious faith. Rather the ad simply criticized the inflammatory views of anti-abortion leaders that Planned Parenthood believed contribute to violence.

While Planned Parenthood's expression of its own first amendment rights can hardly be construed as "censorship," Fournier cloaks a threat within his complaint. He predicted that "The more Planned Parenthood succeeds in censoring the public debate over abortion, the more abortionists are going to die." "The truth about the moral law cannot be suppressed," he declares. "Once a certain element in our society feels that there is no recourse under the law, they will act outside the law." Fournier did not identify that element, although it has been active for nearly two decades, long before legislation and court-ordered injunctions against various forms of clinic blockades and other harassment were necessary to protect people exercising other constitutional rights.

Fournier's red herring is an understandable diversion, since it was the ACLJ's client, Paul Hill, who publicly advocated and ultimately committed murder. The ACLJ also employed Michael Hirsh until

his views—unpopular, but also protected by the First Amendment—
became a public relations problem for Fournier and *his* boss, Pat
Robertson.

Leading institutions of the Christian Right counter-culture,
Reformed Theological Seminary and Regent University have, perhaps inadvertently, produced nationally significant theorists (and at
least one practitioner) of vigilante violence. There may be many
more whose vigilante views were nurtured in these institutions. There
are undoubtedly many more who have been similarly influenced by
their views, and may be organizing for violent action.

John Salvi and the Moral Duty to Act

Michael Hirsh dedicated his suppressed *Regent University Law
Review* article, "Use of Force in Defense of Another: An Argument
for Michael Griffin," to Michael Bray, "Defender of the Unborn, Soldier of the Cross, Hero of the Faith."[30]

Bray, who describes himself as a "Reconstructionist,"[31] is a close
friend of Paul Hill. In the 1980s Bray was convicted, and served 46
months in federal prison for conspiring (scouting the facilities and
helping to plan) to bomb seven women's health centers, as well as
the Washington office of the American Civil Liberties Union,[32] and
the Washington office of the National Abortion Federation.[33] After
serving his time, he published a paper (in 1990) that was a milestone
in the evolution of the theology of vigilantism. In "The Ethics of
Operation Rescue" Bray argued that "Christians who rescue inno-
cents from child slaughter houses are simply extending mercy."[34]

Once Bray determined that OR's illegal and often violent inter-
ventions were theologically justified and necessary as a means of
preventing the "deaths of the unborn," the gears of vigilante logic
were set in motion to endorse violence and murder. Although he had
not yet endorsed vigilante murder in his widely circulated 1990
paper, he did offer a Reconstructionist justification for revolution
under "lesser magistrates" (meaning, "mayors, county executives,
governors") in order to "resist the tyranny of the federal government." Bray saw this as "one of the great political potentials of the
Rescue Movement."[35]

This was just the beginning, however. Following the murder of
Dr. Gunn in 1993, Bray felt that a more thorough examination of

the subject was needed in order to answer "the mindless condemnation of what seemed to be a rational way of following the Operation Rescue dictum: 'If you believe abortion is murder, then act like it.' And so," Bray and his colleague Mike Colvin concluded, "we propose A TIME TO KILL (or some such title) to answer the need for such an investigation."[36] When Bray published this book in 1994, he acknowledged that a section which included his lay legal argument was based in part on Michael Hirsh's Regent University thesis.[37]

Bray also criticizes such fellow Reconstructionists as former *Washington Times* columnist John Lofton and R. J. Rushdoony himself for opposing anti-abortion violence in all of its forms—from clinic blockades to "assassination."[38]

Bray explicitly supports "the principle of revolution and the goal of establishing or preserving a Christian government." "What are patriots to do?" he asks. "Revolution may well be justified in our time of legalized sodomy, and national apostasy (in the name of 'separation of church and state') and taxation to support child slaughter."[39] He does not, however, believe that revolution is currently possible because "American Christians are too morally apathetic to carry out such an enterprise at this time."[40]

Apparently out of respect for one who Bray felt was not apathetic, he named one of his children "Beseda"—after the unrepentant clinic arsonist Curt Beseda. Prior to his sentencing, Beseda underscored his lack of remorse in an article in *USA Today*: "It's Not Terrorism to Stop the Slaughter."[41] The judge gave him twenty years.

During the heady early days of Operation Rescue, Gary North recognized its potential as a revolutionary movement. "[I]n the philosophical war against political pluralism," he writes, "Christian leaders can see where these protests may be headed, even if their followers cannot: to a total confrontation with the civilization of secular humanists."[42] He argues that any "mature" Christian ultimately must become "a revolutionary against Satan's kingdom;" that the battle over abortion is really about "extending the revolution" and that "the abortion question" will never be settled "until Satan's kingdom is obliterated."[43] North describes a series of stages of non-violent protest, including political mobilization and "imprecatory prayer," which means calling the wrath of God down on recalcitrant public officials, which will ultimately lead to "armed revolution."[44] North notes that revolution became necessary "in 1776 in the North American Colonies."[45]

Following the Operation Rescue demonstrations at the 1988 Democratic convention in Atlanta, North expressed what would turn out to be well-founded "serious reservations about where the group may be in a few years, or where its political spin-offs may be."[46] Operation Rescue did indeed splinter, and its various egos and factions have emerged as dangerous proponents of violence.

Randall Terry, the founder of Operation Rescue, has publicly joined the ranks of potential theocratic revolutionaries. Although he has distanced himself from those justifying murder and clinic violence, he told a 1995 Operation Rescue gathering in Kenner, Louisiana that Christians may have to "take up the sword" in order to "overthrow the regime that oppresses them." He called for a theocratic state founded "on the Ten Commandments," and a "culture based on Biblical Law."[47]

One case where the admonition that abortion requires a vigilante response seems to have gripped a fevered mind is the case of John Salvi. Salvi was convicted of first degree murder in the 1995 guerrilla attack on two Boston abortion clinics which left two dead and three wounded. Chip Berlet, the senior analyst at Political Research Associates in Cambridge, Massachusetts, notes that there was literature found in Salvi's apartment that could have been read as a justification of his actions. This included an article by Notre Dame law professor Charles Rice in the John Birch Society magazine the *New American*, that argued that "capital punishment can be seen as a means to restore respect for innocent life…[because the] "willful taking of innocent life is the most abhorrent of all crimes precisely because the right to life is the most precious of all rights." Rice further argued that "God gave us free wills" and the "moral duty to act in accord with the common good." Thus he concludes that there is a "pressing need" to "restore respect for innocent life and to protect innocent members of the community against aggressors, whether abortionists or more conventional killers."[48]

Although Salvi was probably not familiar with it, Rice had previously offered a "necessity defense" for those who destroy clinics, arguing that "Abortuary bombers do not necessarily even violate human law," because "the human law that protects abortion factories is, in that context, as unjust and void as a law that purports to protect murderers against those who would prevent the murder by destroying the property scheduled to be used in the murders." Rice, an advisor to Human Life International, has assisted in the legal defense of individuals who have been convicted of arson and bombings at women's health centers.[49]

A Worldwide Wide Web of Culpability:
"The Beginning of Massive Killing"

The list of anti-choice activists who signed onto the so called "justifiable homicide petitions" included both Catholics and Protestants. Among them was Fr. David Trosch, who after the arrest of Paul Hill became the most prominent spokesperson for the theology of vigilantism. On August 28, 1994, Trosch was interviewed by the *Atlanta Journal-Constitution*. In the interview he stated that "An abortionist, by definition is a murderer. Not by civil law but by moral law." He considered Hill guiltless for his crimes, and suggested that the manufacturers of intrauterine devices and the abortion pill RU-486 might be suitable targets for "killing." Then he further defined a web of culpability.

Q. *You say people will be 'activated' to the point of killing. Do you advocate that?*

A. Do I believe that innocent human people should be defended by all means? Yes. I have no problem with that.

Q. *And that would include [Supreme Court] justices, [Attorney General Janet] Reno, [President] Clinton?*

A. Sure. Anybody who is currently actively involved in abortion. And it wouldn't necessarily have to be at an abortion clinic. It could be at their home. It could be in transport.[50]

A week before Hill's shotgun rampage, Trosch sent a letter to some 1,000 people, including members of Congress and major news organizations, predicting "the beginning of massive killing of abortionists and their staffs." Trosch further argued that abortion advocates at all levels, including the president, judges and abortion rights activists "will be sought out and terminated as vermin are terminated." When Hill received a copy of the letter, he phoned Trosch to say how much he liked it.[51]

Trosch's public statements might reasonably have been taken as threats against the life of the president and other constitutional officers, particularly given his association with other violent felons. One can only imagine the editorial condemnation had such threats been made by a leader of say, the Nation of Islam. Instead, Trosch was, like Hill, treated more like a celebrity by the media. Although Trosch's bishop dismissed him from his duties as a parish priest, he has not been excommunicated. This stands in stark contrast to the actions of the Catholic bishop of Lincoln, Nebraska, who in 1996 excommunicated anyone who was a member of the Masons, Planned Parenthood, or the Catholic dissident group Call To Action, among others.

Militias: Celebrating Baby Jesus With Guns

Rev. Matthew Trewhella made the news when the Planned Parenthood Federation of America released video footage of Trewhella's speech to the small U.S. Taxpayer's Party of Wisconsin (April 1994). He advocated the formation of church-based militias, holding out the example of his own church, comprised primarily of Missionary to the Preborn (MPB) members, and which held firearms classes for its members. He also told his church: "This Christmas I want you to do the most loving thing. I want you to buy each of your children an SKS rifle and 500 rounds of ammunition." He also cryptically declared that "plans of resistance are being made," apparently referring to resistance to the government. Sounding more like a leader of the paramilitary tax-protest movement the Posse Comitatus, or a "freeman," than the stereotype of an anti-abortion activist, Trewhella declared that "We shouldn't have birth certificates, or Social Security numbers...[or] marriage licenses."[52] According to *Newsweek*, an MPB member who lived in Trewhella's basement for five months in 1990 had apparently planned a "guerrilla campaign of clinic bombings and assassinations of doctors." Trewhella claimed no knowledge of these plans.[53]

At the same conference of the USTP of Wisconsin at which

Trewhella spoke, the Party sold a militia manual which stated that an important reason why one should "spring immediately and effectively to arms" is legalized abortion.[54] Trewhella was a member of the USTP National Committee at the time. He also served as a delegate to the USTP 1996 convention in San Diego and cast his ballot for Howard Phillips.

Tim Dreste is a former Operation Rescue leader whose recent leadership activities include a St. Louis militia and the national militant direct action organization, the American Coalition of Life Activists (ACLA). He is best known for picketing at a clinic wearing a hat displaying shotgun shells. Following the 1993 murder of Dr. Gunn, he carried a picket sign that read: "Do You Feel Under the Gunn?" In 1995 Dreste became the chaplain of The Missouri 1st Militia.[55]

The ACLA was formed as a result of a split in the anti-abortion movement over the issue of violence following a leadership summit in Chicago in April 1994.[56] Among the ACLA's leaders are Joe Foreman, Don Treshman, and Andrew Burnett, the publisher of *Life Advocate* magazine (as well as Michael Bray's book, *A Time to Kill*). The group also argues that women who have had abortions, even victims of rape and incest, should be prosecuted for murder "under the same laws that apply to the killing of any other human being."[57] In January 1995, the ACLA unveiled a "deadly dozen" list of doctors who perform abortions. One of the named doctors, Warren Hern of Colorado, said "This is target identification. The American Coalition of Life Activists so-called, death activists I think it should be called, know very well that their ideological colleagues have announced plans to kill doctors who do abortions."[58]

Groups that are best known as militias are also sometimes animated by opposition to abortion. One notable example is the Michigan Militia, which was founded by a Baptist minister and one of his deacons. Investigative journalist Beth Hawkins, writing in the Detroit *Metro Times*, long before the bombing of the Federal Building in Oklahoma City made paramilitary militia groups a national news story, reported that the Michigan Militia Corps (MMC) circulated materials "linking alleged conspiracies to keep abortion legal to the institution of worldwide government, as well as a list of reasons for forming militias that includes protecting the right to life." Hawkins reported that during a July 1994 meeting for prospective recruits, the "brigade's chaplain gave a speech that began with a graphic but dubious description of the in utero decapitation of a fetus for research purposes. The leaders videotaped the talk for inclusion in a training video for other militia start-ups."[59] In the wake of federal investigations into anti-abortion violence, the MMC leaders later downplayed their anti-abortion views.

A 1996 report by the Planned Parenthood Federation of America documented a "convergence" between anti-abortion and militia activism and violence. In July, 1996, the leader of the Oklahoma Constitutional Militia, Willie Ray Lampley, and two accomplices were convicted of conspiring to bomb abortion clinics, gay bars and the offices of civil rights and welfare organizations.[60] Additionally, three alleged members of an underground white supremacist cell, the Phineas Priesthood, were arrested and charged with bombing a Planned Parenthood clinic and the *Spokane Spokesman-Review* newspaper and robbing a local bank. One of those arrested, Jay Merrell, is a Christian Identity minister, originally from Arizona.[61] (Christian Identity holds that Anglo-Saxons are the lost tribe of Israel, and that blacks, Jews and other non-white or non-Christian groups constitute inferior, satanic "mud people" who will ultimately be wiped out, and that God's people, the white Aryans, will rule the world.)[62] The other two arrested are attendees of a Christian Identity church called America's Promise Ministries, headed by David Bartley.[63] Christian Identity is the religious faith of much of the white supremacist movement. Some adherents have adopted parts of the theology of Christian Reconstructionism and Old Testament Biblical law as justification for their goals.

People enter the militia movement for many reasons. While some militia members are pro-choice, and many do not emphasize abortion as an issue, no militia group has so far emerged that has given defense of the constitutional right for abortion as a raison d'être for their militia activities. The implicit and sometimes actual threat from armed paramilitary groups and individuals, which in light of the murder of doctors and staff and the ongoing campaign of terror tactics has compounded the climate of fear surrounding women's health centers, may well pose a longer term problem. The still nascent militia movement could go in any number of directions, and predictions are premature.

Paul Hill told *USA Today* in March 1994 that "I could envision a covert organization developing, something like a pro-life IRA."[64] Similarly, Defensive Action signer Henry Felisone has also advocated the formation of an underground anti-abortion army modeled perhaps on the Islamic terrorist group Hamas, or the Irish Republican Army.[65] Whether there is a revolutionary underground in formation, or already in existence, is a matter of conjecture. However, the climate of fear created by such talk is real enough. Also real is the decade of violence that preceded this threat. The violence continues, largely unabated.

Another Civil War?

One of the most revealing discussions of anti-abortion violence in the U.S. took place on Canadian television. The Canadian Broadcasting Company aired a documentary in December 1994 following the attempted assassination of Dr. Gary Romalis in Vancouver, British Columbia. A sniper with a high-powered rifle and a scope had seriously wounded the 57-year-old physician while he ate breakfast at home.

Don Treshman, leader of the Houston-based Rescue America, (who has since moved to Baltimore) told the CBC that he foresees a civil war. Treshman endorsed the so-called "Army of God" manual, an instruction book which describes how to blockade, bomb, and otherwise attack clinics. Treshman also described the shooting of Dr. Romalis as a "superb tactic." Although Treshman said he had nothing to do with publishing the Army of God manual, he was conversant with its contents.

Host Hana Gartner's interview with Treshman went in part:

Gartner: "It's a self-help manual on how to blow up abortion clinics."

Treshman: "Well, it goes into more than that too. I think it covers actions at the abortionist's home."

Gartner: "It's advocating violence."

Treshman: "Well, I think it's just merely mentioning some ways some people have gone about things."

Gartner: "How to make a better bomb."

Treshman: "Yes. We think that in the spirit of free press it's certainly something that every home should have."

Treshman also stated that "This could be the start of another major civil war" in the U.S. He explained that "There is no common ground with pro-lifers and the abortion industry… and I rebuke the pro-life groups that say we must sit down and talk with the abortionists."[66] Perhaps coincidentally, the manual includes the recipe for the same kind of "fertilizer bomb" that was used to blow up the federal building in Oklahoma City.

Treshman's endorsement of the Army of God manual is significant, because it epitomizes the actual low-level guerrilla war underway in the U.S. The copy now in circulation was dug up by federal agents out of the backyard of Shelly Shannon, who was convicted of the attempted murder of Dr. George Tiller, of Wichita, Kansas, and who engaged in a "year long arson and butyric acid bombing spree across three states."

Anne Bower, editor of the pro-choice magazine the *Body Politic,* wrote in her study of Shelly Shannon and the Army of God that "There is a network of men and women in America who advocate and will attempt violence, even to the point of murder for their cause…these people easily classify as domestic terrorists who should be taken seriously… these individuals see themselves as soldiers in a grand cause, The Army of God."[67]

In a deposition in a case involving clinic blockades during the 1992 Republican convention, Treshman said "I don't feel any compulsion to obey any invalid laws that are not supported by what God teaches us." Prominent, articulate leaders of the violent wing of the anti-abortion movement have been saying similar things for a number of years. What's more, the reason for the activities of these leaders is not just abortion. Michael Bray, Paul Hill, and probably Randall Terry believe a revolution is necessary and justified to implement their vision of society.

Don Treshman and Matt Trewhella dance around the concept, but have endorsed activities consistent with preparing for, and carrying out guerrilla war. They have gotten as far as they have in part by being popularly understood only as anti-abortion activists, fringe characters or extremists. It does not require belief in their capacity to actually win or even mount a revolution to recognize the seriousness of their purpose and consider the implications.

Clinic violence returned to the pattern of previous years in 1995 as this book was being written. The National Abortion Federation documented ten clinic arsons in the first eight months of 1995. In the absence of high-profile assassinations, the ongoing campaign of domestic terrorism went largely unnoticed in the national media. The people who have authored the books and manifestos, issued the statements, given the interviews, are still around and there is no evidence that their beliefs have changed. Furthermore, the militia movement, in its varied forms, is growing.

Yahoo Justice (Making It Up As You Go Along)

One further area of vigilante action which also features a Reconstructionist dimension is the "jury nullification" movement. Reconstructionist theologian David Chilton, who was a columnist for the now defunct *Sacramento Union* newspaper,[68] advocated the doctrine of "jury nullification," which asserts that juries have the right to find the accused not guilty if they disagree with the law under which the accused is charged. Jury nullification is a notion promoted most prominently by the far-right Fully Informed Jury Association (FIJA), based in Helmville, Montana. Interestingly, although FIJA tends to be an anti-elite, often conspiracy-minded collection of activists, much of FIJA's annual budget is provided by the Pittsburgh-based Carthage Foundation, which is controlled by Richard Mellon Scaife, an heir to the Mellon family fortune and the single largest bankroller of conservative institutions in the country—from the Heritage Foundation to Paul Weyrich's National Empowerment Television. The Carthage Foundation provided FIJA with $25,000 each year in 1993 and 1994.[69] Scaife has also been a major contributor to Republican politicians from Richard Nixon to Newt Gingrich.[70]

FIJA activists and advocates generally populate the far right. One Christian Right activist from Georgia told the *Wall Street Journal* that "in our community, we're pretty Christian people, and we want to use that law [jury nullification] to reflect how we feel about these issues." Although he felt that in the wrong hands it could lead to "immoral results," he nevertheless felt that letting the law reflect the standards of a particular community was acceptable.[71] The concept has been percolating through state legislatures for some time. For example, in 1996 Republican Steve Baldwin of El Cajon, California introduced a FIJA-backed jury nullification legislation in the California Assembly, which would have allowed defense attorneys to request that the judge instruct jurors that they could ignore "any other jury instruction and to render a general verdict in favor of the defendant according to the conscience of the individual jurors."[72] Despite the backing of local FIJA activist Jim Harnsberger, Baldwin was unable to move the bill out of committee, and failed to get a single vote.

Reconstructionist author Gary DeMar, in his book *Ruler of the Nations,* urges would-be vigilante enforcers of God's law to infiltrate and hang juries. He says they "must not vote to convict people of crimes that the Bible says are not crimes, no matter what corrupt civil law says." He makes a FIJA-like argument that "Juries must be instructed—as under Common Law and as denied under our current humanistic legal theory and practice—to look to the justice of the law, as well as to the facts of the case. This is absolutely essential if God's law is to be honored." "In the jury room," he concludes, "the jury is sovereign—not the legislature, not the police, and surely not the judge."

Similarly, Gary North and David Chilton argued as far back as 1983 that building a Biblical theocracy means not only studying Biblical law and interpretive commentaries such as Rushdoony's *Institutes of Biblical Law,* but voting "in terms of these laws... We [will] use juries if possible, to nullify the ability of the civil government to impose God-defying laws on our fellow citizens."[73]

DeMar claims that judges who do not adhere to his views are "immoral" liars and urges "the Christian" to "sit silently... and then hang the jury if necessary if the jury votes to convict the defendant of a bad law."[74] DeMar sells his books not only to a wide audience of the Christian Right, but to Christian schools and home schools. DeMar's proposals for abuse of the jury system for political ends are slowly percolating throughout the Christian Right.

The potential implications of jury nullification became evident when anti-abortion activists distributed FIJA leaflets to the jury in the 1995 murder trial of Paul Hill. The jury could have declared Hill not guilty if they decided that the law was irrelevant, and that their version of God's law was more relevant. Fellow Reconstructionist Michael Bray and his colleague Mike Colvin also say that they "agree in principle with the goals of the Fully Informed Jury Association."[75]

(One interesting example of the "family values" of the far right coalition is the Wysong brothers. Harvey Wysong is the Georgia state leader of FIJA. Gordon Wysong is the Cobb County (Georgia) commissioner whose controlling faction made national news by condemning homosexuality, banning abortions through the county public employee health plan, and stopping county funding of the arts, as discussed in Chapter 5. Charlie Wysong, of Chattanooga, Tennessee, is a leader in the American Coalition of Life Activists.)

Like the national ethos of religious equality which the framers of the Constitution sought to establish, there have been specific areas carved out in the law to protect dissident views. There are no penalties if jurors vote their consciences and evaluate the relevance of the law as they see fit, and in fact juries do this all the time. However, FIJA is a right-wing hijacking of the tradition of exceptions created for matters of individual conscience, in order to create a legal and judicial climate which can be exploited to destabilize the judicial system, and fail to protect the rights of other Americans—in this case those exercising their constitutional rights to have, and to perform abortions.

This movement has grown over time as the ideas of Reconstructionism have been more widely disseminated and adopted by the Christian Right. Would "fully informed" Christian Right jurors find wife batterers not guilty in the interest of preserving "the family?" Would they find those charged of violating the civil rights of minorities in hiring not guilty because, as R.J. Rushdoony writes, an employer has the "property right to prefer whom he will in terms of color, creed, race or national origin"?[76]

Significantly, there are people not associated with the Right who also sympathize with FIJA, including libertarians, advocates of the legalization of marijuana and progressives such as Alexander Cockburn, a columnist for the *Nation* magazine. The idea of jury nullification has been closely linked to the "necessity defense" which has occasionally been used, for example, by attorneys arguing on behalf of anti-nuclear protesters, or women accused of killing their violent husbands. However, the "necessity defense" was also used by Michael Hirsh as a key point in his hypothetical defense of Michael Griffin, as well as by others committing anti-abortion violence, such as convicted clinic bomber John Brockhoeft. Similarly, David Trosch believes that a Christian has the "obligation to become a juror" in order to subvert "unjust civil law that is in opposition to God's will."[77]

What society is prepared to consider to be "necessary" is likely to be an ongoing dispute. However, there is a difference between a necessity defense offered by a defense attorney and the judge's instructions to a jury about their duties.

The appropriate balance between orderly judicial procedure and citizen/juror conscience is beyond the scope of this discussion. However, those concerned about such matters should be wary of an organization that is substantially bankrolled by the same Richard Mellon Scaife who has been the major funder of the Heritage Foundation, as well as others that would severely restrict the civil and constitutional rights of Americans.

An Uncommon Threat to Constitutional Law

Meanwhile, self-appointed "common law courts," are becoming a further extension of vigilante law, and are popping up all over the country. Generally, although not always, they are associated with white supremacist and Posse Comitatus groups. These groups consider the laws of the United States and the court system itself to be generally invalid. The most dramatic example of such views emerged in early 1996, during the standoff between the FBI and the self-described "Freemen," in Jordan, Montana. The notion of the "freeman" is commonly understood in Posse Comitatus, anti-government circles. Rev. Matthew Trewhella, in his infamous speech to the USTP of Wisconsin, not only embraced such tenets of freemanship as failing to register for everything from marriage licenses to Social Security, but specifically said that he is teaching his son "to be a freeman." Members of the Montana Freemen refused to have drivers licenses and plates, and to pay income taxes. They passed bogus checks, filed phony property liens against public officials and threatened a federal judge and other officials who crossed them, and established a "common law court" in which they tried and convicted public officials of a variety of supposed crimes. They also claimed sovereignty over government-owned land that had been rented to local farmers and ranchers—who say the Freemen threatened them.

Property liens have also been a favorite tactic of the Posse Comitatus, according to an IRS report, to "clog the court system, and to embarrass, impede, and obstruct the trial courts in the administration of justice."[78] In January, 1996, a local minister went to visit the Freeman compound. Members of the group explained that they adhere to "Christian Identity" beliefs: white males are the pinnacle of creation, and the U.S. is run by a satanic conspiracy of Jews. "We have established Heaven on Earth," she was told, "by establishing God's Law on Earth at Justus Township. We are there. All that's left is the cleanup."[79]

If the kangaroo courts of the "common law" movement and the judicial monkey-wrench gang of FIJA further gain in popularity, they could gain the capacity to undermine confidence in the judicial system of the United States (which is certainly their goal). The long-range consequences of the patriarchal growth of this movement could be that smaller units of the country seek greater latitude in deciding what "community standards" of justice might be. Even such matters as abortion and civil rights become state or even local matters in such a scenario. Radically decentralist movements like this epitomize the multidimensional strategy of straining the system with "resistance" of various forms, advocated by elements of the Christian Right, Reconstructionists, anti-abortion revolutionaries, neo-Nazis, and many others.

CHAPTER 8

The Fight for the Framework

Resetting the Terms of Debate

The Christian Right has been active in American politics for hundreds of years. It has, in recent years, developed a very effective electoral strategy that enables a minority to win big in both local and national elections.The latter was marked by their stunning control of the GOP at the party's 1996 convention. (The import of this was missed by the mainstream media's focus on how well-behaved the delegates were.) Its scholars have created a coherent body of written work that lays out their ideology and vision of Biblical law. Its activists have worked to disrupt and destroy such important democratic institutions as jury trials and public schooling. They have demonized their opponents to provide justification for their activites. And some are acting on that justification to carry out terrorist violence and assassinations as the first shots in what they hope will be a new civil war to overthrow democracy.

Unless the movement can dent the commitment to democratic values held by the majority in this country, its ultimate impact may be limited, but the progress Christian Right activists and scholars have made in controlling the terms in which these issues are debated is as impressive—and alarming—as are their other accomplishments. Even a relatively small but well organized and ideologically unified movement can dramatically affect politics and culture in any society, whether or not it becomes the dominant faction.

Two of the most prominent books that have informed mainstream discussion of the resurgent Christian Right over the past few years have actually been significant sources of the misinformation that has misdirected the response to the Christian Right. One of the authors of these "must read" books is a closeted partisan of the Christian Right, and the other cares so much about protecting religious expression from creeping secularism that he largely misses the threat posed by contemporary theocratic movements.

James Davison Hunter's 1991 book, *Culture Wars: The Struggle To Define America*, was an alternate Book of the Month Club Choice, and was treated as a "neutral" description of the "culture war" by a wide and prominent spectrum of opinion. A companion volume which was published in 1994, *Before the Shooting Begins,* also received considerable attention.

Stephen Carter's 1993 book, *The Culture of Disbelief: How American Law and Politics Trivialize Religious Devotion,*[1] was publicly endorsed by President Clinton prior to publication and thus became an important text in mainstream discussions about religion and public life.[2] Yale Law School, where Carter teaches, hung a photo of President Clinton holding a copy of the book.

Few books that deal with the Christian Right ever reach such a mass audience, making these two especially important.

Hunter's Wars

James Davison Hunter, a professor of the sociology of religion at the University of Virginia writes, he says, out of concern that tensions between what he calls the "orthodox" and "progressive" communities could result in violence and civil war.

Hunter views the disagreements "that fire the culture war" as "deep and perhaps unreconcilable." He emphasizes that *"these differences are often intensified and aggravated by the ways they are presented in public... At stake,"* he concludes, *"is how we as Americans will order our lives together"*[3] (italics in the original). In this spirit, Hunter details how the communications and fundraising industries distort and corrode civil discourse through demonization, sensationalization and polarization, since both industries feed on conflict and scare tactics. He summarizes some major issue areas, and describes how civil discourse ought to function. These are useful discussions for all who aspire to a civil and pluralist society.

Additionally, Hunter writes "I have worked very hard to keep my own opinions about the issues of contemporary public dispute to myself...I have made every effort to be neutral in my analysis of particular issues and fair in understanding all sides...."[4] For all the media hype about Hunter's professed neutrality in the culture wars, he is not the Switzerland of scholarship that he seems to be. As will become clear, there is an important difference between making honorable efforts to consider arguments on both sides and hiding one's own affiliations. Sometimes the failure to disclose such affiliations means there is something to hide.

Hunter's Scholarship: Don't Ask, Don't Tell

Early in the book, Hunter offers short profiles of several people who, in his view, epitomize the culture war. These are presented as instructive and human portraits of worthy adversaries. The first profile is of Rev. Charles McIlhenny, perhaps the leading anti-gay crusader in San Francisco, who, as Hunter reports, pastors a small Orthodox Presbyterian Church "not far from the Golden Gate Bridge,"[5] and who, with his family, lives in real fear because of his controversial stands.

What we do not learn from Hunter is how McIlhenny emerged as a major public figure when he fired his church organist, Kevin Walker in 1978, for being a "practicing homosexual." When the man sued McIlhenny for discrimination, R.J. Rushdoony put his "friend", McIlhenny, in touch with attorney John Whitehead, who represented him in this case that made both of them famous.[6] Rushdoony and Whitehead (and Christian Right financier Howard Ahmanson) later founded the Christian Right legal foundation called the Rutherford Institute. McIlhenny described his 1980 victory: "Two diametrically opposed religions had clashed in the courtroom: secular humanism, the religion of our dominant American culture, and orthodox Christianity."[7] McIlhenny, who declared that "there is no neutrality here," attacked the constitutional doctrine of separation of church and state in favor of "God's authority over the civil magistrate."[8] McIlhenny, as has been previously discussed, believes that a "religious war" is underway, and is, if not a Reconstructionist himself, very close to the movement philosophically.

Although Hunter did not probe McIlhenny's views very deeply, he indicates that for McIlhenny "homosexuality is just the tip of the iceberg," of his political vision. "If I want a godly society," Hunter quotes McIlhenny as saying, "then I must advocate godly candidates… I want a Christian society, so I'll advocate Christians running for office." However, what these "Christians" would do to create a Christian society, Hunter doesn't ask, and McIlhenny didn't tell.

It's clear McIlhenny isn't advocating that just any Christians run for office. The most recent presidents are professing Christians, but that is clearly not what McIlhenny has in mind.

R. J. Who?

Hunter obscures the role of the most important American theocratic theologian, R.J. Rushdoony himself, even while relying on a quote from Rushdoony to define the "orthodox" notion of "justice," in a section titled "competing moral visions." However, Hunter fails to identify and explain Rushdoony's significance.

"As R.J. Rushdoony makes clear," writes Hunter, "justice can only be understood in terms of the law, which in its highest form is 'theocentric and is a manifestation of the nature and life of the ontological Trinity.'"[9] In the same section in which he quotes Rushdoony, he also quotes from Reconstructionist writers Rus Walton and Peter Marshall, as well as Charles McIlhenny.[10] This is especially odd, since earlier in the book, he accurately reports, (sans citations) that Reconstructionists "favor a more theocratic model of governance derived from Old Testament law," yet off-handedly dismisses the Reconstructionists by saying "their numbers are very small."[11] Perhaps unintentionally, Hunter's own reporting is emblematic of how the significance of Reconstructionism has been in the influence of their ideas, rather than their numbers.

Hunter also dodges opportunities to discuss the theocratic elements of the Christian Right. He reports, for example, that editorial writers and interest groups sometimes accuse elements of the "orthodox alliance" of being theocratic. However, this observation comes in the context of his discussion of mutual demonization in the culture war. By way of example, he describes an editorial in the *Chicago Tribune* as relating "activism in the orthodox alliance to the Crusades, the Spanish Inquisition, the 'intolerant theocracy' of the Massachusetts Bay Colony, Islamic fundamentalism, and Jewish fundamentalism in contemporary Israel."[12] But characteristically, he makes no comment on whether any of this editorial rhetoric is true. By letting the quote dangle without explanation, he implies that it is not.

Don't Worry About the Occasional Bombing

Hunter uses abortion as the primary case example by which to examine the "culture war." However, in doing so he ignores the terrorism at women's health centers, engages in a propagandistic attack on non-profit abortion providers, and obscures his own relationship to an important anti-abortion organization.

As was discussed in Chapter 7, this terrorism is real and pervasive, something I gained first-hand understanding of in my work researching the anti-abortion movement and the wider religious right with the national office of Planned Parenthood Federation of America in New York, during 1994-1995. For example, I was one of the staff on hand when anti-abortion zealot John Salvi shot up two clinics in Brookline, Massachusetts—one was a Planned Parenthood clinic. In all, two people died and five were wounded. I worked late that day and for many days afterwards dealing with the many aspects of these crimes. As chilling, in its own way, was a call I made some months before the Salvi shootings to a Planned Parenthood public affairs director in the midwest. I asked her how she was. "We had a bomb threat today," she said matter of factly. "You did?" I asked, shocked and concerned, "what happened?" "Oh, we evacuated the building for an hour while the bomb squad checked it out and then we went back." I was thunderstruck. This happened with such frequency that she was used to it. It was *routine*. It was this moment, perhaps more than the dramatic acts of violence, that taught me the meaning of this terrorism. It is in part this very record which compelled me to begin work on this book not long after I left PPFA.

That is why I found Hunter's assertion in *Culture Wars* particularly striking: "Physical violence is notably absent from the contemporary culture war, (despite accusations for example that Planned Parenthood leaders are 'baby killers' and pro-life activists in Operation Rescue are 'terrorists.') It is true that abortion clinics have been bombed on occasion."[13] Exchanges of volleys of invective from both sides notwithstanding, the actual violence is real, more than occasional, and far more significant than name calling. The Federal Bureau of Alcohol, Tobacco and Firearms recognized 99 bombings and arsons during the nine years[14] preceding the 1991 publication of *Culture Wars*. In addition to the official figures of bombings and arsons, incidents of attempted arsons, death threats and bomb threats, stalking and harassment number in the hundreds, perhaps thousands annually.[15]

Hunter continued to obscure clinic violence in his (1994) "companion and follow-up" book, *Before the Shooting Begins: Searching for Democracy in America's Culture Wars.* "Some would say the shooting has already begun," Hunter declares in the first sentence. "Pro-choice activists…" he continues, "point to the shooting of abortion providers David Gunn in Pensacola, Florida, and George Tiller in Wichita, Kansas, not to mention the vandalizing of abortion clinics…."[16] Although Hunter, a sociologist, makes extensive use of survey data in both books, he cites no sources, presents no data, and analyzes no trends regarding clinic violence. Weasel words such as "bombed on occasion," and "some would say," substitute for facts, which were readily available from the obvious sources in law enforcement, the pro-choice community, and the media. In the years between the publication of his two books, 1991-1993, the National Abortion Federation reported a total of 38 arsons and bombings against abortion providers.[17]

Deafening Silence on Anti-Gay/Lesbian Violence

While Hunter doesn't report the one-sided violence of the abortion issue, he does claim that "gays firebombed Chuck McIlhenny's church and house and harassed him ceaselessly with death threats."[18] Interestingly, McIlhenny himself does not identify the source of these crimes and Hunter does not document his claim.[19] Nevertheless, this is the only occasion when Hunter addresses the issue of violence as it relates to homosexuality and the "culture wars."

As in the case of clinic violence, there was documentation of anti-gay violence readily available. Thus, contrary to Hunter's claim that "physical violence is notably absent from the contemporary culture war," what is actually "notably absent" is any acknowledgment by Hunter of the scope and severity of the one-sided violence. The National Gay and Lesbian Task Force (NGLTF) has issued annual reports on anti-gay violence since 1985. Although much of the data for the first few years was anecdotal or based on press reports, and limitations in data collection have meant incomplete figures, the seriousness of the problem is clear: dozens of grisly anti-gay murders, thousands of assaults, and dozens of bombings and arsons of homes, business, and churches. The NGLTF reports offer not only numbers but also the stories of some of the victims of violence—and it is chilling reading.

In 1989 NGLTF documented 15 specifically "anti-gay" murders, and another 47 "gay related" murders in which local groups or the police believed that the sexual orientation of the victim was a factor, but anti-gay prejudice was not clearly present. There were also 11 arsons, and 82 bomb threats.[20]

As in the case of clinic violence, Hunter obviously knows that anti-gay violence is a problem, but he left it out. This is a particularly obvious omission because in *Culture Wars* he writes about the "struggle over the passage, in 1990 of the Hate Crimes Statistics Act, requiring the federal government to collect statistics on crimes motivated by prejudice based on race, ethnicity, religion or 'sexual orientation'…" There was a "struggle," in large part, because the Christian Right opposed its passage with the inclusion of sexual orientation as a category. Even though he quotes from the NGLTF's statement that the act, (which was ultimately signed into law by then-President George Bush)[21] was "the most significant lesbian and gay rights victory in the history of the U.S. Congress," Hunter does not explain why the legislation was so urgently needed[22]—although there was evidence enough of the need for Congress to pass and the president to sign the legislation. NGLTF's 1990 annual report on violence stated that "NGLTF's annual tallies, along with other research, provided an undeniable body of evidence that demanded official measures to counteract anti-gay crimes—including the federal Hate Crimes Statistic Act and numerous state and local laws directed at crimes based on sexual orientation."[23]

Thus Hunter's concern about the excesses of rhetoric on both sides as *possibly* leading to violence seems disingenuous in light of the actual violence he ignores. From Charles McIlhenny to Pat Buchanan, key leaders of the "orthodox" alliance believe that a religious war—not a culture war—is already underway. Many fully expect there to be more violence. As has been discussed, it is a war of aggression from the side that Hunter generally supports.

Violence (and the threat of violence) has been, and continues to be an every day reality for family planning clinics, abortion providers, and people seeking health services, as well as for gay men and lesbians.

"Industry" As Epithet

Hunter also engages in propagandistic labeling of the sort that he criticizes in *Culture Wars*. Hunter adopts a favorite label of the anti-choice movement, and sticks it on his target. Hunter calls the provision of abortion services an "industry," the implication being that abortion doctors are driven by greed to perform this routine, if controversial, procedure, while the motives of anti-abortion forces are somehow purely religious. There are many for-profit medical facilities that provide abortions, just as for-profit medicine dominates health care in the United States. But this is not really the issue. The crafty Dr. Hunter uses the label "abortion industry" as a basis for ascribing "powerful economic incentives"[24] to, and thus questioning, the non-profit tax status of some abortion providers.

Hunter asserts that it is "disingenuous for a group like Planned Parenthood to say that it is a non-profit organization," because "salaries are paid, clinics and family planning centers advertise, and the national headquarters is funded in part on the revenue generated by abortion. In the end," he concludes, "the championing of abortion rights of some organizations on the pro-choice side of this controversy is inseparable from their economic interests."[25]

While non-profit health care providers have the obligation to sustain and even advance their missions as charitable agencies, and this involves fiscal responsibility, it is not the same as having a profit motive, or satisfying the bottom line interests of investors who ultimately control the direction, staffing, and activities of a company. Hunter offers no evidence that Planned Parenthood's tax status is undeserved.

In 1993, while PPFA provided 131,000 abortions nationwide, they also provided pre-natal care to over 9,000 women, and made almost 96,000 referrals for prenatal care. In other words, there were almost as many clients or referrals for pre-natal care, as there were abortion clients. But then, Hunter would never accuse PPFA of being part of the "pre-natal care industry."[26] Planned Parenthood is more comparable to other non-profit health care providers, including those that do not perform abortions such as Catholic hospitals, than it is to any advocacy group.

Since 1992 more PPFA affiliates have become abortion providers—a period in which many non-PPFA abortion providers have been driven out by harassment and intimidation from militant anti-abortion groups. Epitomizing this kind of strategy was the 1992 publication of *Firestorm: A Guerrilla Strategy for a Pro-Life America* in which the author, Mark Crutcher, of the Texas-based anti-abortion group Life Dynamics, declared: "Today, we have opportunities before us which, if properly exploited, could result in an America where abortion may indeed be perfectly legal, but no one can get one."[27]

Stealth Partiality

Hunter's non-scholarly outburst may seem less surprising in light of his professional association with a leading anti-abortion organization. He crafted the questions for a major survey, conducted in 1990, of public attitudes on abortion, which he acknowledges (deep in the chapter notes at the end of the book) "was commissioned and underwritten by Americans United for Life"[28]—a leading anti-abortion strategy organization, headquartered in Chicago, whose annual budget of over $2 million is plowed into research, legislation and litigation.

The Gallup polling organization did the actual leg work for the study, and described its role in a statement when AUL released the original findings: "Reporting, analysis and interpretation of the survey findings was performed by Dr. James Rogers, Quantitative Research Fellow for AUL...." Gallup's role in "the Abortion and Moral Beliefs Survey was limited... Specifically, Gallup designed the survey sample, conducted the survey interviews and tabulated the survey findings. Gallup played no part in selecting the questions to be asked in the survey, nor in reporting, analyzing or interpreting the findings."

AUL released its findings at a press conference at The Heritage Foundation on May 23, 1991, and distributed them, in the classic mode of Washington interest groups, to every member of Congress. The *Washington Times* seized the opportunity to claim that Americans hold to a "pro-life consensus, as depicted by the Gallup survey."[29] The newspaper sought to inoculate the study against criticism by invoking Gallup as if it was the arbiter of impartiality: "the poll was conducted by the most highly respected polling company in the United States."

Although he featured a re-examination of data from the AUL survey in his 1994 book, *Before the Shooting Begins*, Hunter still refers to it as "the Gallup survey" or "the Gallup study."[30] In the buried chapter note, however, Hunter tells a somewhat different story, explaining that neither Gallup nor AUL played any part "in the analysis, interpretation, or reporting of the findings here."[31] Hunter took the data Gallup had gathered in response to the questions he had designed. AUL did the original analysis. This represented a new interpretation. If Gallup played no part, then why call it the Gallup survey in the text?

He buries his own role in the original study as well. In introducing the subject in the text he writes, "There are many... surveys that we will refer to, but we key on an unusual one conducted by the Gallup Organization in the summer of 1990. What makes this survey unique is that *it was designed* (emphasis added) to probe in greater depth than ever before the complexities of American public opinion on the subject."[32] What he does not say (until the chapter notes) is that he and a colleague, Carl Bowman of Bridgewater College, were the designers.[33] The use of the passive voice in "it was designed" conceals the name of the designers. (To offer a Biblical example, the first line of the Bible might read, "In the beginning, the heavens and earth were created.")

It is not the purpose here to compare the AUL's interpretation of the data with Hunter's re-interpretation in *Before the Shooting Begins*. At issue are Hunter's efforts to obscure his relationship to AUL, and the original propagandistic use of the survey data. Hunter knows that such things matter. In the same book he discusses similar problems of bias in journalism, observing "that when personal prejudices or class interests find their way into news reporting, they do so under the pose of neutrality and fairness."[34]

Hunter was not alone in the laundering of the AUL connection. Rev. Richard John Neuhaus, a member of the AUL board of directors at the time of the survey, penned a glowing review of *Before the Shooting Begins* in the *National Review*. Neuhaus praised Hunter's chapter based on the abortion survey data as a "model of sociological sophistication," which was based "on work [Hunter] previously published in *First Things*" (a neo-conservative magazine edited by Neuhaus).[35] Neuhaus disclosed neither his nor Hunter's relationship to AUL, and the original survey.

In the *First Things* article, which appeared in 1992, Hunter is remarkably more open about his anti-abortion sympathies. In fact, his article is actually a strategy memo for the anti-abortion forces, based on his analysis of three separate public opinion surveys commissioned by anti-abortion groups following the *Webster* decision of the Supreme Court (among them, the AUL survey). Although this time he identified the AUL's sponsorship of the Gallup survey in the text, he does not disclose his role in the original study. Instead, he mentions only that he and Carl Bowman later did a "reexamination of the Gallup survey."[36] Hunter's efforts to obscure his relationship to AUL are consistent with the anti-abortion propaganda that infects *Culture Wars*.

Interestingly, Neuhaus, Hunter's partner in this affair, has also been a principal of the Washington, DC-based Institute on Religion and Democracy (IRD)—a small group of conservative and neo-conservative activists bankrolled by millions of dollars from right-wing foundations.[37] IRD was founded by secular conservatives in an apparent effort to neutralize the foreign policy views of mainstream Protestant denominations and the National Council of Churches which was at odds with U.S. policy on issues ranging from South Africa to El Salvador. The IRD played an important role in the 1980s in attacking, and often neutralizing, liberal religious and political expressions of mainstream Protestantism—that is to say, the expressions of views with which they disagreed.

IRD was started in 1980 by the Coalition for a Democratic Majority (CDM), which was founded in 1972 by conservative Democrats (many of whom later defected to the GOP) to counter the takeover of the party by liberals associated with presidential candidate George McGovern. IRD was originally run by CDM chief Penn Kemble—a political activist who did not attend church. IRD was originally funded almost entirely by the same right-wing foundations which bankrolled the major infrastructure of the conservative movement in Washington, DC, including the Heritage Foundation and National Empowerment Television.[38]

Hunter Fingers the Bogeyman

"The Gallup survey" was not the first time Hunter obscured his personal connections to events on which he reported. In *Culture Wars,* he discusses a famous 1986 "Alabama Textbook Case" in which a legal arm of Pat Robertson's organization represented conservative Christian parents who sued the Mobile, Alabama school board. At issue was the supposed promotion of the supposed religion of "secular humanism" through school textbooks. Hunter was a key witness for the plaintiffs. His views were cited by the judge who ruled in the plaintiffs' favor. The decision was overturned on appeal.

Hunter explains in *Culture Wars* that "the case pitted a coalition of Evangelical Protestants, conservative Catholics and other 'theists' against the Mobile Board of Education, which was backed by, among others, the American Civil Liberties Union and People for the American Way." Hunter concludes that "this one case by itself...illustrates clearly the polarization of orthodox and progressive interests and ideals over how religion should be defined for establishment purposes."[39]

However, Hunter not only fails to disclose his role, but he does not disclose the final disposition of this important case or that he was a key witness for the losing "orthodox" side. The adventurous reader who makes it all the way to the chapter notes learns that Hunter "was one of the expert witnesses called to testify in this case."[40] But called by whom? Hunter implies (once again using the passive voice) that he was called by the court. In fact, he was hired by Pat Robertson's legal team to produce two background papers, to review some elementary school social studies text books, and to serve as one of their expert witnesses to undergird their theory that "secular humanism" is not only a religion but that it is somehow advanced by the textbooks at issue.[41] In his deposition he testified that "The material is presented in such a way that is consistent with the tenets of secular humanism."[42] And during the trial itself, Hunter further testified that his studies "persuaded me that a secular humanism of a sort is a dominant ideology of public school textbooks, at least the ones reviewed."[43] Because some of the texts omitted important historical references to religion in American history, Hunter argued that the "secularization" of public life generally, and education specifically, is epitomized by the omission of certain references to religion.[44]

Under cross examination by George H. Mernick III of the Washington, DC law firm of Hogan and Hartson, Hunter was asked "Is it a tenet of secular humanism, that history be portrayed inaccurately?"—and had to acknowledge that it was not.[45] Mernick also compelled Hunter to concede that he had found no passages in the elementary social studies books he had reviewed that "were consistent with secular humanism," rather that the books "advance a secularistic view of their world. Not a humanistic, but a secularistic."[46]

District Court Judge Brevard Hand's opinion, which significantly relied on Hunter's testimony, ruled that the Mobile school board had unconstitutionally established secular humanism as a religion and thus violated the rights of the complaining individuals through the use of the textbooks at issue in the case. "The factual inaccuracies are so grave as to rise to a constitutional violation," declared Judge Hand in his decision. "The Court's (Judge Hand's) independent review of the books confirm Dr. Hunter's testimony in this regard. Religion, especially theistic religion, is never placed in context by these books."[47]

The upshot of the case was, however, that just because some text books were deficient did not mean that humanism, secular, religious or otherwise was responsible.[48] The appellate court wrote, in reversing Judge Hand's decision, that "We do not believe that an objective observer could conclude from the mere omission of certain historical facts regarding religion or the absence of a more thorough discussion of its place in modern American society that the State of Alabama was conveying a message of approval of the religion of secular humanism."[49]

Impartiality or Stealth?

Hunter's efforts to obscure his relationship to his prominently partisan clients suggest that up-front disclosure might have undermined his image of impartiality. At issue is more than just his client list. Hunter apparently shares the basic beliefs of his clients, as his testimony in the Alabama textbook case and his inflammatory accusations against Planned Parenthood suggest. A careful reading of *Culture Wars* with this in mind leaves little doubt. Additionally, Hunter's warning that "culture wars precede shooting wars," would have been a lot less neat if he had had to acknowlege and elucidate the 'shooting' that has been going on for a long time.

Hunter apparently anticipated criticism of his ties to partisan interests. In the preface to *Before the Shooting Begins*, he wrote: "some will undoubtedly read this book with the chief purpose of linking it to the agenda of one social issue or another. So be it. But those who focus on this will miss the book's central concern: the possibilities of (and problems facing) substantive democracy in our historical moment."[50] These are not mutually exclusive concerns, however. Hunter's links, and the lengths he goes to obscure them, are essential to evaluating his scholarship and the sincerity of his plea for civility.

All this is particularly unfortunate, because Hunter has had useful things to say about the nature of civil discourse. Speaking at a 1993 symposium sponsored by the *Columbia Journalism Review*, he said "The idea that civil society—and the press in particular—could inform the citizenry far better than it does presently sounds idealistic and academic until we consider the options." He called for a "substantive" instead of a "shallow democracy," in which "the search is not for the middle ground of compromise, but for the common ground in which rational and moral suasion regarding basic values and issues of society are our first and last means to engage each other."[51]

Nevertheless, knowledge of his actual commitments helps to explain why, as several reviewers noted, Hunter allows the "orthodox" agenda to define the moral universe in which the culture war is supposedly waged. Abortion, homosexuality, the National Endowment for the Arts, school vouchers, and the like are featured prominently. There is little discussion of such issues as the environment, civil or labor rights, or the consequences of the gulf between rich and poor that animate what Hunter calls the "progressive" side. "So too the market," wrote David Earle Anderson, in *Christianity & Crisis*. "Not a word here (in *Culture Wars*) of the role of corporations in value forming or value shattering, such as what a plant closing does to a family, neighborhood, education—all presumably positive values in the unchanging hierarchy of the orthodox worldview." [52] Also almost completely absent are the issues of race that have defined the American experience since the arrival of slaves and the murder of Native Americans from the earliest days of colonial America. These issues continue to compel the attention of those who aspire to a moral vision of society, and generate considerable controversy in the context of the "culture war"—but not in the moral universe according to Hunter.

Despite his apparent desire for civility, he believes that "*In the final analysis, each side of the cultural divide can only talk past each other*" (emphasis in the original). The reason? Because, he claims, "the organizing principle of American pluralism" has shifted from a standard of how "one stands vis a vis Jesus, Luther, or Calvin," to how one stands in relation to the philosophers of the "secular Enlightenment of the eighteeth century."[53] Hunter's claim, that the culture wars are rooted in an irreconcilable conflict between orthodox Christianity and secular humanism is indistinguishable from McIlhenny, Rushdoony, Robertson, or virtually any leader of the Christian Right.

What's more, "pluralism" has never been defined in terms of one's relationship to Jesus and the theologians of the Protestant Reformation. Rather, the shift in American government was generally from orthodox theocracies, which promoted and enforced religious bigotry, to constitutional democracy, which promoted and protected (if imperfectly) the rights of individual conscience and more broadly, religious equality. Then as now, the leadership of "orthodox" Protestantism adamantly opposed the ideas of the Enlightenment and would never claim that orthodoxy has anything to do with pluralism.

Thomas Jefferson and others made quite clear that the religious equality (eg: "pluralism") they sought, as Jefferson drafted in the Statute of Virginia for Religious Freedom in 1777, must be extended not only to Christians, but to everyone, including "the Jew, the Mahometan, and the Hindoo."[54] Jefferson, who was U.S. Ambassador to France when Governor James Madison finally pushed the bill through the Virginia legislature in 1786, felt it was not only a political victory, but as Jefferson scholar Charles Sanford writes, "enhanced the cause of the Enlightenment abroad and the reputation of America among European intellectuals."[55]

Hunter's books are not the only ones that skew the discussion about the role of religion in politics and the future of democratic pluralism.

Intellectual Cover for Clinton
(and for the Christian Coalition!)

Stephen Carter entered the ranks of celebrity scholars after President Clinton read an advance copy of *The Culture of Disbelief* while on vacation in 1993. Speaking to a group of religious leaders upon his return, Mr. Clinton publicly urged them to read *The Culture of*

Disbelief. The resulting media frenzy led one reviewer to observe that this became a "cultural event" resulting in "more reviews" and more "discussion in the general media" than any recent book by a law professor.[56]

The president, apparently seeking to defuse the "anti-Christian" themes used against him by the Christian Right, had used the book as a prop for complaining that America has become too secularized and that religious expression is rightfully within the realm of public discourse.

Bill Clinton has, in fact, had a long history as a practicing Christian, and during his first term often and effectively used this to deflect attacks on his moral character and the unfair rhetorical assaults of the Christian Right. Clinton told a national prayer breakfast audience in 1994 that "we should all seek to know and do God's will, even when we differ."[57]

Carter's book claimed that religious expression is stifled, trivialized and ridiculed in public discourse in the U.S. While there are certainly excesses by government and other elements of society at all levels, Carter presents no evidence of anything new, beyond his own impressions. Yet his work is important to our discussion because of how its framework helps the Christian Right advance its cause.

Many, such as neo-liberal commentator Michael Kinsley, found Carter's general thesis unsupported, at best. Kinsley wondered whether Americans who "take their religion seriously" are really, as Carter claims, "consigned 'to the lunatic fringe'... Are those who 'pray regularly' forced to keep it a 'shameful secret'?" Kinsley asks. "Not in any America I recognize."[58]

Robert S. Alley, professor of the Humanities at the University of Richmond, wrote that "Carter offers no evidence that the prevailing 'political culture' is afraid of religious ways of looking at the world,"[59] and that "Carter appears to draw strength for his assertions largely from commentary and observations by church-state accommodationists supportive of the Religious Right such as Richard John Neuhaus."[60]

Although Carter is popular among some liberals, perhaps because of President Clinton's opportunistic (even if authentic) endorsement, Carter's thesis shoehorns neatly into a major theme of the Christian Right itself—the cry of religious persecution when encountering resistance to their efforts to promote their political *and* their religious agenda in public life, and through public institutions. (When, for example, the Christian Coalition was sued by the Federal Election Commission in 1996, for allegedly violating federal election laws, Marilyn Scola the state director of the Christian Coalition in Massachusetts said that the government was trying to "silence people of faith." She said to a reporter, "You've heard of religious bigotry haven't you? I think this is an example of that.")[61] Jay Sekulow of Pat Robertson's American Center for Law and Justice was delighted with the book. Although he disagrees with Carter on such issues as abortion and homosexuality, Sekulow wrote that Carter's is a "voice crying in the wilderness," which provides "a refreshing examination of the role of people of faith in society today."[62]

Although Carter is generally no friend of the Christian Right, mere religiosity seems to hamper his analysis. "The error" in much criticism of the Christian Coalition according to Carter, "is to suppose that the Christian Coalition's *religiosity* rather than its *platform* is the enemy."[63] Later in the book he similarly stresses that "what was wrong with the 1992 Republican convention was *not* the effort to link the name of God to secular political ends. What was wrong was the choice of secular ends to which the name of God was linked. Thus Pat Buchanan's world view might be objectionable to the secular liberal, but it should not be more objectionable because he offered a religious justification for it."[64]

This is an easy straw man for Carter to knock down since religious justification for political action is not now, nor has it ever been a central issue. But Carter misses the central issue: the advancement of a religious agenda is part of the political agenda of the Christian Right—which has never limited itself to secular goals. Thus it is reasonable and necessary to examine and be critical of those parts of a program that cleverly promote a religious agenda and threaten the constitutional rights of others. To do so does not mean criticizing religion per se, nor the religiosity of anyone or any group. Yet neither are we required to turn a blind eye towards religious doctrines that underlie political programs that are in turn dressed up with religious language as a shield against criticism. An organization that calls itself the Christian Coalition, and self-identifies its political agenda as distinctly "Christian" is sending an unmistakable message, one that we are not required to ignore.

Carter makes an extraordinary and utterly unsupported declaration early in the book that offers a telling insight into his method. "What is going on here in America," Carter rhetorically asks, "where religion was once thought so important that the Constitution was amended to protect its free exercise?…What has happened can be captured in one word, abortion."[65] Let us pause here for a moment. Carter is about to blame the supposed suppression of religious expression in America on *Roe v. Wade* and the legalization of abortion. If a woman's right to choose an abortion constitutes a constraint on someone else's religious freedom, we should expect at the very least a detailed argument—copious data, scholarly citations, perhaps thoughtful reflections from knowledgeable commentators. However, Carter presents no data, no scholarly citations, no thoughtful reflections, no proof.

Pamela Maraldo, Planned Parenthood president at the time, scored Carter's hyperbole as consistent with the campaign to "paint us as anti-religion."[66] While this was probably not Carter's intention (since he says he is pro-choice), it is certainly the effect, and an excellent example of how the arguments of the theocratic right are sometimes unwittingly internalized. In fact, Carter's general thesis is one of the litmus tests of what it means to be "Christian Right."

Ralph Reed, the executive director of the Christian Coalition, like Bill Clinton, made the most of the opportunity presented by Carter's book. Reed declared in his 1996 book *Active Faith* that "the issue most important to many religious conservatives [is] the creation of what Stephen L. Carter has called a 'culture of disbelief.'"[67] Reed draws heavily on Carter's argument that liberals have abandoned religious motivation for political action, as well as expression of religious conviction. He also uses Carter's unsupported exclamation on abortion as intellectual cover from which to attack the religious and civic integrity of liberals. Reed writes, "As Yale law professor Stephen Carter has observed, abortion played a central role in marginalizing the voice of faith in our public discourse, helping create a 'culture of disbelief.'"[68]

Playing into the Hands of the Theocrats

Carter's defense of religious expression in public life is undermined when he fails to recognize that the contemporary threat to religious freedom comes not primarily from secular elements, but from some of the very people who profess deep religious beliefs.

For example, he writes that "After the 1992 Republican convention, which filled the air with the kind of cruel and divisive rhetoric that gives religions a bad name, Tom Wicker of the *New York Times*, was led to draw an analogy between the antics of the religious right and the Salem witch trials of three centuries past. The comparison was apt," Carter continues, "for the Salem trials, most historians now agree, rested on a societal distaste for those who were different, particularly when those who were different were women."[69] While that "distaste" was one factor, the witch trials were possible in the first place because Salem was a theocracy in which social and religious differences were defined and punished by a singular religiously-based governmental authority. There were laws on the books calling for the execution of Jesuit missionaries, if any turned up. Far from being an exception, witch trials took place all over New England, and were based on the idea that witches were supernatural agents of Satan. Executions were not limited to Salem, nor to witches. Official religious intolerance in the Massachusetts theocracy led to the passage of anti-Quaker legislation in 1656. Many Quakers were whipped and four were hanged on Boston Common.[70]

Wicker's comparison is perhaps more "apt," than Carter realizes since Pat Robertson, who gave a prime-time speech at the 1992 GOP convention, actually praised the Massachusetts Bay Colony as a model of Christian governance in his 1989 book *The New World Order*. (Carter does not mention any of Robertson's books in *The Culture of Disbelief*, although he does refer to James Davison Hunter's "fine book," *Culture Wars*.[71])

Similarly, Carter's analysis of how mainstream press reporting trivializes religion often misses the mark. He cites, for example, the "general cultural amusement" over the mass weddings presided over by Rev. & Mrs. Sun Myung Moon.[72] Carter is correct that some bemused reporting may trivialize the faith of those who subordinate themselves to clerical authority in this way. However, Carter ignores the serious issues raised by the theocratic goals and practices of the Unification Church and how the mass weddings figure into the church's larger plans to eliminate democracy, pluralism, and religious freedom.

As was discussed in Chapter 3, Sun Myung Moon has declared that he and his wife, Hak Ja Han Moon, "are the True Parents of all humanity... we are the Savior, the Lord of the Second Advent, the Messiah."[73] And that "when it comes to our age, we must have an automatic theocracy to rule the world." He has further explained that his aim is the "subjugation of the American government and population."[74] There is copious literature on Moon's record of predatory recruiting and indoctrination practices, his 30-year record of anti-democratic pronouncements and activities,[75] the billions of dollars of assets of mysterious origin, the central role this small church plays in American life through its media, and on its business and political empire. In this light, Carter's focus on the trivialization of the Unification Church by the superficial reporting on Moon's mass weddings is breathtakingly shallow and fundamentally misguided.

Carter also fails to distinguish between oppressive attacks on religion aimed at curtailing religious expression, on the one hand, and critical debate about religion generally, and specifically religion in politics, on the other. Debating the latter issues is healthy in a country where active theocratic movements are working to undermine the principles of the enlightenment vital to meaningful democracy.

The Christian Right: Weak and Divided?

Carter extends his concern from the supposed excesses of secular society to how society should view the Christian Right. However, this discussion is hampered by his apparent lack of knowledge of the history, ideology and players of the Christian Right. Although Carter was shocked by the Christian Right's performance at the 1992 Republican national convention in Houston, he was unable to explain either how this came about or what it really meant. In the first chapter of *The Culture of Disbelief* he derided the "expression of some loud fears about the influence of the weak and divided Christian Right."[76] Oddly, the final chapter's discussion of the new-found political strength of the Christian Right is titled "Religious Fascism." Unfortunately, Carter failed to define what he meant by religious fascism, let alone its relevance to his discussion.

Still, Carter's concern for religious expression is rooted in the best of American contributions to advancing this principle. He calls not for "mere tolerance," but for religious "equality," because tolerance is extended at the whim of the majority and can be withdrawn. "[I]n a nation where 85 percent of adults identify themselves as Christians," he explains, "it may seem easier to speak of toleration of Jews and other non-Christians than to speak of equality of any practical sort. But the language of tolerance is the language of power."[77] Non-Christians, he points out, "rightly object to language suggesting that Christians (or anyone else) should 'tolerate' them. The fundamental message of the First Amendment is one of religious *equality*—a message to which the idea of majority and minority religions should be bitter anathema."[78]

One glaring example of Carter's good intentions thwarted by his superficial approach is a too-brief discussion of the 1992 flap over Mississippi Republican governor Kirk Fordice's public claim that the U.S. is a Christian Nation.[79] Carter summarizes the episode as it appeared in the media, but makes no mention of the Christian Nationalist authors, leaders and constituencies that give the term its contemporary meaning. Senior politicians rarely make declarations about such things unless they are speaking to and for a significant constituency. There was much that could have been said in this context, for example, about the role of the Christian Coalition in Fordice's election, or the significance of such Christian historical revisionists as David Barton and Gary DeMar.[80]

Nevertheless, "It is painful to me as a Christian," Carter concluded, "to watch the perversion of [Christ's message of love and inclusion]... by the far right wing of my own faith, into a call for holy war—a call which even if metaphorical, can only raise the terrifying imagery of the wholesale slaughter of the crusades."[81] While the specter of religious warfare is painful for everyone, Carter does not address the role of Christian Nationalism as an integral and animating doctrine of the Christian Right, and thus much more than a metaphor, that could lead to just such a 'holy war.' Indeed, it was precisely the grim history of religious nationalism, religious warfare and Christian persecution, of not only minority religions but fellow Christians, that led the framers of the Constitution to seek to create a constitutional structure for, and national ethos of, religious equality.

It is the cultivation (if not always successful implementation) of this ethos of religious equality over the past 200 years that has been one of the most extraordinary cultural projects in the history of the world. The Christian Nationalists of the 18th century didn't like the Constitution when it was written, and their political and theological descendants don't like it today.

The Defeat of the Christian Right?

Carter correctly concludes that the "defeat of the Christian Right—if indeed defeat is to be" will be a matter of alerting "a sufficiency of one's fellow citizens of the danger, creating a democratic counter insurgency. And then, harder still, one must get this majority to the polls on election day."[82] However, political victory over the formidable Christian Right requires knowledge and accurate assessments of its positions and prospects—something Carter does not much provide. For example, early in *The Culture of Disbelief*, he argues that "one must be wary of attributing too much influence to the emergent religious right. The Reverend Pat Robertson's efforts to gain the 1988 Republican presidential nomination was of interest mainly to the mass media…"[83]

As argued in the chapter "Neither Juggernaught nor Joke," he is correct that it is important not to unwarily "attribute too much influence" to the religious right. But it is just as important not to naively—and inaccurately—dismiss their actual strength and potential.

Indicative of a larger problem in Carter's reporting is his use of the word "Reverend" in reference to Pat Robertson. Robertson resigned his Baptist ministry to run for president in 1988, and does not, nor is he entitled to, use the honorific, "Reverend." More importantly, it is well known that Robertson has for many years been positioning himself to exert political power in the U.S. The run for president was integral to the building of a political movement, and thus was of far more than passing interest to those who follow religion and politics, especially in the GOP. Robertson actually beat George Bush in the Iowa Republican caucuses in 1988, and did well in the disputed Michigan precinct caucuses. Although the campaign unraveled after Robertson's poor showing in the "Super Tuesday" primaries in the South, Iowa and Michigan provided clues about Robertson's long- term political significance.

The Robertson campaign served as an experiment and a building block in much the same way that Barry Goldwater's unsuccessful 1964 campaign for president served as the cornerstone of the modern conservative movement. In light of Carter's claim that Robertson's 1988 campaign was a creature of the media, it is important to note that the same media generally missed the story of the rise of the Christian Coalition until well into the 1992 campaign season. Carter's lack of knowledge of the on-the-ground history of this and related political phenomena undermines his media criticism and mis-directs his "attitude" about religion in public life—which he says is the main subject of the book.[84]

The problem with Hunter's and Carter's books is not that they don't have useful thoughts and information in them. These influen-tial books pose special challenges to those who are committed to democracy, pluralism and religious freedom. Hunter is a partisan scholar from the Christian Right who is generally committed to civil-ity, but who uses a facade of neutrality to mask that he's stacking the deck of his argument. Carter is a legal scholar who disagrees with the Christian Right on most things,[85] but hasn't really studied it, and thus fails to locate the original and current threats to religious free-dom from theocratic movements.

As long as such books are major sources of intellectual guidance to which people turn for insight into the Christian Right, misdirec-tion, misinformation, misreporting and political mistakes will be the norm for every segment of society that follows them.[86] James Davi-son Hunter offers some sound advice in this regard in *Culture Wars*. "As with military campaigns, cultural warfare is always decided over the pragmatic problems of strategy, organization and resources... The factions with the best strategies, most efficient organization, and access to resources will plainly have the advantage and very possi-bly, the ultimate victory."[87]

Thus great care must be taken when reading material that will inform the strategy of a movement.

CHAPTER 9

Promise Keepers

The Death of Feminism?

While this book details the threat to democracy posed by theocratic political movements, especially the Christian Right, a closely linked cultural movement called the Promise Keepers has added an unexpected dimension to this still growing movement. On the surface, the Promise Keepers seems to simply assemble Christian men in sports arenas to pray, to improve their family life, and to purge themselves of the sin of racism. Many may wonder, what could possibly be wrong with that? As has been the story of the Christian Right and its major institutions and sub-movements, there is both more and less than meets the eye amongst the Promise Keepers.

Since its first event in 1991 the organization has become a social phenomenon with the capacity to fill sports stadia in major cities with tens of thousands of evangelical Christians seeking new meaning in their lives. However, the Promise Keepers' offer to be a catalyst in the search for meaning and family is but bait on the hook for the Christian Right. In fact, this lead agency of the "Christian men's movement" is part of a larger struggle for religious supremacy being waged by the leaders of the Promise Keepers that will emerge more strongly as they gain power and momentum.

However if such matters entered the minds of the 38,500 men inside the Carrier Dome in Syracuse New York, in June 1996, they kept it to themselves.[1] By all appearances they came to study the Bible, listen to nationally known preachers, hold hands, sing songs, roar approval at the right moments, and stand in line for expensive hot dogs and super size Cokes. Preachers clad in matching blue and purple polo shirts exhorted them to become better husbands, better fathers, to abandon the sin of racism and to obey God's Word. They prayed. They repented. They batted around beach balls. They went back to their communities. Many will join personal accountability cell groups to carry the message forward. For five years the Promise

Keepers had staged dozens of similar events all across the country. Although ostensibly apolitical, replete with soft sell appeals to new and improved marriage relationships, fatherhood and racial brotherhood, the Promise Keepers also functions as a front and recruiting agency for the Christian Right.

The Denver, Colorado-based organization has grown from an original gathering of seventy-two convened by former University of Colorado football coach Bill McCartney to filling sports arenas with as many as 72,000 men. A staff of 400 spent a projected $115 million to draw over perhaps one million attendees to nearly two dozen stadium rallies in 1996, including one in New York's Shea Stadium in September.

Most of the attendees are in their 30's and 40's, although many are in their 20's. They range from lower to upper middle class, but the dress code—sports informal—blurs class distinctions. They also tend to be overwhelmingly white, despite outreach efforts aimed at racial minorities, and particularly at African-Americans. Tickets range in cost from about $18 to $60, depending on the size of the arena; churches can buy discounted blocks of tickets. Attendees come from hundreds of miles around the regional hub where the stadium events are held and many come with their sons.

Promise Keepers events are smartly packaged, mediagenic and may be the slickest religious consumer product since televangelism. Perhaps it's the packaging, but the media rarely and barely get beyond the surface of the story and tend to cover the Promise Keepers rallies like a sporting event. The coverage is almost as superficial as explaining the Catholic Church by reporting on a Papal Blessing for the tourists in St. Peter's Square. Syndicated columnist Norman Solomon thinks that the "news coverage of Promise Keepers has been more like advertising than journalism." In 1995, ABC News cheered "a Christian men's movement devoted to reviving faith and family," and a front page story in the *New York Times* was headlined: "Men Crowd Stadiums to Fulfill Their Souls." Similarly *Time* magazine hyped the movement as: "Full of Promise."[2]

Political leaders with fingers ever to the wind are certainly assessing the breezes. President Clinton is no exception. Bill Hybels, a member of the Promise Keepers speaking team, has been a frequent jogging partner and spiritual counselor to the president. Hybels is also a former member of the board of directors of Focus on the Family, (headed by Promise Keepers director James Dobson) which is the largest and most influential organization on the Christian Right.[3]

PK Heads

Media coverage of Promise Keepers is distorted by factors similar to those which affect coverage of the wider Christian Right. In fact Promise Keepers seems almost perfectly designed to exploit media stereotypes by providing a showy event that lends itself to shallow analysis. The Promise Keepers have been the beneficiary of media and opposition tendency to exaggerate the strength of Christian Right entities. The assemblage of large numbers of men leads easily to conclusion jumping—that there are millions of "members" of the Promise Keepers—but attendance is different from membership. For example, many Promise Keeper attendees have been to more than one event, thus reducing the official total of individuals who have attended Promise Keepers events. In fact many of the ticket holders at Promise Keepers events are not unlike the "Dead Heads"—the loyal followers of the Grateful Dead rock band who would attend numerous concerts on every tour. "PK Heads" also tend to buy the requisite Promise Keepers hats and sweat shirts emblazoned with the "PK" logo.

Thus in some senses, the Promise Keepers movement is less than meets the eye. It is a clever re-packaging of elements of the evangelical (particularly the Pentecostal) movement. While the Promise Keepers is indeed a significant development in itself, it follows strongly in the tradition of tent revivals and stadium rallies, of evangelists Oral Roberts, Billy Graham, and many others which do not come to the attention of a wider public. Just as some men go to more than one conference, or go year after year, many of these have also gone forward at many an altar call.

Additionally, the Promise Keepers offers a flashy new answer to the mundane old problem of church life. Men go to church in far fewer numbers than women. Promise Keepers is the latest effort to get men to go to church. In modern America, men who work all week are generally unwilling to give up a large part of their weekend. In the Pentecostal and charismatic churches, one effort to keep men in the fold has been the Full Gospel Businessmen's Fellowship International (FGBFI); instead of luring men to church, they brought the church to the men. They would organize breakfast meetings at local restaurants before men went to work so they could keep in touch with God without sacrificing their weekends. At its height FGBFI had some 1,800 chapters in the U.S., a $6.5 million budget and a significant following in the military. The organization has declined in recent years following the death of the founder, Demos Shakarian, and one of the beneficiaries, according to *Charisma* magazine has been the Promise Keepers.[4]

It is unclear how many 'PK Heads' there are, and just as elusive is the percentage of the Promise Keepers attendees who actually join PK cell groups when they return home. What's more, it is impossible to establish how much of the ambitious social and political agenda is taken home. Indoctrination is not instantaneous, and many rally attendees may never do more than attend a rally. The process is differently paced and more subtle than either the Promise Keepers themselves or some of their critics contend. The importance of Promise Keepers need not be minimized, but its significance is elsewhere.

Replacing the "Anti-Biblical Feminist Movement?"

Promise Keepers is a Pentecostal revival organization and recruiting arm for the Christian Right. The venue has been updated from tents to sports arenas for what they hope will be nothing less than a twentieth century scale Great Awakening and the advent of the Christian Nation. But there are many baby steps to be taken on the long march to the Christian Nation. That's why these weekend conclaves are homey, fun, and designed to create a middle class comfort zone for male bonding into what it means to be a "Christian man." Unstated is the long-term meaning of being a Christian man in the context of the evolving Christian Right.

The founding text of the group, *Seven Promises of a Promise Keeper*, is published by Focus on the Family. The book is a compilation of essays on each of the "promises"—which are like a Boy Scout oath for evangelicals.

A Promise Keeper commits to:

1. "honoring Jesus ... and obedience to God's Word"
2. "pursuing vital relationships with a few other men... to help him keep his promises"
3. practice "spiritual, moral, ethical and sexual purity"

4. build "strong marriages and families through love, protection and biblical values"
5. "support the mission of his church… and praying for his pastor"
6. "reach beyond any racial and denominational barriers to demonstrate the power of biblical unity"
7. be "obedient to the Great Commandment (Jesus direction to love God and love thy neighbor as thyself) and the Great Com mission" (to evangelize and Christianize the world.)

There are no statistics on the number of the men who actually commit themselves to these promises. However, it is clear that most attendees are already evangelicals and most—eighty-eight percent according to one survey—are married. Only twenty-one percent have been divorced, which is well below the national average.[5]

Promise Keepers emphasizes that the definition of gender is not a secular matter. Gender is explained and affirmed strictly in the context of a theological patriarchy: God the Father, Jesus the son; male pastors; fathers and sons. Rev. Jerry Falwell wrote of a Promise Keepers rally he hosted at his Liberty University in 1995, "It appears that America's anti-Biblical feminist movement is at last dying, thank God, and it is possibly being replaced by a Christ centered men's movement…"[6] Promise Keepers leader Rev. Tony Evans in a much quoted passage from the *Seven Promises of a Promise Keeper* underscored the authoritarian nature of "Reclaiming Your Manhood." He wrote, "I can hear you saying, 'I want to be a spiritually pure man. Where do I start?' The first thing you do is sit down with your wife and say something like this: 'Honey, I've made a terrible mistake. I've given you my role. I gave up leading this family, and I forced you to take my place. Now I must reclaim that role.' Don't misunderstand what I'm saying here," Evans concluded, "I'm not suggesting that you *ask* for your role back, I'm urging you to *take it back*." (emphases in the original.)[7] In Syracuse, Promise Keepers leader Bill Bright, head of the Campus Crusade for Christ, said wives should be treated with love and respect and included in decision making, but the man is "the head of the household and women are responders."

Rev. Velma Brock, the Associate Pastor at the University United Methodist Church in Syracuse, wanted to see and hear Promise Keepers for herself. She also wanted to test McCartney's claim that women, particularly clergy, are not excluded, they are just not invited. Wearing her clerical collar and Promise Keepers ID bracelet for which she had paid, she got in. Once inside, she noticed that the "volunteers" who were almost all women, "were doing hard labor, such as pushing carts full of food and books." While she got into the main event, Brock was barred from sales tents; they were "for men only."

While Promise Keepers and the broader Christian Right seeks the death of feminism as Jerry Falwell wistfully declared, male domination is offered as the antidote. Lee Quinby, a feminist and professor of English at Hobart and William Smith Colleges who has studied PK, believes that the apocalyptic theology of PK leaders and much of the Christian Right induces a kind of "gender panic." If the Bible or its interpreters insist on particularly dominant roles for men in marriage, the church, and broader society, and reinforce the doctrine with some of the extraordinary images and stories from the Book of Revelation (which describes the end of the world), questions of male identity deepen—and PK leaders are there to provide answers. The "bouts of gender panic" induced in this way are answered "by efforts to quell it by reinstituting male authority." Quinby specifically references the 144,000 men (no women) who in the Book of Revelation are allowed triumphal entry into the holy city, "the New Jerusalem," because they "follow the lamb" and because they are not "defiled of women."[8] With Pat Robertson, among others, promoting the notion that biblically prophesized "end times" are upon us, believers are preparing themselves to play their respective roles.

Writer and political organizer Suzanne Pharr is disturbed by the PK's "call for the 'leadership' of men over their wives and families, for the submission of women to this leadership that holds no shared decision making, no shared power, and no equality. They base their authoritarian vision on one verse of the Bible that suggests that as Christ is to the church, man is to woman...This notion of righteous hierarchy is taught to young men as they are organized into the 'Promise Seekers.'"[9]

From Racial to Religious Supremacy

Promise Keepers rallies combine elements of the mass psychology of arena sports, tent revivals, rock concerts and political rallies. They are well paced with blues, jazz, gospel songs, evangelical songs, and even a mainline hymn, and still share some of the spirit and iconography of a rock concert tour—the 1996 "Break Down the Walls" theme even has a logo emblazoned on the program, the T-shirts, and other paraphenalia. The Promise Keepers crowd in Syracuse sang a bouncy anthem "Let the walls fall down," several times over two days—once via satellite hook-up with a Promise Keepers gathering of 10,000 in Boise, Idaho. This theme is directed to Promise #6—to reach beyond "racial and denominational barriers to demonstrate the power of biblical unity."

The Promise Keepers' call for "racial reconciliation" is similar to other genuine efforts underway in some evangelical denominations. McCartney and others speak and write movingly of "repenting the sin of racism." However, they also present "racial reconciliation" like they invented it. What's more, their approach to race glosses over racial and economic injustice past and present, blames men for their circumstances, and turns a blind eye to the major actors in society, and the major sources of solutions. Rev. Tony Evans, who is African-American and chaplain of the Dallas Mavericks professional basketball team, writes in *Seven Promises of a Promise Keeper* that, "Families today lack roots because they lack purpose and direction. They jump from place to place, job to job, looking for the good life. Their plans for the future are a muddle of self-centered whims."[10] Promise Keepers' literature and speakers make no mention, however, of the displacement of families by corporate downsizing, the export of manufacturing jobs, family crises caused by illness and death, the lack of access to adequate health care, or the destruction of neighborhoods by toxic waste dumping.

At the Syracuse rally Rev. Tom Claus, a Mohawk evangelist, introduced the theme. Wearing a full feathered headdress, he declared that despite the history of broken treaties and genocide against native peoples, he does not hate the white man because the white man brought him to Jesus and he would "rather have Jesus than all the land in the U.S." This was met with wild cheering, as was *de rigueur* whenever a speaker found a dramatic way to demonstrate that he had his priorities straight. Similarly, if less dramatically, the head of Promise Keepers' Native American outreach effort, Jon Lansa, an Arizona Hopi, told the 1996 rally in San Diego that "The most important thing is relationships: our vital relationship with Christ, and our relationship with brothers of other colors."[11]

One of the songs sung at the Syracuse rally featured a lyric that epitomizes the Promise Keepers message—that of becoming "one Holy race." The notion of membership in a "holy race," in this context, suggests transforming any actual or latent attitudes of racial supremacy into one of religious supremacy which is consistent with the Christian Nationalist goals of the Christian Right.

Half of the speakers on the stage are racial minorities. Promise Keepers started a minority outreach division in 1995 and as part of this effort, Bill McCartney systematically met with groups of minority pastors, particularly African-American pastors, during 1996. Although they claimed a minority attendance of 25 percent in St. Petersburg, Florida,[12] their outreach efforts have generally fallen short. In Syracuse, there was perhaps one face of color per hundred attendees. At the 1996 rally in Oakland, Promise Keepers claimed sixteen percent minority turnout but a writer for *Christian Century* magazine who was there reported that only one in thirty were men of color. Even Promise Keepers' vice president of reconciliation, Raleigh Washington, admits that audiences have been overwhelmingly populated by white evangelicals. A "pastors conference" of 40,000 in Atlanta noted for its minority attendance drew only 10 percent minority participants.[13]

Rev. Velma Brock, an African-American, is suspicious of Promise Keepers. She notes that African-Americans have been divided from their families and their communities since they were brought to America as slaves. "African-Americans," she says, "do not need one more source of division, particularly between men and women," who need to have relationships founded "on an equal basis." Brock saw the rally as a "means to justify their hidden agenda, which is the takeover of the political system in America."[14]

Indeed, Promise Keepers' minority outreach is part of a wider recruiting drive for the conservative movement. A special issue on black conservatives in the May 27, 1996 issue of *Citizen* magazine (issued by Promise Keepers director James Dobson's Focus on the Family) featured a discussion of Promise Keepers' outreach to African-Americans.[15] Dobson is a member of the Alexandria, Virginia-based Council for National Policy,[16] a secretive, conservative leadership group which meets quarterly and is comprised of several hundred top strategists, funders and political operatives including Howard Ahmanson, Bill Bright, Jerry Falwell, Beverly and Tim

LaHaye, Kay Cole James, Peter Marshall, Gary North, Howard Phillips, Larry Pratt, R.J. Rushdoony, Ralph Reed, Pat Robertson, Paul Weyrich, Don Wildmon and others discussed in this book. The 1996 CNP president was former Attorney General Ed Meese. Dobson co-chairs (with Phyllis Schlafly) the CNP Committee on the Family. Morton Blackwell is the executive director. While members do not necessarily agree on all things, this is one leadership forum where strategies, for recruitment of minorites for example, can be discussed debated, and planned.

The Promise Keepers should be viewed in the context of the political and social goals of the members of the Council for National Policy; it is in that context that what's wrong with the Promise Keepers becomes clear. Author Russ Bellant who has done the most definitive reporting on CNP writes that the secretive group "was inspired by business and political leaders who were also leaders of the John Birch Society. The CNP is attempting to create a concentration of power to rival and eventually eclipse traditional power centers in the U.S."[17] Unsurprisingly, such CNP and Christian Right leaders as Jerry Falwell, Pat Robertson, and D. James Kennedy have promoted Promise Keepers through their extensive media empires. As such, Promise Keepers is seen as a vehicle for promoting the wider goals of the secular and Christian Right, from the dismantling of the public shools, to the criminalization of abortion and homosexuality, the radical deregulation of every major consumer and environmental protection initiative of the federal government, and the weakening, if not elimiantion of civil rights laws protecting the interests of women and minorities.

Ralph Reed's Painful Truth

White evangelicals have traditionally held views on racial and economic justice that stand in contrast to those of the ecumenical movement in mainline Protestantism. The National Council of Churches and the World Council of Churches have been at the forefront of the struggle for racial and economic justice, actively supporting the civil rights movement, standing up to neo-Nazi violence, and working against South African apartheid. The wider religious community of the U.S., including the U.S. Catholic Conference of Bishops and Reformed Judaism, have made historic stands opposing racial prejudice and its institutional manifestations in legislation and litigation. White evangelicals have generally been either neutral or actively opposed to these efforts.

This is now acknowledged by Ralph Reed, executive director of the Christian Coalition. Reed writes in his 1996 book *Active Faith*, that the Promise Keepers, the Christian Coalition, and "other pro-family groups are making the inclusion of African-Americans and Latinos in their ranks a major priority."[18] Reed also admits that the Christian Right has "moral blind spots on issues ranging from anti-Semitism and anti-Catholicism to racial injustice…The painful truth is that religious conservatives must confront in their general disdain of modern liberalism is this: liberals have been correct throughout history on issues of social justice while we have been neglectful or derelict in applying the Christian principles of our faith to establish justice in a fallen world. When it came to racism, where were conservative evangelicals? They were not only on the sidelines, but on the wrong side of the most central cause of social justice in this century."[19]

Reed is sometimes capable of such remarkable words, but the political calculation behind them is clear. When Reed ruefully acknowledges the moral failures of white evangelicals, he seems less remorseful than regretful that the Christian Right "has had a difficult time achieving moral resonance in the broader society" as a result.[20] "The sad record of religious conservatives on race," Reed complains, "gives liberals reason to hurl charges of bigotry and intolerance at us."[21]

The Christian Right's answer to this problem of moral credibility and political viability is to attempt to hijack the moral and spiritual authority of the American civil rights movement. "It would be a clear distortion," Reed writes in *Active Faith*, "to compare the recent political involvement of the white evangelical church with the black church as a political force."[22] Then he spends the better part of a chapter doing just that.

John Perkins, head of John Perkins Ministries in Pasadena, California, is one of the leading proponents of the doctrine of "racial reconciliation," the conservatives' new approach to race. An African-American and member of the Promise Keepers speaking team, he was featured at the 1996 Promise Keepers "pastors conference" in Atlanta, and his work is recommended in *Seven Promises of a Promise Keeper*. Interestingly, Perkins' principal backer, contributing $800, 000 in recent years, is a leading Christian Right financier and strategist,

Howard Ahmanson. Ahmanson is also the longtime bankroller and director of the Chalcedon Foundation, a Reconstructionist think tank, and a member of the Council for National Policy.[23] Perkins and other featured black speakers at PK rallies have also been active in the theocratic Coalition on Revival[24] (which was discussed in Chapter 5).

Certainly a high point—if not the definitive moment of the Christian Right's campaign for moral and racial credibility—will be the fundamentalist, multi-racial "million man march" on Washington, DC in the Fall of 1997 which the Promise Keepers have been planning since early 1995. The Promise Keepers and the wider Christian Right that supports them hope to seize the mantle of moral authority held by the civil rights movement and erase the image of the white fundamentalist as hypocrite and bigot. Regardless of how the march is ultimately interpreted by the media, the Promise Keepers' experienced staff, big budget, well crafted messages, and media-savvy staging will make this an historic event. Promise Keepers leaders are insisting, however, that it is not going to be a political event.

Undermining Christian Denominations

Significantly, Promise #6 causally equates racism with religious denominations as if they were problems of the same kind. Promise Keepers views racism as a barrier to unity in the "body of Christ" and sees denominational structures—and of course different accepted theologies—as also standing in the way of their goals. This can mean controversy within individual congregations when the stadium veterans return home and start Promise Keepers cells in their churches, attend Promise Keepers leadership training sessions or even take special Promise Keepers courses at conservative seminaries in Denver and Orlando. The cell group leaders or "Key Men" report to area "Ambassadors," who in turn report directly to Promise Keepers headquarters in Denver. John Swomley, a professor emeritus at the St. Paul School of Theology in Kansas City, warns that Promise Keepers "is particularly dangerous because of the divisions it seeks to create within mainline churches" that do not accept Promise Keepers' fundamentalist theology and politics.[25]

Although it is not widely reported, there is actually a "Promise Keepers Statement of Faith," which includes the fundamental notion of fundamentalism: that the Bible is the literal word of God, "We believe that the Bible is God's written revelation to man and that it is verbally inspired, authoritative, and without error in the original manuscripts."[26] McCartney himself writes that "We are going to break down the walls that separate us so that we might demonstrate the power of biblical unity…"[27] This vague notion of "biblical unity" is actually the pivotal idea that sets the stage for the attack on traditional denominations and social institutions. Further, if Promise Keepers is able to successfully instruct its followers to conduct their lives and marriages according to Promise Keepers standards, they may also be able to dictate the specifics of their religious beliefs. Promise Keepers is a strategy on the part of biblical fundamentalists and right-wing political operatives to appeal to the social and spiritual needs among the middle class before bringing them more deeply into the religious and political whirlwind they seek to set in motion.

However, there are also issues of outside accountability within the marriage. Members of PK cells are required to submit intimate aspects of their lives from their sex lives to their finances to the group to be judged as to whether they are conforming to Promise Keepers' standards. Journalist Russ Bellant who has tracked the connections of McCartney, Ryle and other Promise Keepers leaders to the cultic "shepherding discipleship" movement, notes that this controversial cultic cell group structure is not well known even within the evangelical community. "[M]any would be deeply offended," writes Bellant, "if they experience the degree of manipulation and control (to which they may be 'submitting' themselves and their families) that has occurred in many shepherding/discipleship situations."[28] Promise Keepers' own seminal text *Seven Promises of a Promise Keeper* mentions the shepherding strain within the movement noting that "Some Christian traditions speak of spiritual directors, shepherds, or even spiritual fathers." While the term "shepherd" is in some senses generic, in this community it has very specific meanings regarding the authoritarian hierarchy of leaders and followers.

The Politics of an Apolitical Movement

Despite frequent claims of being apolitical, the hot button "social issues" of the Christian Right regularly percolate through the Promise Keepers events. For example, Rev. James Ryle in his Syracuse altar call sermon listed a series of consequences of what he called the glorification of "the self" over Christ. These included "murder," "drug" addiction and "the gay movement." McCartney himself directed one Promise Keepers rally to "Take the nation for Jesus Christ;" at another he said battles would be waged, "Wherever truth is at risk, in the schools or legislature...We will win."[30]

Outside of PK rallies, the leaders are active in American political life. Ryle participated in a secret 1994 conference to plan anti-gay electoral strategies in Colorado. There he addressed "the crisis of homosexuality" which he sees as part of a "cultural revolution, which has poised our nation precariously on the brink of moral chaos...."[31] McCartney has addressed gatherings of Operation Rescue, and campaigned for Colorado's Amendment 2, which would have barred local civil rights ordinances protecting gays and lesbians. The referendum on the Amendment passed, but was declared unconstitutional by the U.S. Supreme Court.

The conferences themselves provide a cultural staging area to deepen the political consciousness and involvement of those who respond to the PK appeal. For example, although Promise Keepers leader Bill Bright's speech in Syracuse did not drift off into political matters, less than a football field away, organizers were selling his new book, *The Coming Revival: America's Call to Fast, Pray and Seek God's Face*. In it, Bright denounces the teaching of evolution instead of the "biblical view of creation" in the schools[32] and Supreme Court decisions which he believes too "sharply defined the separation of church and state,"[33] banned state sponsored prayer in the schools,[34] legalized abortion,[35] and "misinterpreted the Constitution."[36] He also denounces "the homosexual explosion," and blames gay rights initiatives on "anti-Christian forces."[37]

Such declarations are particularly disturbing because the words of Promise Keepers leaders, like those of other Christian Right leaders, are filled with military metaphors for their activities. Often they are not simply metaphors, but direct comparisons. Bill McCartney has said "The first principle of war is unity of command. The second principle of war is unity of effort..."[38] Similarly, PK speaker Dr. Steven Farrar declared that "If you don't understand that a war has been declared on the biblical family, then you are missing the boat. We are at war in this nation. War has been declared." Also, PK co-founder David Wardell unsubtly announced that "We're drawing a line in the sand here...There has already been controversy about abortion and homosexuality. I hope there won't be physical confrontation but look at Amendment 2 and the Act-Up people and the foreign religions coming in here."[39]

Rev. James Ryle has a dramatic and disturbing vision of the future of PK. Ryle who is Bill McCartney's personal pastor and a director of Promise Keepers, explained to Russ Bellant that he believes Promise Keepers is the fulfillment of a biblically prophesied end-times army which will destroy sinners and unbelievers. "Never have 300,000 men come together throughout human history," he said, "except for the purposes of war."[40] In this context, it is particularly unsettling that there are a number of former military officers (including Special Forces veterans), serving as top PK leaders.[41]

This pre-millenialist vision is not unlike Pat Robertson's. He foresees a world war "motivated by demonic spirits," in which two billion people will die during a period of "tribulation."[42]

For an organization that bills itself as building "men of integrity," there is a great deal of opportunistic double talk. Love your wife, (but demand submission). Serve your pastor, (but undermine his denomination). Seek racial unity, (but only among the biblically correct). March on Washington, DC, (but claim it's not political). Bring Christian love to the world (and prepare for war). Promise Keepers President Randy T. Phillips wrote in the Syracuse program book for example: "Before us, we have the opportunity to see this generation, this nation, and this world transformed." But these transformations, as we have seen, involve much more than showy rallies in football stadiums and much more than self-improvement.

The Stadium Shopping Network

But as Phillips knows better than any one, on the road to the apocalypse, there is still an organization to run. Thus one critical component of the business of Promise Keepers is business. This is a significant part of the cultural and financial success of the movement. In Syracuse, New York, the downtown business community was thrilled that Promise Keepers was coming to town. Every hotel and motel room in the area had been booked for months. The Syracuse *Post-Standard* put out a special conference edition of the paper headlined: "WELCOME PROMISE KEEPERS!"

Promise Keepers is a sophisticated nonprofit business, generating considerable income from ticket sales and the merchandising of Promise Keepers products (as well as the offering taken up at each stadium rally). But with the sexual and financial scandals of Pentecostal televangelists Jim and Tammy Bakker and Jimmy Swaggart still so fresh in people's minds, Promise Keepers is careful to sell an image of "purity." One Promise Keepers backer observed that all it would take would be one sex or financial scandal "and the whole organization will come apart like a cheap suit."[43] While this may be overstating the case, Promise Keepers' play book does seem to owe more to the soft-sell of upscale companies like Land's End than to Swaggart.

Promise Keepers not only has its own catalog and web site, but successfully markets through Christian book stores. In Syracuse, Promise Keepers set up three big tents, the largest of which was 100x200 feet, next to the Carrier Dome, on the grounds of Syracuse University. Promise Keepers' products and services are modeled on and in many respects are extensions of those offered by Focus on the Family—the big Christian Right "ministry" of radio psychologist James Dobson. Focus on the Family filled one tent. A second tent featured exhibits of other ministries, mostly foreign missions. Most of what they offered was free.

The Promise Keepers tent displayed row after row of Promise Keepers merchandise on cafeteria tables—PK baseball hats, PK football jerseys, PK golf shirts, PK jackets, and PK sweats—all available in several different styles. There were PK mugs, pens, books, videos, and CDs and cassettes of the greatest hits of past Promise Keepers rallies.

Promise Keepers is at or near the cutting edge in the marketing of products which link the identity of the individual with the product and the corporate image. They have apparently learned to use catalogs and retail outlets from observing the likes of Pepsi, Disney and Marlboro Gear. The official PK edition of the New Testament, *PK: Man of His Word* makes the Good Book look like a cross between a product catalog and *Sports Illustrated*. Interspersed among the books of the Bible are personality profiles of Christian athletes. And at the end, right after the Book of Revelation, there are ads and tear-out cards for PK products — including an opportunity to "Save on Promise Keepers New Testaments by the Case." (They are priced to sell—$35 per case of 20, $75 per case of 50)

Finally, there was a PK merchandise mart on the floor of the Carrier Dome, roped off on two sides with a banks of cashiers on either end. At one point, Bob, the MC for the event, waded down from the stage for a live televised guided tour, which we watched on giant TV screens visible from every part of the stadium. Bob showed off some of the Promise Keepers books, videos, and CDs for your home improvement "tool box." Then the crowd rushed down to shop. The loss leader designed to help get men on the program is the hard cover of *The Seven Promises of a Promise Keeper*, priced at only $5.

Stop Religious Warfare Before It Starts

The Promise Keepers movement is the most dynamic element of the Christian Right in the mid-1990's. How long it can sustain its appeal with stadium rallies as expensive as football games remains to be seen. It is important to view it as but one manifestation of a growing cultural and political movement. Like the rest of the Christian Right, it is far from a juggernaut. There is a coarse and unappealing aspect to its unstated but transparent appeal to religious supremacism as replacement for racial supremacism. Political analyst Chip Berlet has pointed out that Promise Keepers is also a crass appeal to the boys club of gender supremacism. "Power in America has traditionally been accorded to straight white men," he says. In the case of Promise Keepers, Berlet observes that "the boys club has been expanded to include people of color. When push comes to shove," he asks, "what's more important, race or gender?"[44] Similarly, Lee Quinby, writes that "From my angle of vision, the movement looks more like power keepers."[45]

If the Promise Keepers are properly understood and their agenda properly articulated by those who question or oppose the Christian Right, there are many opportunities to expose the the movement before it infuses hundreds of thousands of new activists into the Christian Right. The religious bigotry and overt Christian nationalism that is integral to the cultural and political agenda of Promise Keepers and the wider Christian Right is one of its least noticed features. However, it is the crucial seed of the growing theocratic political movement in the U.S. and the tap root of the religious warfare sprouting from this movement, which is still in its early stages.

CHAPTER 10

Defending Democracy

Rethink the Strategy

As the preceding chapters make clear, the threat posed by the Christian Right comes not from a few extreme elements but from well-organized cadres, both political and paramilitary, dedicated to overthrowing democracy. What responses are appropriate?

The Christian Right is successfully exploiting the larger crisis of democracy—the extraordinary lack of participation by most Americans in electoral politics specifically, and in political life generally. Although the Christian Right often functions as a disciplined minority bloc of voters, it is not nearly as large, unified, or powerful as it often appears, and it does not have the numbers to politically prevail. Thus the answers to much-asked questions about what to do about the Christian Right lie not so much in polls, focus groups and "message" politics, as they do in the basics of participatory democracy and constitutional government.

Among the obstacles to an effective response to the Christian Right is political opportunism in the form of collaboration with the Christian Right by elements of both major parties, especially the Republicans. Other obstacles previously discussed include terminological gridlock and overestimation and underestimation of the Christian Right. Such obstacles must be eliminated or greatly reduced in order to reverse the march to power by the Christian Right.

In any case, a prerequisite for thwarting the Christian Right is a fundamental rethinking of the strategy. There are people named in this book whose hostility to democracy is indeed eternal, and who seek to destabilize the normal functioning of government and society at all levels, from the school board to the White House. Some are anti-abortion terrorists. Others seek to undermine or abolish the public schools. Others seek armed theocratic revolution. Still others may be content to gain political power in order to obtain social control in the near future. All are some variety of Christian National-ist. Any strategy to deal with these elements must take into account their common goals. Many members of the Christian Right see themselves as engaged in a religious war and are intent on undo-ing what the framers of the U.S. Constitution accomplished over 200 years ago. Countering this assault will require a knowledge of the strategy and goals of the Christian Right beyond the single issues that dominate the so-called culture war.

The ancient Chinese military philosopher Sun Tzu stated in his classic *The Art of War*, "what is of importance in war is to attack the enemy's strategy." This concept was discussed 15 years ago by Christian Right theorists Gary North and David Chilton in an arti-cle that foreshadowed much of the contemporary tactics of the Chris-tian Right. They explained that it is necessary to understand the strategy of the opposition in order to appropriately counter it. Much of the Christian Right's strategy is based on sound political think-ing, grounded in reality, although they also keep a weather eye on the supposed satanic conspiracy which they claim is responsible for "humanists" disestablishing the churches and creating pluralist civil orders in the U.S. and Europe. "Satan and his forces understood the strategy of Christians," they wrote, "… better than Christians under-stood Satan's strategy."[1] To the extent that the claims of being engaged in religious warfare are not just the stuff of direct mailing fundraising promotions, it is necessary to determine what the oppo-sition's strategy actually is.

The Strategy of the Christian Right

Four key elements of the strategy of the Christian Right by which they have achieved considerable political power are: increased ideological unity; exploitation of ignorance about their movement for political advantage; exploitation of the theme of reli-gious freedom and persecution for political advantage; and mobi-lization of a disciplined voting bloc with which to take over the Republican Party and ultimately to attain hegemonic political power in the U.S.

1. Increasing ideological unity

In terms of theology, this unity is manifested by the factions of the Cristian Right being able to agree to disagree in order to pursue a common political game plan and implement a common political agenda. Their plan includes indoctrinating constituents with revisions of American history designed to justify the Christian Right's contemporary political activities and agenda.

2. Exploiting ignorance about the movement for political advantage

While "stealth tactics" contribute to the ignorance, simple lack of knowledge about many aspects of the Christian Right on the part of otherwise well-informed people in the media and public life remains a major advantage for the movement. For example, more than a few people routinely say "the Christian Coalition" when they mean the broader Christian Right. This is more than a casual slip by politically literate people. It's like saying the Boston Red Sox when you mean baseball.

3. Exploiting the themes of religious freedom and religious persecution

The Christian Right motivations for invoking religious freedom are to silence liberal critics of their political agenda, to create a cohesive sense of destiny among their constituents, and to gain disproportionate latitude to exert their religious agenda in public affairs, and in public spaces and institutions.

4. Mobilizing a disciplined voting bloc

The main near-to-mid-term objective for mobilization is to take over the Republican Party from the inside, systematically achieving political power by running for political offices at all levels, beginning with lower level offices. This is based on the theory that it is possible to exert political influence disproportionate to their numbers. So far it is working.

Defending Democracy and Pluralism: Five Core Elements

How can the four elements of Christian Right strategy—ideological unity, exploiting ignorance, misappropriating the banner of religious freedom, and a disciplined voting bloc—be countered? Any effective program must, as Sun Tzu states, attack the strategy of the theocratic right and should incorporate the following:

1. Reclaim American History, and the Theme of Religious Freedom

Religious freedom means equality and pluralism, not as R.J. Rushdoony argued when the Rutherford Institute was founded, merely more space for Christian evangelism and political activities to fight "the battle against statism and [for] the freedom of Christ's Kingdom."[2] Major Christian Right initiatives should be examined in the light of Christian Reconstructionist intentions to utilize the culture of pluralism and religious freedom in order to systematically gain the political power necessary to erode and abolish religious freedom.

Christian Nationalism lost decisively when the Constitution was ratified. Not only did the framers vote to ban religious tests for public office, they did so unanimously: Deists, Anglicans and Calvinists alike. They realized that this was the best means of inoculating against the religious warfare and persecution that had wracked Europe for centuries. In order to defeat the Christian Right, it will be necessary to intellectually reconnect with the roots of religious freedom in the United States.

Progressives have long been the leaders in opposing bigotry in all facets of American life—beginning with religion and conscience and subsequently including race, gender, ethnicity, and sexual orientation. The right to difference begins with the right to individual conscience. The former would not have been possible without the latter. Progressives must reclaim this heritage, envision its contemporary meaning, and become vigorous, knowledgeable defenders of religious freedom.

Religious freedom is a concept that has often been marginalized as something of concern primarily to minority religions—whether Jews, Muslims, or "new religions." The effective defense of religious freedom recognizes that the theocratic worldview barely distinguishes between the Christians and non-Christians who do not share the particular distinctives of their theology. Come the theocracy, the religiously incorrect may all be subject to being charged with such capital offenses as heresy, apostasy, idolatry and propagating false doctrines. The insufficiently Christian, the public freethinker, and the theologically suspect will not be "tolerated." Those who support religious freedom against bigotry have a far greater claim to the "original intentions of the founding fathers," and should draw on the history and philosophical origins of constitutional law and the national ethos of religious pluralism. The historical high ground belongs to the pluralists and is available to thwart the Christian Right's efforts to capture the mantle of history as a contemporary means of legitimation.

2. Register and Mobilize Voters

It should be axiomatic that participatory democracy is defined by participation. The Christian Right has successfully exploited the current low voter participation crisis of democracy. Part of the answer to this crisis is locally focused voter registration and mobilization campaigns, which should target certain constituencies and certain institutions. Key to such efforts are integration of voter identification and registration into the daily life of democratic institutions. The Christian Right, which has sought to maximize its political clout by creating a disciplined voting bloc, to date has largely succeeded by changing the political and electoral culture of their key institutions—individual churches. Voter registration and identification are carried out by the Christian Coalition year round, with the information systematically computerized for later use. Similarly, the Christian Coalition and Focus on the Family conduct leadership schools year round. Activist churches in the network carry out "in pew" voter registration drives on designated Sundays prior to the registration deadline.

Similar political development programs can be logical outgrowths of existing institutions, consistent with their aims and organization. For example, voter registration could be part of the membership functions of local chapters of organizations like the Sierra Club and the YWCA, as well as churches and religious institutions that oppose Christian Nationalism and support the separation of church and state.

These activities need to be carried out systematically across the election cycles and not crammed into the six months before biannual elections, then revved up yet again 18 months later. The necessary resources and expertise are probably available locally, so there is no need to wait for leadership from national organizations. Exhortations to "VOTE!" are always insufficient. Detailed information such as dates of primaries and candidate filing deadlines can be published in organizational newsletters and posted on bulletin boards. Most importantly, such things must be normal, not exceptional. If a range of organizations and individuals undertake an initiative to change the political and electoral culture—beginning with their own organizations— it will be easier to learn from each other's experiences and create a mutually reinforcing base from which to respond to the Christian Right.

One result of integrating the culture of civics and electoral politics into the daily life of an organization will be a larger pool of volunteers and professionals with evolving expertise in non-traditional forms of voter mobilization. It is out of such activated constituencies that prospective candidates for office will likely be identifed, offered any appropriate training and resources, and provided with a political base on which they can rely. All this will be essential in ongoing electoral contests with the Christian Right—and in building an electoral base that is not necessarily controlled by the political parties. The Christian Right's compilation of local voter files can be easily emulated and the result utilized by new hybrids in political and cyberspace skills.

Although there is "motor voter" registration in most places now, sometimes people, particularly young people and renters, move more often than they change drivers licenses. It is important to maintain the eligibility of voters committed to democratic values by updating their addresses with the local board of elections, ensuring that absentee ballots are obtained in time and ensuring that newcomers are registered, know the location of the polling place, and have access to transportation. All this may require some specific, but modest, investments in training, research and organizational infrastructures to achieve the necessary pool of knowledge and skills. More simply put, organizations may develop volunteer voter education and mobilization committees, and perhaps even assign staff to such projects.

As Christian Right theorist Gary North wrote in the mid-1980s, "our job is not to 'throw the rascals out' in one glorious national election. Our job is to replace them steadily by our own competence."[3] The real strength of the Christian Right has come in this way—through competent organizing—although the high profile growth spurts brought on by the Christian Coalition or Operation Rescue have gotten most of the attention and the credit. The latter would not be possible without the former.

One tactical use of voter mobilization could be to help thwart the specific Christian Right goal of taking over the Republican party infrastructure, by stopping Christian Right candidates in the primaries. In states with "open primary" laws such as California and Virginia, the disciplined voting bloc of the Christian Right can be countered by turning out non-Republican voters in normally low-turn-out primaries. Democrats and independents can vote against Christian Right candidates in the primary and vote as they choose in the general election. For example, crossover voting in the GOP primary for the 1996 nomination for U.S. Senator from Virginia appears to have been a factor in the victory of moderate John Warner over Christian Right-backed candidate James Miller.

3. Research

There is no substitute for knowledge of the players and institutions, *local* as well as national, of the Christian Right. This may be acquired by coming to understand the culture of the Christian Right, whose key local and regional institutions are usually churches, bookstores, and radio stations. Since the Christian Right is a church-based political network, it stands to reason that there is a core network of activist churches which provide the activists, the candidates, the campaign workers, the meeting space, and the core of the local voting bloc. Wherever there is an active Christian Right, there will very likely be a Christian bookstore that serves as a political community center of sorts. Sometimes it is freestanding, sometimes connected to a church. This is where political meeting notices, newsletters and other useful information can be picked up, usually for free. There is, for example, a free directory available in many communities called *The Shepherd's Guide*, which, while not exclusively about the

Christian Right, is a helpful resource to anyone researching the local or regional Christian Right. Often, too, a Christian radio station that covers public affairs may have a local talk show or community calendar worth monitoring. By listening in and selectively taping, one can learn of significant Christian Right speakers coming to town, and document the unvarnished views of local figures who often speak more freely on "Christian radio" than in other formats. Any sensible counter strategy must be based on making an accurate assessment of the local Christian Right. These simple monitoring activities are the necessary minimum.[4]

Although knowledge of the opposition is critical to the formulation of good strategy, few state or national organizations of the center or the Left do much in the way of systematic opposition research. There are a number of small research organizations that do fine work, and help to inform a growing network of community-based groups that have sprung up to fight the Right in San Diego and Sacramento, California; Colorado Springs, Colorado; Kansas City, Kansas; New Haven, Connecticut; and Northampton, Massachusetts, to mention but a few. The Mainstream Voters Project (MVP) in San Diego originally came together to try to understand what had happened in the San Diego Surprise of 1990, when a slate of stealth candidates took over first the GOP central committee, then 60 of 90 local offices open in the November elections. Since then, the bi-partisan MVP has been an influential source of information and analysis about candidates and organizations in the San Diego area, publishing a four-page monthly newsletter, doing public speaking and serving as a source for reporters nationwide. In an information age, MVP has proven that political information counts.

Many of the characters discussed in these chapters have long track records, and very often their views and activities are a matter of public record. Too often, however, valuable information is unavailable to the defenders of democratic values and when it is available, it is under utilized. One remarkable example is that Larry Pratt's connection to the militia movement and to white supremacists was exposed by Lenny Zeskind in *Rolling Stone* magazine six months before it became a campaign issue in the New Hampshire presidential primary campaign of Pat Buchanan.[5] Although media exposure of the controversial views of Christian Right leaders is important to the development of long range political responses, dedicated constituencies may not be influenced by media they consider to be too secular or "anti-Christian" in the first place. Actual political power comes more from being able to deliver votes and candidates than clips and bites.

There is much to be learned from the successes—and the failures—of the Christian Right. Obviously, there is much that is not replicable in any community but their own. Since they are far from monolithic, they cannot always replicate their own successes any more than they can avoid certain obvious failures. They have done some things very well, and there are important political lessons to be learned, and applied.

4. Identify and Expose the Christian Right's Contradictions and Weaknesses

This is a logical outgrowth of political research. Although theological and political unity are some of the great achievements of the Christian Right to date, their coalition, like any other in American politics, is an often uneasy alliance, full of flaws and contradictions. Extreme statements about a range of issues are not hard to find. However, useful information and analysis can be gleaned from the internecine ideological battles within the Christian Right.

Theocratic purists, for example, are often critical of the Christian Right which is, after all, a political movement, attempting to gain influence with a wider public than actually supports its vision and many of its programs. Theocrats like these say that they are simply not willing to compromise on God's "standards," and are often the sharpest critics of the more "mainstream" Christian Right. There is much to be learned from the critiques of movement insiders who share many of the same goals, but different means.

For example, Rev. Michael Bray, an anti-abortion leader from Bowie, Maryland, is frustrated by the "immaturity" of the Christian Right, which, he feels "has no vision for administration of government by the Almighty's standards."

"Were a popular revolution to occur over—let's say taxes, what kind of government would be put in place?" Bray asks. He wonders whether "the various groups who whine about the loss of national 'values' are ready to define which 'values' are good and which are evil?" Bray questions, for example, whether Concerned Women for America has "a position on what the penalty shall be for abortion when it is outlawed?"—knowing full well that they probably don't. The reason that they don't is that no one is challenging Beverly LaHaye and her sidekick, Jim Woodall, to come up with one. Such subjects are awkward for Christian Right leaders since so many women in their own constituency have had abortions and continue to get them, and since there are far more women who attend church on Sunday than men. That is one reason why the focus on stopping abortions excludes the discussion of what the penalties would be if their movement succeeds.

Reconstructionist author Gary DeMar of Atlanta, who urges the death penalty for "abortionists and parents who hire them," counsels "consistency" in the thinking of the Christian Right. He says "If abortion is murder, then we must call for the death penalty. If abortionists are not supposed to be executed, then they are not murderers, and if they are not murderers, why do we want to abolish abortion?"[6] DeMar's logic is impeccable. Those who insist that abortion is murder ought to be challenged with the public policy implications of their views. If, in Gary DeMar's scenario, abortion providers and would-have-been parents are to be executed, how far would the web of culpability extend in terms of accomplices and co-conspirators? Politicians could be asked, if abortion is murder, then who are the culprits? If abortion were criminalized in this way, how many prisons would be needed to accommodate all the new criminals serving long sentences for accomplice to murder? How would the politicians propose to pay for these facilities and to staff and supply these facilities?

Michael Bray wonders about the Christian Coalition's "position on the just penalty for sodomy?" Robertson and his staff are strong on denouncing the things of which they do not approve, but vague on exactly what ought to be done about them. They don't say, because their final solutions might jeopardize their efforts to achieve "mainstream" legitimacy. While the sheer invasion of privacy would probably appall most Americans, the bizarre priorities such policies would establish in already overextended law enforcement budgets are the stuff of which late night comedy is made.

Bray also wonders if the moderate evangelical magazine *Chris-*

tianity Today has, for instance, "a position on the reestablishment of Christendom in these United States or does it advocate 'pluralism' as an ideal? Were the constitutions of the individual colonies (expressly declaring themselves to be Christian) a bad idea?"[7] Such questions, asked of the major figures of the Christian Right, usually lead to rapid dissembling. Some would also have a hard time explaining their endorsement of Christian theocracy, or of key aspects, such as "Christian oaths" for pubic office, in their books and articles. In previous chapters, Michael Farris, the 1993 GOP candidate for Lt. Governor of Virginia, Pat Robertson, and televangelist D. James Kennedy were quoted expressing these views.

Such beliefs and opinions are openly published by the theocratic right and are actively discussed in Christian Right circles. For example, Christian Right attorney Michael Hirsh's graduate thesis at Pat Robertson's Regent University Law School, which justified the murder of abortion providers, was not only considered within the respectable range of views that qualified him for graduation from law school, but was no barrier to his being hired by Pat Robertson's answer to the ACLU—the American Center for Law and Justice—which is located at the law school.[8]

There are many even more obvious points of hypocrisy and contradiction in Christian Right organizations that should be explored. Pat Robertson and Ralph Reed frequently completely contradict one another on matters such as the separation of church and state and Christian Nationalism.[9] Robertson takes the extreme view; Reed comes on TV like a moderate. The Christian Coalition cannot have it both ways any more than any other interest group can have its top two figures in obvious public contradiction about issues central to its mission and identity. They have gotten away with these inconsistencies because their opponents have been insufficiently alert or equipped to take advantage of the opportunities presented by such obvious weaknesses. Additionally, the media has permitted a double standard by ignoring or under-reporting such significant matters while thoroughly airing schisms elsewhere in political and religious life. Facts in hand, it is possible to hold the media accountable for such lapses.

The political fault lines between the unabashed Christian Nationalists and those who dissemble into bland pronouncements about "family values"are very unstable. Different fault lines exist around such issues as the role of women in society, religious freedom, anti-abortion violence, and the viability, even the desirability of public schools and even of democracy itself.

Mother Jones magazine detailed one such hypocrisy, which could become a fault line in the Christian Right. The "pro-life" organizations and the broader Christian Right generally either oppose, or have no position on, efforts to curb smoking—even though one medical journal published a survey of the existing medical literature and found that smoking may be linked to over 100,000 "miscarriages" or "spontaneous abortions" annually in the U.S. alone. Anti-abortion activist Pat Mahoney of the Christian Defense Coalition says he worked for a year to no avail to engage the major anti-abortion groups on the issue. "It's hypocrisy," Mahoney correctly declares. Part of the reason for the schism is that the Republicans generally, as well as key politicians specifically, are also allied with the tobacco industry. Mahoney observes, for example, that "It's obvious that Sen. Helms is more concerned about contributions from Philip Morris than standing for the dignity of human life."[10] Similarly, Don Wildmon's American Family Association attacks corporate conglomerate Philip Morris for sponsoring television programs which depict homosexuality in a context of normalcy, but turns a blind eye to how the company presents smoking as a normal and acceptable lifestyle choice.[11]

5. Practice Democratic Values

The style of democratic practice should be consistent with democratic values. Defending democracy and pluralism requires avoiding the tactics of demonization and demagoguery that have generally propelled the theocratic right. Members of the Christian Right will continue to also be members of our communities—regardless of the outcome of the political struggles of the day. They may be people we see at the supermarket, the Little League game or just around the neighborhood. Most people on all sides are sincere and honestly—motivated people who have much more in common with one another than the divisive demagogic rhetoric of Christian Right leaders would suggest. The tools of division can be neutralized, in part, by practicing democratic values in an effort to *de-demonize* all sides. It is necessary to respect the religious rights of all people, including political opponents, and to vigorously defend those who are the targets of religious bigotry. Defense of religious freedom also should not be relegated exclusively to members of the clergy. All political leaders must become at least as articulate about religious freedom and religious bigotry as they are about matters of race, gender, and sexual orientation. Madison and Jefferson understood rights of conscience to be synonymous with religious rights. Thus, defending the right to non-belief is as vital as defending the right to believe. And the right to believe differently is equal to the right to self-proclaimed orthodoxy.

Part of the value of political research is that actual knowledge reduces the unfounded fears and false assumptions that lead to demonization and misdirected political strategy. Actual knowledge allows one to arrive at fair and accurate conclusions, and leads to the confidence required to make strong charges stick in public.

A few years ago, a group of researchers and activists (including the author), subsequently called the Blue Mountain Working Group, met to discuss the challenge of the Christian Right and released "A Call To Defend Democracy & Pluralism."[12] This expression of democratic values states in part, "The leaders of the anti-democratic right wave the flag, wrap themselves in the cloak of religion, and claim they speak for God and country. We are not attacking God when we confront those who pridefully presume to speak for God. We are not attacking religion when we challenge those who imply that only persons who share their specific narrow theological viewpoint can claim religious or moral values. We are not attacking our country when we rebuke those who peddle a message of fear, prejudice, and division...The time has come to stand up and vigorously defend democracy and pluralism against the attacks orchestrated by cynical leaders of the anti-democratic right."

Mobilization For Democracy

The time has come to mobilize for democracy. The Christian Right's cynical analysis and exploition of the crisis in democracy—epitomized by the lack of voter participation—is a serious threat. This well-disciplined minority is able to exert political power greatly disproportionate to their numbers and resources. Of course, our fellow citizens have every right to do so. However, that does not mean that they have the right to go unchallenged. That is a privilege extended to them by the rest of society in failing to adequately defend democratic values and the public policies and institutions that reflect them. The defense of democratic values against the theocrats will require the development of a sizable and knowledgeable constituency to generate effective political responses in public life generally, and electoral politics specifically. Political participation must not be limited to the voting booth, but must include active participation in political and electoral life across the calendar year. Business and politics as usual cannot prevail. While the theocratic right is eminently beatable, it will take a well-informed strategy and a major mobilization to win. Although most of the creative and effective responses to the Christian Right have been local and regional, eventually national organizations must transform the way they do business in order to defend and advance democratic values. The pivotal role that national leaders and organizations must play is offering a revitalized vision of democratic society, plausible means of achieving it, and energetic efforts to mobilize the near majority which does not participate in electoral politics. This will mean creating a culture in which political and electoral participation is considered valuable, instead of an onerous responsibility, a culture in which positive outcomes seem, and are indeed, possible, a culture in which the vote is not reduced to merely a choice for the lesser of two evils.

The threat is great and the time is now—and probably for the rest of our lives.

Appendix: Resources

This is a sampling of useful materials on the anti-democratic right in the U.S. For a more comprehensive reading list, contact Political Research Associates (see below.)

The Anti-Abortion Movement and the Rise of the Religious Right: From Polite To Fiery Protest, by Dallas Blanchard, Twayne Publishers. An important study of the anti-abortion movement from 1973 to 1993. (Available by mail from *The Body Politic*–see below).

Challenging the Christian Right: The Activists Handbook, by Frederick Clarkson and Skipp Porteous, Institute for First Amendment Studies, The Ms. Foundation, 1992. The first activist handbook to address the new Christian Right. Organizes articles by the authors and others into a narrative to explain and document the rebounding of the Christian Right, especially the Christian Coalition. Profiles the top ten Christian Right groups.

Combatting Cult Mind Control, by Steven Hassan, Park Street Press, 1988. An explanation of how cultic groups work, what friends and families can do to prevent people from entering totalist groups, and how to encourage them to leave if they get involved. Hassan is a former leader in the Unification Church and has worked as a family counselor for over ten years.

The Coors Connection: How Coors Family Philanthropy Undermines Democratic Pluralism, by Russ Bellant, South End Press, 1991. One of the definitive works on the right in the U.S. The story of the politics and political reach of the Coors beer family. Published in cooperation with Political Research Associates. Telephone V/MC orders: 1-800-533-8478.

Eyes Right! Challenging the Right-Wing Backlash, edited by Chip Berlet, South End Press, 1995. A fine compilation of essays about the ideology, agenda, and strategy of the anti-democratic right in the U.S. Includes a comprehensive resource and reading list, and articles by Russ Bellant, Sara Diamond, and Loretta Ross, among many others. Published in cooperation with Political Research Associates. Telephone V/MC orders: 1-800-533-8478.

Facing the Wrath: Confronting the Right in Dangerous Times, Sara Diamond, Common Courage Press, 1996. A compilation of articles by one of the best analysts of the Christian Right. Telephone V/MC orders: 1-800-497-3207. Fax orders: 207-525-3068.

From Abortion to Reproductive Freedom: Transforming a Movementt, edited by Marlene Gerber Fried, South End Press, 1990. An essential anthology of essays about politics, diverisity and reproductive rights.

House of God?: The Religious Right Aims to Take the Presidency, by Adele M. Stan, *Mother Jones* magazine reprint. (November/December 1995.) The single best magazine treatment of the rise and significance of the Christian Right. Postpaid copies are available for $1.95 each for 1-9 copies; $1 each for 10-24; 75 cents each for 25-99; 50 cents each for 100 or more. Send orders to Mother Jones Reprints, 731 Market Street, Suite 600, San Francisco, CA 94103.

The Most Dangerous Man in America? Pat Robertson and the Rise of the Christian Coalition, by Robert Boston, Prometheus Press, 1996. The most important study of Pat Robertson, Ralph Reed and the Christian Coalition, and the contrast between the actual views of Pat Robertson and the public relations persona of Ralph Reed. Available for $14.95 from Americans United for Separation of Church and State.

A New Rite: Conservative Catholic Organizations and Their Allies, by Steve Askin. Periodically updated. Profiles the major organizations of the Catholic Right. Order directly from Catholics for a Free Choice, 1436 U Street NW, Suite 301, Washington, DC 20009-3916. 202-986-6093.

A Newsroom Guide to Abortion and Family Planning, by David E. Anderson, Communications Consortium Media Center, 1996. A guide to the major terms, issues, and history of abortion, family planning and anti-abortion violence. Order by check or money order, ($10.95) directly from the publisher: CCMC, 1200 New York Avenue, NW, Washington, DC 20005.

The Religious Right and the Assault on Tolerance & Pluralism in America, by David Cantor, Anti-Defamation League, 823 United Nations Plaza, New York, NY 10017. An excellent primer on the threat to religious freedom posed by the theocratic right. Not available in bookstores, order directly from ADL.

The Religious Right in Michigan Politics, by Russ Bellant, Americans for

Religious Liberty, 1996. A fine study of the religious right in one state where James Dobson's Focus on the Family plays a major role. Includes Bellant's award-winning investigation of the Word of God community, a Catholic charismatic shepherding cult, and details its ties to such Christian Right groups as the Puebla Institute. Available from the author. $10.55 plus $2.00 shipping and handling. P.O. Box 02363, Detroit, MI, 48202.

Roads to Dominion: Right-Wing Movements and Political Power in the United States, by Sara Diamond, The Guilford Press, 1995. The major scholarly work on the history of the post WW II right in the U.S. Includes much discussion of the Christian Right in the wider contexts of the right and its factions. Telephone Amex/V/MC orders: 1-800-365-7006.

Without Justice For All: A Report on the Christian Right in Sacramento and Beyond, Jerry Sloan and Tracey Jefferys-Renault, Planned Parenthood of the Sacramento Valley, 1993. A groundbreaking 90-page model study of the structure, players and financing of the anti-democratic right in California. Updated in 1996. Order from Planned Parenthood, Public Affairs Department, 2415 K Street, Sacramento, CA 95815-5001. 916-446-5037.

Why the Religious Right is Wrong about Separation of Church & State, by Robert Boston, Prometheus Press, 1993. An essential explanation and debunking of the myths and misinformation promulgated by the Christian Right about American history and the Constitution. Includes a useful section on ideas for activists. Telephone orders: 1-800-421-0351.

ORGANIZATIONS

This is a sampling of local, state, and national activist and research groups that are excellent sources of information about the anti-democratic right in the U.S.

Americans for Religious Liberty

P.O. Box 6656
Silver Spring, MD 20916
301-598-2447

Publishes books, reports, pamphlets, and quarterly newsletter, *Voice of Reason*, $20. Specializes in education issues, notably vouchers.

Americans United for Separation of Church & State
1816 Thomas Jefferson Place NW
Washington, DC 20036
202-466-3234
http://www.netplexgroup.com/americansunited/

A national advocacy organization that supports religious freedom and opposes the theocratic agenda of the Christian Right. Publishes *Church & State* magazine, an essential 24 page monthly. $18/yr. Sells books by mail.

The Body Politic
P.O. Box 2363
Binghamton, NY 13902
607-648-2760

A national monthly magazine on the politics of reproductive rights. Frequently covers the activities of the anti-choice movement and the broader anti-democratic right. Features interviews with pro-choice leaders, thinkers and activists. $22/yr. Sells books by mail.

The C.C. Watch Electronic News Service
3741 NE 163rd Street, Suite 311
Sunny Isles, Florida 33160
305-751-5001
http://www4.ncsu.edu/unity/users/r/rfaggart/ccwatch

Tracks and reports on the activities of Pat Robertson and his many enterprises—especially the Christian Coalition. Delivers 4-5 timely reports per week directly to subscribers' e-mail boxes. Provides information/documentation to like-minded organizations and to the media.

Center for Democratic Renewal
P.O. Box 50469
Atlanta, GA 30302
404-221-0025

A national community-based coalition fighting hate group activity. Many resources, including *The Monitor*, a quarterly newsletter, $35/yr, and *When Hate Groups Come to Town*, an essential guide for community response to hate-motivated violence and intimidation. Affiliated groups nationwide.

Civil Liberties and Public Policy Program

Hampshire College
Amherst, MA 01002
413-582-5645
clpp@hamp.hampshire.edu
http://hamp.hampshire.edu/~clpp/index.html

Hosts an annual spring conference for pro-choice student and community activists from all over the country. Web site includes information on the annual National Young Women's Day of Action, links to other pro-choice web sites, newsletters to print out and much more. Publications include a free newsletter for student activists published 3 times a year, *The Fight for Reproductive Freedom.*

Coalition for Human Dignity

P.O. Box 21266
Seattle, WA 98111-3266
(206) 233-9775
chdpdx@aol.com
http://www.chd-seattle.org/chd/

Research and action organization that monitors hate group activity, primarily in the pacific Northwest. Publishes occasional studies and a regular newsletter, *Northwest Update.*

Coalition of Concerned Citizens

70 Crown Street
Bridgeport, CT 06610
203-368-9126

Community group originally established to fight the takeover of the University of Bridgeport by a front group of the Unification Church of Sun Myung Moon. Publishes an occasional newsletter, *Moon Watch.*

Council for Secular Humanism

P.O. Box 664
Amherst, NY 14226-0664
716-636-7571

Publisher of *Free Inquiry*, a quarterly magazine which discusses aspects of the struggle between democracy and theocracy in every issue. $28.50/yr; $6.95 for a single issue. Telephone V/MC orders: 1-800-458-1366.

Common Courage Press

P.O. Box 702
Monroe, ME 04951
207-525-0900

Publisher of several titles—including this book—about the anti-democratic right and related issues. Write for the current catalog. Organizations may order discounted bulk copies of books. Telephone V/MC orders: 1-800-497-3207. Fax orders: 207-525-3068.

Connecticut Coalition for Democracy
129 Whitney Avenue
New Haven, CT 06510
203-865-5158

Statewide bi-partisan coalition of education, labor, civil rights, and women's organizations, headquartered at Planned Parenthood. Sponsors educational events.

The Data Center
464 19th Street
Oakland, CA 94612-2297
510-835-4692
culturewatch@datacenter.org
http://www.igc.org/culturewatch/

A multifaceted research organization. Publishes *Culture Watch* a unique, synopsis of essential clips by and about the anti-democratic right. ($35/10 issues) Comes with an order form to purchase copies of often hard-to-find material.

Fairness and Accuracy In Reporting (FAIR)
130 West 25th Street
New York, NY 10001
212-633-6700
http://www.fair.org/fair/

A progressive media watchdog organization. Has effectively campaigned against "hate radio" such as the nationally syndicated talk show of host Bob Grant. Publishes an excellent bimonthly magazine, *Extra!* $19/yr. Also sells books.

Institute for Alternative Journalism
77 Federal Street
San Francisco, CA 94107
415-284-1420

http://www.alternet.org/an/demworks.html

IAJ publishes a news service called AlterNet, primarily for alternative weeklies. IAJ's home page, Democracy Works, features the resources of a variety of pro-democracy organizations, and research on the anti-democratic right.

Institute for First Amendment Studies
P.O. Box 589
Great Barrington, MA 01230
413-528-3800
http: //www.berkshire.net/~ifas/

Publisher of the *Freedom Writer* newsletter, ($25/11 issues) and other important resources including a 1995 documentary film, *Onward Christian Soldiers,* on the "rise of the Radical Religious Right." (VHS, $24.95 plus $3.50 S&H. Mass. Residents add 5% tax). Sells mail order books.

Interfaith Alliance
1511 K Street NW, Suite 738
Washington, DC 20005
202-639-6370

A national organization of mainstream religious leaders who oppose the religious right, and stand for democracy and pluralism.

Mainstream Voters Project
Box 19966
San Diego, CA 92159-0966
619-464-4417

The prototypical local bi-partisan research group formed in 1991 in response to the successful stealth tactics of the Christian Right. Publishes *MVP Bulletin!* $25/yr.

National Campaign for Freedom of Expression
1402 Third Avenue, Room 421
Seattle, WA 98101
206-340-9301

National advocacy organization opposed to censorship, particularly of the arts. Quarterly *NCFE Bulletin* regularly features information and analysis about the anti-democratic right. $25/yr.

National Gay & Lesbian Task Force
2320 17th Street NW

Washington, DC 20009
202-332-6483
http://www.ngltf.org

Has active "fight the right" teams organizing in several states. Publishes an excellent *Fight the Right Action Kit*, and an annual report on anti-gay violence, among many other resources.

Paper Tiger Television
339 Lafayette Street
New York, NY 10012
212-420-9045
http://flicker.com/orgs/papertiger

Producers of a useful introduction to the politics of the Christian Right and the uses of technology, from televangelism to the internet. *Narrowcasting: Technology and Tte Rise of the Christian Right.* 1996, 29 minutes, color, VHS. $60 rental; $125 purchase.

People for the American Way
2000 M Street NW, Suite 400
Washington, DC 20036
202-467-4999

National constitutional rights organization and publisher of numerous resources on the Religious Right. Write for a current list. Produced a report on the San Diego Surprise, and a video documenting how pro-democracy elements of the community fought back. *The San Diego Model: A Community Battles the Religious Right*, $6.95; and *Vista: A Battle for Public Education*, $29.95. Helps establish local "coalitions for democracy" to challenge the Religious Right.

Planned Parenthood Federation of America
Clinic Defense and Research Project
810 7ᵗʰ Avenue
New York, NY 10019
212-261-4459
http://www.ppfa.org/ppfa

Publisher of *Front Lines Research*, an investigative newsletter on the anti-choice movement and the broader Christian Right.

Political Research Associates
120 Beacon Street, Suite 300
Somerville, MA 02143-4304

617-661-9313
http://www.publiceye.org/pra/
gopher://gopher.publiceye.org:7021

Publishes *Public Eye*, a quarterly journal of analysis of the players, agenda, tactics and history of the anti-democratic right. $29/yr. Also publishes excellent studies and bibliographies. Web site is an excellent entry point to right-wing web sites.2

Pro-choice Resource Center
174 East Boston Road
Mamaroneck, NY 10543-3701
914-381-3792
perc682-4936@mcimail.com

Advocates political and electoral mobilization to defend reproductive rights and fight "the ultra-conservative opposition." Publishes an *Opposition Primer* for challenging the right on issues of welfare reform, gay and lesbian rights, tax reform, censorship, and education as well as reproductive rights. $15.00.

Project Tocsin
P.O. Box 163523
Sacramento, CA 95816-3523
916-381-3115
http://home.earthlink.net/~pkelley/index.html

Monitors the role of the Christian Right in California politics, particularly campaign finance. Publishes short, easy-to-use booklets and fact sheets.

Right-Watch
P.O. Box 844
Chicopee, MA 01021-0844
413-585-1293

A gay, bi-sexual and trans-gendered lesbian-oriented group that monitors and researches the Religious Right in Western Massachusetts. Holds educational programs and assists other communities contending with Religious Right initiatives. Helped found a wider local coalition called the Progressive Alliance.

Sterling Research Associates
Suite 404
177 East 87th Street

New York, NY 10128
212-423-9237
103406.532@compuserve.com

A consulting firm that conducts strategic research on the religious and secular right, both domestically and internationally. Sterling manages the Center for Democracy Studies of the The Nation Institute (affiliated with *The Nation* magazine). Produces research reports and videos, including a 1996 study and accompanying video on the Promise Keepers.

Western States Center

522 SW Fifth Avenue, Suite 1390
Portland, OR 97204
503-228-8866

Research and activist group specializing in the anti-environmental "wise use" movement. Publishes numerous resources including *The Covert Crusade: The Christian Right and Politics in the West*. $8.00

Notes

Chapter 1: Eternal Hostility: The Born-Again Struggle

1. There is a fine line between theocracy and theonomy, which is a society ordered, rather than governed, by God's laws. The latter is sometimes used to deny that one advocates theocracy, although the terms are not mutually exclusive.

2. Gary North, Afterward, "What Are Biblical Blueprints?", in Gary DeMar, *Ruler of the Nations: Biblical Blueprints for Government*, Dominion Press, 1987. p. 270.

3. John Wilson, "Church and State in America," in *James Madison on Religious Liberty*, Robert S. Alley, editor, Prometheus Books, 1985. p. 99.

4. Robert Boston, *Why the Religious Right is Wrong About Separation of Church & State,* Prometheus Books, 1993. p. 87.

5. Dumas Malone, *Jefferson the President: First Term, 1801-1805*, Little, Brown & Company, 1970. p. 190.

6. Charles B. Sanford, *The Religious Life of Thomas Jefferson,* University Press of Virginia, 1984. p. 1

7. Ibid., p. 83.

8. Ibid., p. 2.

9. Ibid.

10. *Christian Beware...To vote for Bill Clinton is to sin against God,* undated, circa, Fall 1992. Other endorsers included, Rep. Robert Dornan (R-CA); Rev. George Grant; Rev. Paul Schenk, Operation Rescue; Rev. Keith Tucci, Director Operation Rescue National; Joseph Scheidler, Executive Director, Pro-Life Action League; Rev. Rod Aguillard, and Fr. Louis Marx. Interestingly, Lou Sheldon's group, the Traditional Values Coalition, received $25,000 from the California Republican Party during the 1994 election campaign.

11. Rob Boston, "Pulpits, Politics and the IRS: Why A New York Church Lost Its Tax Exemption—And How Pat Robertson's Lawyers Plan to Get it Back," *Church & State,* June 1995. Randall Terry offers his version of events in his book, *Why Does a Nice Guy Like Me Keep Getting Thrown in Jail?,* Huntington House Press and Resistance Press, 1993.

12. Ibid.

13. *Faith & Freedom '95*, Conference Program.

14. Donald Lambro, "GOP Senators Urge Clinton to Disown Attack: Democrats Hit Religious Right," *The Washington Times*, June 24, 1994.

15. For example, Pat Buchanan, "Christian Bashing Time," *The Wanderer*, June 30, 1994. Buchanan suggested that a Jewish conspiracy was also involved. He claimed that there is a "double standard; and yes, the Christian bashing appears orchestrated." He noted that a book by the Anti-Defamation League and a direct mail letter by the American Jewish Committee came "at the same time."

16. Ralph Reed also discusses this episode in his book *Active Faith*, The Free Press, 1996. pp. 79-80. Ralph Reed and staffers from the Christian Coalition attended a Fazio press conference and passed out materials calling Fazio's attack "hate mongering, name calling, and religious bigotry."

17. Paul Weyrich, *The Weyrich Insider*, June 29, 1994.

18. Lambro, op. cit.

19. Michael Lind, "Rev. Robertson's Grand International Conspiracy Theory," *The New York Review of Books*, February 2, 1995.

20. Frederick Clarkson, "On the Road to Victory?" *Church & State,* January 1992; See also Frederick Clarkson, "Inside the Covert Coalition," *Church & State*, November 1992.

20. Weyrich, op. cit.

22. Sara Diamond, *Roads To Dominion: Right-Wing Movements and Political Power in the United States,* The Guilford Press, 1995. pp. 5-6.

23. David Cantor, *The Religious Right: The Assault On Tolerance & Pluralism In America,* Anti-Defamation League, 1994. The ADL dealt with this issue by using the term religious right. They explained that although the term is a "promiscuous media concoction that has sometimes lent itself to caricature and derogation... it is fair when it is specific: in this report it refers to an array of politically conservative religious groups and individuals who are attempting to influence public policy based on a shared cultural philosophy that is antagonistic to pluralism and church/state separation. The movement consists mainly of Protestants, most of them evangelical or fundamentalist, a far smaller number of Catholics, and a smattering of Jews." p. 7.

24. See *Eyes Right: Challenging the Right-Wing Backlash*, South End Press, 1995. Chip Berlet, ed. p. 16.

25. Ibid., Blue Mountain Working Group, "A Call To Defend Democracy & Pluralism, p. 316-326.

26. John W. Whitehead, *The Separation Illusion: A Lawyer Examines*

the First Amendment, Mott Media, 1977, third printing 1982. p. 92. Forward by R. J. Rushdoony.

27. David Barton, *The Myth of Separation: What is the Correct Relationship Between Church and State?*, WallBuilder Press, 1992, p. 44.

28. Cantor, op. cit., p. 42.

29. Ibid., p. 40.

Chapter 2: Neither a Juggernaut nor a Joke: How Overestimating and Underestimating Helps the Christian Right

1. Frederick Clarkson, "On The Road To Victory?" *Church & State*, January 1992; Joe Conason, "The Religious Right's Quiet Revival," *The Nation*, April 27, 1992.

2. Reed has acknowledged some of this debt. Part of the Christian Coalition organizing plan, he writes, was "modeled after the leadership schools of Morton Blackwell." Ralph Reed, *Active Faith*, The Free Press, 1996, p. 13.

3. George Grant, *The Changing of the Guard: Biblical Principles for Political Action*, Dominion Press, 1987. p. 145-146.

4. Ibid., p. 16.

5. Ibid., pp. 148-151.

6. Frederick Clarkson, "The Making of a Christian Police State," *The Freedom Writer*, September/October 1991.

7. Frederick Clarkson, "The Christian Coalition: On The Road To Victory?" *Church & State*, January 1992.

8. Ibid.

9. Frederick Clarkson, "Inside the Covert Coalition," *Church & State*, November 1992. Robertson himself briefly discusses the Coalition's role in the Helms campaign in his book, *The New World Order: It Will Change The Way You Live*, Word Publishing, 1991. p. 260.

10. Joseph L. Conn, "Judgement Day," *Church & State*, September 1996.

11. John O'Connell, "Republican Official Challenges Caucus Vote," *Springfield* (MA)*Union News*, May 10, 1996

12. See for example, Frederick Clarkson, "Wildmon Kingdom," *Mother Jones*, November/December 1990.

13. Randall Terry, "Why do Christians use Birth Control?," *Crosswinds*, Winter, 1992.

14. Michael Bray, *A Time to Kill*, Advocates for Life Publications, 1994. pp. 22-23.

15. For an account of one such pitch, see Matthew Fleischer, "Slaying The Christ Killers," *The Village Voice*, December 26, 1995.

16.   Robertson, op. cit., p. 246.

17.   Ralph L. Ketcham, "James Madison and Religion, A New Hypothesis," in *James Madison on Religious Liberty*, Prometheus Books, Robert Alley, ed., 1985, p. 177.

18.   See Frederick Clarkson, "On the Road to Victory?" and "Inside the Covert Coalition," op. cit., and David Cantor, *The Religious Right: The Assault on Tolerance & Pluralism in America,* Anti-Defamation League, 1994. pp. 45-46.

19.   Cantor, Ibid.

20.   Stephanie Kraft and Frederick Clarkson, "Liberals In Body Bags: The Christian Right Likes David Duke Better Than Weld," *The Springfield Advocate*, February 27, 1992.

21.   "Ralph Reed's Missing Million: Christian Coalition Numbers Drop," *Church & State*, January 1996.

22.   These points were first discussed in Frederick Clarkson, "Neither a Juggernaut Nor A Joke," *The Freedom Writer,* October/November, 1993.

23.   Dan Balz and Ronald Brownstein, "Among the Believers: Ralph Reed's Christian Soldiers," *The Washington Post Magazine*, January 28, 1996. p. 11.

24.   Colonel Doner, *The Samaritan Strategy: A New Agenda for Christian Activism*, Wolgemuth & Hyatt, 1988. pp. 11-12.

25.   Paula Xanthopoulou, *CC Watch,* January 1996. *CC Watch* monitors the Christian Coalition, see Resources.

26.   Pam Belluck, "Conservative School Board Gains Turned Out To Be No Revolution," *The New York Times*, April 29, 1996.

27.   Heidi Schlumph, "How Catholic Is The Catholic Alliance?", *Christianity Today*, May 20, 1996.

28.   The media watchdog group Fairness and Accuracy In Reporting (FAIR) consistently called the media to task on this point, even putting out a special report on Buchanan's views.

29.   Balz and Brownstein, op. cit.

30.   Andrew Sandlin, "Why Contra Christian Coalition?" *The Christian Statesman,* July/August 1994. pp. 4-5. Sandlin also edits the monthly newsletter of R.J. Rushdoony's Chalcedon Foundation, *Chalcedon Report*.

31.   William Einwechter, "Christian Politics: Contending for the Faith," *The Christian Statesman,* July/August 1994. p. 11.

32.   Niles S. Campbell, "A Response From Christian Coalition," *The Christian Statesman,* July/August 1994. p. 19

33.   Ibid.

34. Randall A. Terry, "Selling Out The Law Of Heaven," *The Washington Post*, September 18, 1994.

35. Frederick Clarkson, "Christian Right Is Born Again," *The Freedom Writer,* November/December 1991.

36. Robertson, op. cit., p. 204.

37. Ibid., p. 205.

38. Ibid., p. 200.

39. Quoted in Cantor, op. cit., p. 108.

40. Joseph L. Conn, "The Airwaves Ayatollahs," *Church & State*, March 1994.

41. *Money, Power and the Radical Right in Pennsylvania*, Planned Parenthood Association of Pennsylvania, 1996. 717-234-3024.

42. Tracey Jefferys-Renault and Jerry Sloan, *Without Justice for All: A Report on the Christian Right in Sacramento and Beyond*, Planned Parenthood of Sacramento Valley, 1993.

43. Russ Bellant, *The Religious Right in Michigan Politics*, Americans for Religious Liberty, 1996.

44. Conn, op. cit.

45. Frederick Clarkson "Reclaiming America for Christ?" *Church & State*, March 1994.

46. Sidney Blumenthal, "Christian Soldiers," *The New Yorker,* July 18, 1994.

47. See Frederick Clarkson, "Focusing: Correcting Dangerous Myths about the Christian Right," *The Freedom Writer*, June 1993; See also Frederick Clarkson, "Don Wildmon: He's No Jim Bakker," *In These Times*, July 4-17, 1990.

48. For a concise analysis of the early history of the Wildmon organization, see Kate Waracks, "Chronology of a Censor: How Rev. Wildmon Has Changed the Cultural Climate," *Extra!*, May/June 1991. See also Frederick Clarkson and Skipp Porteous, *Challenging the Christian Right: The Activists' Handbook*, Institute for First Amendment Studies, 1992. pp. 145-148.

49. Clarkson, op. cit.

50. See Russ Bellant, "Council for National Policy: Stealth Leadership of the Radical Right," *Front Lines Research,* August 1994.

51. Frederick Clarkson, "Culture Buster," *The Village Voice,* October 10, 1989. For example Cardinal O'Connor, unlike several other ranking Catholic leaders failed to disassociate himself from Wildmon, in light of remarks which were widely viewed as anti-Semitic.

52. Cantor, op. cit., p. 86.

53. See Bill Dedman, "Bible Belt Blowhard," *Mother Jones,* Novem-

ber/December, 1992; and Bill Dedman and Art Harris, "Don Wild-mon Is A Liar And A Fraud, *Penthouse*, September 1993.

54. David Elliot, "AFA Calls For Boycott," *The Texas Triangle*, January 5, 1996.

55. For a discussion of the economic impact of the Nestlé boycott of the late 1970s and early 1980s, see Frederick Clarkson, "The Taming of Nestlé: A Boycott Success Story," *Multinational Monitor*, April 1984.

56. Ibid.

57. Dedman, op. cit.

58. Jean Hardisty, "The Resurgent Right: Why Now?," *Public Eye*, Fall/Winter 1995.

Chapter 3: Americans for Theocratic Action: Rev. Sun Myung Moon, "Family Values," and the Christian Right—One Dangerous Theocrat.

1. In March 1994 in Toronto, for example the Women's Federation for World Peace and CARP (Collegiate Association for the Research of the Principle) hosted a program aimed at teenagers on AIDS prevention at a public library. There was, as usual, no mention of who was really behind it. Ross Laver, and Paul Kaihla, "Sun Myung Moon Embraces The High And Mighty," *Maclean's* October 23, 1995.

2. Robert Boettcher, *Gifts of Deceit: Sun Myung Moon, Tongsun Park, and the Korean Scandal,* Holt, Rinehart, and Winston, 1980.

3. Frederick Clarkson, "God is Phasing Out Democracy," *Covert Action Quarterly*, Spring, 1987. See also Boettcher, op. cit., p. 38.

4. See John Judis, "Rev. Moon's Rising Political Influence: His Empire is Spending Big Money Trying to Win Favor With Conservatives," *U.S. News & World Report,* March 27, 1989.

5. Excerpt from *New Hope News*, November 25, 1974. Reprinted in Frederick Miller, *Confusion At The Fronts, Part 3*, True Light Educational Ministry, 1996.

6. Boettcher, op. cit.,Ibid., pp. 55 and , 157. See also, Frederick Clarkson, "God is Phasing Out Democracy," *Covert Action Quarterly*, Spring, 1987.

7. Jon Lee Anderson and Scott Anderson, *Inside the League: The Shocking Expose of How Terrorist, Nazis, and Latin American Death Squads Have Infiltrated the World Anti-Communist League,* Dodd, Mead & Company, 1986.

8. Press statement by Allen Tate Wood, November 15, 1979

9. *Ripon Forum,* January 1983.

10. Fraser Report p. 320

11. Boettcher, op.cit. p. 166.

12. Quoted in Frederick Clarkson, "Behind The Times: Who Pulls The Strings At Washington's #2 Daily?", *Extra!*, August/September 1987.

13. Cheshire made this observation at a panel discussion with former Moon media executives James Whelan, the founding editor and publisher of *The Washington Times*, and Michael Warder, the former editor of the now-defunct *New York News World*, at the annual conference of the (also defunct) Cult Awareness Network, November 1-3, 1990. His remarks were reported in "Cults and the Media," *Cult Awareness Network News*, December 1990.

14. Jolen Chang, *Asian Fortune,* March 1995.

15. "Bush and '1M From Moonies,' *Daily Mail,*, September 5, 1995.

16. Kevin Sullivan and Mary Jordan, "Moon Group Paying Bush for Speeches," *The Washington Post*, September 6, 1995; Andrew Pollack, "Bush Host In Japan Tied To Rev. Moon," *The New York Times*, September 4, 1995; Andrew Pollack, "Bushes Speak At Tokyo Rally Of Group Linked To Moon Church," *The New York Times*, September 15, 1995.

17. "Another Queasy Experience," *Newsweek,* September 25, 1995.

18. Lisa Gray, "Honor Thy Parents", *Washington City Paper*, September, 1995. See also Robert Boston, "Unholy Matrimony" *Church & State*, October 1996.

19. *Ripon Forum*, op. cit.

20. Boettcher, op. cit., p. 44.

21. Kevin Sullivan and Mary Jordan, "Moon Group Paying Bush for Speeches," *The Washington Post,* September 6, 1995. Bush spokeswoman Jean Becker said Bush is "unaware of any connection, " between WFWP and the Unification Church.

22. Peter McGill, et al, "Ed Schreyer and the Moonies, *Maclean's*, October 23, 1995; see also Andrew Pollack, "Bush Host in Japan Tied to Rev. Moon," *The New York Times,* September 4, 1995.

23. Ibid.

24. Frederick Clarkson, "Heaven and Helms," *Washington City Paper*, August 18, 1989

25. Frederick Clarkson, "The Republicans, Rev. Moon, and the Media," *Extra!* October/November, 1988.

26. Robert Boston, "Unholy Matrimony," *Church & State*, October 1996.

27. By Marc Fisher, "Bill Cosby, Scowling at the Moons: Unsmiling Comic Performs At Church-Related Forum," *The Washington Post*, August 1, 1996

28. Joanna Molloy and George Rush, "Moonie Convention is Cos for Indignation," *New York Daily News,* July 31, 1996.

29. Kevin Sullivan and Mary Jordan, "Once-Generous Japanese Become Disenchanted With Moon's Church," *The Washington Post,* August 4, 1996.

30. Ibid.

31. Ibid.

32. For a discussion of the issues surrounding the Moon takeover, see Glenn Scott Davis, "Dissolution or Survival: The University of Bridgeport and the Unification Church," in *Nonprofit Boards and Leadership: Cases on Governance, Change and Board-Staff Dynamics,* Mimiam M. Wood, editor, Jossey-Bass Publishers, 1996

33. Dr. Richard L. Rubenstein, "Bridgeport University Honors Rev. Moon," *Unification News,* October 1995; See also Joseph Berger, "U. Of Bridgeport Honors Rev. Moon, Fiscal Savior," *The New York Times,* September 8, 1995.

34. See Frederick H. Miller, *Confusion at the Fronts,* True Light Educational Ministry, 1994. See note 19. Jefferson is also a director of Massachusetts Citizens for Life, and Americans United for Life.

35. See Frederick Clarkson and Larry Zillioux, "Sex, Lies, and Slide Shows: Rev. Moon and Sex/HIV Education," *Front Lines Research,* February 1995. Richard Panzer was also listed as speaker on the conference program.

36. Maura Reynolds, "So-Called San Marcos 'Miracle' Actually May be Just a Myth," *The San Diego Union,* December 19, 1991.

37. *The Private Plague,* Slide Program Manual, p. 23.

38. Dr. Tyler Hendricks, "Sex Ed In Westchester County," *Unification News,* February 1994.

39. Richard Panzer, promotional letter, Free Teens USA, Autumn, 1992.

40. Robert Hanley, "Fears of Link to Rev. Moon Slow a Celibacy Program," *The New York Times,* March 22, 1995. These retractions occurred as the result of the work of Frederick H. Miller, Director, True Light Educational Ministry, P.O. Box 310 Shirley, NY 11967-09310. His report "Confusion at the Fronts" is a detailed investigation of the relationship between the Unification Church and the Free Teens program.

41. Jessica D. Matthews, "Board Votes To Discontinue 'Free Teens, USA' Program," *Review Press-Reporter,* April 13, 1995.

42. John H, Sutter, "Anti-AIDS Group Pushes Abstinence Over 'Russian Roulette' of Condoms," *New York City Tribune,* November 29, 1988.

43. Hanley, op. cit.., Clarkson and Zillioux op. cit.

44. For a discussion of Merrimack in the context of the GOP presidential politics of 1996, see, Adele M. Stan, "House of God? The Religious Right Aims to Take the Presidency," *Mother Jones,* November/December 1995. Shelly Uscinski was a featured speaker and workshop leader at the Christian Coalition's *Faith and Freedom '95* conference in Syracuse, NY, as well as the Coalition's national *Road To Victory '94* conference in Washington, DC. Uscinski served as an alternate delegate for Pat Buchanan at the 1996 GOP convention. She then defected and gave a seconding speech for Howard Phillips, the presidential candidate of the far-right U.S. Taxpayers Party.

45. Ken Coleman, press release, "Radical Right Invades Merrimack," April 26, 1996.

46. Jill Smolowe, "The Unmarrying Kind: Focusing on Local Targets, Religious Conservatives Wage a Fervent Campaign to Stomp Out Gay Rights," *Time*, April 29, 1996.

47. Rene Sanchez, Sex Education: "The Debate Continues, Only Now, The Question is Whether Anything Should be Said About Homosexuality," *The Washington Post, National Weekly Edition*, May 20, 1996. pp. 30-31

48. Rod Paul, "New England Town Rejects Religious Right," *San Francisco Examiner*, May 5, 1996.

49. "Radical Right Loses Control of NH School: Antigay Measure Defeated," *Sojourner,* June 1996.

50. "Pro-War Rally Near Lady Liberty: 'Let Freedom Ring' 400 Activists Told," *Bergen County Record*, February 10, 1991.

51. Wood, op. cit; see Frederick Clarson, "God is phasing out Democracy," op. cit.

52. See Frederick Clarkson, "Money Talks, But Whose Voice Is it?", *In These Times*, January 20, 1991. The leaders of the Coalition also included registered Kuwaiti agent William Kennedy, the former publisher of *Conservative Digest*, Scott Stanley a former editor of John Birch Society publications, David Keene of the American Conservative Union, and direct mail entrepreneur Richard Viguerie.

53. Sara Diamond, *Roads to Dominion: Right-Wing Movements and Political Power in the United States*, Guilford Press, 1995. p. 400; Frederick Clarkson "Kuwaitgate?" *Washington City Paper*, July 17, 1992. Mary Jordan, "Conservative Group Lobbies for Gulf Policy," *The Washington Post*, November 30, 1990..

54. "Kuwaiti Ties With U.S. Official Disclosed," Baghdad INA, September 8, 1990; translated and published by FBIS, September 11, 1990.

55. Frederick Clarkson, "Kuwaitgate?", *Washington City Paper*, July 17, 1992. Significantly, WJLA, the ABC affiliate in Washington DC, which ran Zakhem's ads on *Nightline*, refused to run ads opposed to the Gulf War which had been produced by the Military Families Support Network, whose purpose was to graphically demonstrate the human costs of war.

56. Ibid.

57. Mary Jordan, "Conservative Group Lobbies for Gulf Policy," *The Washington Post*, November 30, 1990.

58   Sue Lindsay, "Federal Case Against Zakhem Slowly Crumbling Away," *Rocky Mountain News*, October 24, 1994.

59. Sue Lindsay, "'Justice and Truth Prevailed,' Zakhem Says After Acquittal Ex-Ambassador is Cleared of 2 Tax Charges; 8 Others Dismissed by Prosecutors as 4-Year Ordeal Concludes", *Rocky Mountain News,* March 8,1995.

60. Thomas Cromwell, interview, "I Gave Up Everything to Go Back to Live as a Free American," *The Middle East Times*, October 17, 1987.

61. Frederick Clarkson, "Heaven and Helms," and "Moon's Man in Bahrain," *City Paper,* August 18, 1989

62. John S. Saloma III, *Ominous Politics: The New Conservative Labyrinth*, Hill and Wang, 1984, p. 46.

63. Boettcher, op. cit., p. 47.

64. Boettcher, op. cit., p. 322.

65. Walter Hatch, "Jail Time Was Start of Try for Legitimacy," *The Seattle Times*, February 13, 1989.

66. For a discussion of the case, see Frederick Clarkson, "The Manifest Sins of Sun Myung Moon," *Christianity & Crisis*, October 28, 1985.

67. Proceedings of the 7th World Media Conference, November 19-22, 1984.

68. The Moon case is discussed in detail in Frederick Clarkson, "The Manifest Sins of Sun Myung Moon," *Christianity & Crisis*, October 28, 1985; see also, *The New Republic*, August 26, 1985.

69. *Seattle Post Intelligencer,* September 27, 1986.

70. On a Coalition for Religious Freedom letterhead, letter by CRF President Greg Dixon dated October 3, 1984, for example.

71. One brochure, long after exposure of issues of Moon control domination of the Coalition for Religious Freedom had driven others away, listed the "Executive Committee" as: Dr. Paul Crouch, Dr. Robert Grant, Dr. E.V. Hill, Rev. Rex Humbard, Dr. Jess Moody, Author Hal Lindsey, Dr. Joseph Lowery, Evangelist James Robison, and

Rev. Donald Wildmon. " The "Advisory Board" included Dr.
Richard Rubenstein, who would later be named president of the
Moon controlled University of Bridgeport.

72.   Ibid., *Coalition for Religious Freedom: Who We Are And What We Stand For,* brochure..

73.   See Frederick Clarkson "God Is Phasing Out Democracy," *Covert Action Quarterly*, Spring 1987.

74.   See John Judis, "Rev. Moon's Rising Political Influence: His Empire is Spending Big Money Trying to Win Favor with Conservatives," *U.S. News & World Report,* March 27, 1989.

75.   Much of this section is based on Frederick Clarkson, "The Fine Hand of Rev. Moon's Church," *St. Louis Journalism Review*, September 1989.

76.   Steven Hassan, *Combatting Cult Mind Control*, Park Street Press, 1988. p. 197.

77.   David G. Racer, *Not For Sale: The Rev. Sun Myung Moon And One American's Freedom*, Tiny Press, P.O. Box 6446, St. Paul MN 55106, p. ii.

78.   Ibid., p. 20, 68-70.

79.   Ibid., p. 74. "Nothing would destroy the conservative movement faster than to be linked inextricably to the Rev. Moon."

80.   Sara Diamond, *Roads to Dominion: Right-Wing Movements and Political Power in the United States*, Guilford Press, 1995. p. 242.

81.   Colonel V. Doner, *The Samaritan Strategy*, Wolgemuth & Hyatt, 1988. pp. 224. Doner, who assembled ACTV for the Reagan/Bush campaign, and later got out of national politics, obliquely referred to the Moon scandal "I am afraid that if we continue on our present course of trying to build ill-fitted alliances and strange bedfellows for the purpose of trying to impose our agenda on an unreceptive public, all we will reap is one gigantic and well-deserved backlash." p. 214.

82.   Ibid., pp. 22-23.

83   Ibid.

84.   Carolyn Weaver, "Unholy Alliance," *Mother Jones*, January 1986.

85.   David Cantor, *The Religious Right: The Assault on Tolerance & Pluralism in America*, Anti-Defamation League, 1994. p. 64.

86.   Mike Mokryzcki, *Associated Press*, June 24, 1996..

87.   Cynthia Lilley, "My Daughter Lived A Nightmare," *Connecticut Post*, July 7, 1994

88.   Haven Bradford Gow, "Separate Church From State?", *Unification News*, October 1995.

89.   Robert Boston, *Why the Religious Right is Wrong About Separation*

of Church & State, Prometheus Books, 1993. pp. 67-68, 222.

90. A.E. Dick Howard, "James Madison and the Founding of the Republic," in *James Madison on Religious Liberty*, Robert S. Alley, editor. Prometheus Books, 1985. p. 26.

91. Quoted from Robert S. Alley, "The Protestant Establishment," Ibid., p. 253.

92. Charles Sanford, *The Religious Life of Thomas Jefferson*, University Press of Virginia, 1984. pp. 30-31.

Chapter 4: Laying Down the (Biblical) Law: Christian Reconstructionism by the Book

1. For another view on this point, See Sara Diamond, *Spiritual Warfare: The Politics of the Christian Right*. South End Press, 1989. p. 138.

2. Gary Scott Smith, ed., *God and Politics: Four Views on the Reformation of Civil Government*, Presbyterian and Reformed Publishing, 1989. p. 18.

3. H. Wayne House and Thomas Ice, *Dominion Theology: Blessing or Curse? An Analysis of Christian Reconstructionism,* Multnomah Press, 1988. p. 352.

4. Ibid., p. 65.

5. R. J. Rushdoony, *Institutes of Biblical Law*, Presbyterian and Reformed Publishing Company, The Craig Press, 1973. p. 113.

6. Ibid., p. 93.

7. Gary North, Prologue XV, to Greg Bahnsen, *By This Standard: The Authority of God's Law Today*, Institute for Christian Economics, 1985.

8. Gary North, Preface xiii, from Gary North and Gary DeMar, *Christian Reconstruction: What It Is, What It Isn't*, Institute for Christian Economics, 1991.

9. Rushdoony, op. cit., p. 4.

10. Ibid., pp. 235, 402.

11. Ibid., p. 38.

12. Gary North, *Political Polytheism*: *The Myth of Pluralism*, Institute for Christian Economics, 1989. p. 627

13. Rushdoony, op. cit., p. 237.

14. Rev. Ray Sutton, *That You May Prosper: Dominion by Covenant*, Institute for Christian Economics, 1987. p. 188.

15. Ibid.

16. Rushdoony, op. cit., p. 237.

17. Gary North, *The Sinai Strategy: Economics and the Ten Commandments*, Institute for Christian Economics, 1986, pp. 121-123.

18. Greg Bahnsen, *By This Standard: The Authority of God's Law Today*, Institute for Christian Economics, 1987. p. 280.

19. Kathey Alexander and Gayle White, "Focus on 'American Vision': Reconstructionists Advance A 'Radical' Christian Belief That Includes Support For Cobb's Anti-Gay Resolution," *The Atlanta Journal-Constitution*, July 5, 1994

20. Gary DeMar, *Ruler of the Nations: Biblical Principles for Government*, 1987, Dominion Press, Ft. Worth, Texas. p. 212.

21. Ibid., p. 218.

22. Ibid., p. 217.

23. Sutton, op. cit., p. 115.

24. R. J. Rushdoony, *The Nature of the American System*, The Craig Press, vi., 1965.

25. Ibid., pp., 2-3.

26. Leo Pfeffer, *Church, State and Freedom*, Beacon Press 1967. p. 254 (revised edition).

27. Albert J. Menendez, *No Religious Test: The Story of Our Constitution's Forgotten Article*, Americans United for Separation of Church & State, 1987. p. 11.

28. Gary DeMar, *America's Christian History, The Untold Story*, American Vision, 1993. pp. 88-89.

29. Garry Wills, *Under God: Religion and American Politics*, Simon and Schuster, 1990. p. 383.

30. Robert Rutland, "The Courage to Doubt in a Secular Republic," in *James Madison on Religious Liberty,* Prometheus Books, 1985. p. 208.

31. Ibid., p. 209.

32. Michael Novak, ibid., p. 300.

33. North, *Political Polytheism*, op. cit., pp. 681-685. A non-Reconstructionist advocate of the "Christian Nation" doctrine, Harold O.J. Brown, agrees with North. "America made a mistake in the year 1787. Officially, government...broke with Christianity," *God and Politics, Four Views on the Reformation of Civil Government*, Gary Scott Smith, ed. Presbyterian and Reformed Publishing, 1989. p. 132.

34. North, ibid., p. 568.

35. Ibid., p. 265.

36. Ibid., p. 227.

37. Ibid., p. 569.

38. Rushdoony, *Institutes*, op. cit., p. 747.

39. Larry Abraham, *Call It Conspiracy*, Double A Publications, revised edition, 1985.

40   Joseph Morecraft III, *Liberty and Justice for All: Christian Politics Made Simple*, Onward Press, Sevierville, TN, 1991, p. 160.

41.   Robert Thoburn, *The Christian and Politics*, Thoburn Press, 1984. p. 124.

42.   House & Ice, op. cit., p. 20.

43.   Earl Lee and Scott Forschler, "Bearing Gifts: How Librarians Deal with Gift Books and Gift Givers," *Journal of Information Ethics*, Fall 1992.

44.   North, *Political Polytheism*, op. cit., p. 133.

45.   Ibid., p. 621.

46.   Rushdoony, *Institutes*, op. cit., p. 92.

47.   Press conference interview with the author, U.S. Taxpayers Party convention, August, 1996.

48.   Rodney Clapp, "Democracy As Heresy," *Christianity Today*, February 20, 1987.

49.   Sara Diamond, "Patriot Games," *The Progressive*, September 1995.

50.   Ibid. Sileven currently pastors the Faith Baptist Church in Houston, Missouri.

51.   Charles D. Provan, *The Church Is Israel Now: The Transfer of Conditional Privilege*, Ross House Boods, 1987. Quotes are from a summary on the back cover.

52.   House & Ice, op. cit., p. 66.

53.   Chuck & Donna McIlhenny, *When the Wicked Seized a City: A Grim Look at the Future and a Warning to the Church*. Huntington House Publishers, 1993. p. 59-60. This book was written with Frank York, "a writer and editor in the Public Policy Department with Focus on the Family." Unsurprisingly, there are many references to Focus on the Family sprinkled throughout the book. Further, McIlhenny writes that Dobson (who has featured McIlhenny on his radio show) and "his entire organization have been continually supportive and encouraging, and we are grateful to them." p. 121.

54.   Ibid.

55.   Ibid., p. 231.

56.   Robert L. Thoburn, *The Christian and Politics,* Thoburn Press, 1986. p. 55.

57.   Rev. Joseph Morecraft, "Biblical Obedience to Civil Government, " speech at Biblical World View & Christian Education Conference, August 31, 1993. (audiotape)

58.   Rushdoony, *Institutes,* op. cit. p. 294.

59.   Ibid., p. 510.

60.   David Cantor. The Religious Right and the Assault on Tolerance &

Religious Pluralism in America, Anti-Defamation League, 1994. pp. 122-123.

61. Rushdoony, op. cit., p. 76.

62. Gary North and David Chilton, "Apologetics and Strategy," *Tactics of Christian Resistance*, Geneva Divinity School Press, Tyler, Texas. p. 111.

63. "The Religious Right," Firestorm Chats, Howard Phillips Interviews Gary North, February 10, 1989. (audiotape).

64. Like Rushdoony, Schaeffer also studied with Cornelius Van Til at Westminster Theological Seminary in Philadelphia 1935-1937. See Gary North, *Christian Reconstruction*, op. cit., p. xiii.

65. Wills, *Under God*, op. cit., p. 324.

66. North, *Political Polytheism*, pp. 206-207.

67. Ibid., pp. 166-167; See also Sara Diamond, *Roads to Dominion: Right Wing Movements and Political Power in the United States,* The Guilford Press, 1995. p. 247.

68. John Whitehead, "The Separation of Church & State: Myth or Fact?" speech at Third Annual Conference on Christian Reconstruction, May 14, 1983.

69. Whitehead, op. cit.

70. Ibid.

71. Jerry Sloan and Tracey Jeffreys-Renault, *Without Justice For All: A Report On The Christian Right In Sacramento And Beyond,* Planned Parenthood of the Sacramento Valley, 1993. p. 70. Also an undated Chalcedon fundraising letter, states that "with the help of Chalcedon, the Rutherford Institute was founded...".

72. McIlhenny, op. cit., pp. 49-50.

73. Ibid.

74. John Whitehead in Gary DeMar, *Ruler of the Nations*, op. cit., *xix.*

75. Skipp Porteous, "Special Profile: The Rutherford Institute," *The Freedom Writer*, June 1994. Similarly, although Whitehead has been listed in materials distributed by the Reconstructionist oriented Coalition On Revival, Crow says he was never involved.

76. See Frederick Clarkson, "Only Christians Need Apply: Religious Freedom and Michael Farris," *The Freedom Writer*, August 1993. Like John Whitehead, Michael Farris has had to distance himself from the Coalition On Revival. He admits he was involved in 1984 and 1985, but claims he left because "it started heading to a theocracy... and I don't believe in a theocracy." Peter Baker, "Farris Asserts His Religious Tolerance," *The Washington Post*, October 18, 1993.

77.   Michael Farris, *Where Do I Draw The Line?*, Bethany House Pub-
       lishers, 1992, p. 25.
78.   Ibid., p. 26.
79.   Ibid.
80.   Ibid.
81.   B. Drummond Ayers Jr., "Christian Right Splits GOP in South," *The
       New York Times*, June 7, 1993.
82.   Harvey Cox, "The Warring Visions of the Religious Right," *The
       Atlantic Monthly*, November 1995.

Chapter 5: Theocrats in Action: From Theory to Practice

1.   For an extended discussion of COR, see Frederick Clarkson, "Hard-
       COR," *Church & State*, January 1991.
2.   Ibid.
3.   Jay Grimstead, August, 1991 *Report*, Coalition On Revival.
4.   Clarkson, op. cit.
5.   Author's interview with Rev. Tim LaHaye, January 1991.
6.   Albert James Dager, *Vengeance Is Ours: The Church in Dominion*,
       Sword Publishers, Redmond, WA, 1990, p. 250.
7.   House & Ice, op. cit., p. 20.
8.   Exceptions are books and articles by this writer, as well as Russ Bel-
       lant, Chip Berlet, Sara Diamond, and Skipp Porteous, whose work
       is cited throughout these notes. See also the author's two part-dis-
       cussion of Reconstructionism in *Public Eye*, March and June 1994.
9.   Ralph Reed, *Active Faith*, The Free Press, 1996. p. 261.
10.   "Christian Coalition Peddles Book Touting Death Penalty For Homo-
       sexuals," *Church & State*, July/August 1996. The book is *Legislating
       Immorality: The Homosexual Movement Comes Out Of The Closet.*
11.   Gary North and Gary DeMar, *Christian Reconstruction: What It Is,
       What It Isn't*, Institute for Christian Economics, 1991. p 176.
12.   Colonel V. Doner, *The Samaritan Strategy: A New Agenda For
       Christian Activism,* Holgemuth & Hyatt Publishers, 1988. p. 38.
13.   Gary North, *When Justice Is Aborted: Biblical Standards for Non-
       Violent Resistance*, Dominion Press, 1989. p. 49.
14.   Frederick Clarkson, "The Making of a Christian Police State," *The
       Freedom Writer*, September/October, 1991.
15.   Frederick Clarkson, "Wildmon Kingdom," *Mother Jones*, Novem-
       ber/December, 1989.
16.   Billy Falling, *The Political Mission of the Church*, Christian Voters
       League, 1990. From the Introduction.
17.   The National Coordinating Council seems to have withered after

exposure of its agenda, and the apparent defection of COR leaders over the issue of Reconstructionism, and militias. See Frederick Clarkson and Skipp Porteous, *Challenging the Christian Right: The Activists Handbook*, Institute for First Amendment Studies, 1992, in which the document that outlines the entire NCC agenda is reprinted.

18. Frederick Clarkson, "Wildmon Kingdom," *Mother Jones*, November/December 1990.

19. Interview with the author.

20. Lawrence D. Pratt, "Tools of Biblical Resistance," in *Christianity & Civilization, Tactics of Christian Resistance,* Gary North, ed.; Geneva Divinity School Press, 1983. p. 442.

21. See Leonard Zeskind, "Armed and Dangerous: The NRA, Militias and White Supremacists are Fostering a Network of Right Warriors," *Rolling Stone*, November 2, 1995.

22. Pratt was baptized by Reconstructionist pastor Robert L Thoburn. See Robert L. Thoburn, *The Christian and Politics*, Thoburn Press, 1986. p. 132.

23. Pratt, op. cit. One of the Family Foundation's subsidiary projects is English First, which opposes bi-lingual education in the U.S.

24. Lee Shepherd, "U.S. Probes Operation Rescue," *Press & Sun Bulletin*, March 3, 1990; Lee Shepherd, "Terry To Shut Down Headquarters," *Press & Sun Bulletin*, November 13, 1990; Lawrence W. Pratt, fundraising letter, Committee to Protect the Family Foundation, July 16, 1990.

25. Zeskind, op. cit.

26. Anthony Flint, "Report of Racist Affiliates Forces Buchanan Aide From Campaign," *The Boston Globe,* February 16, 1996; Richard L. Berke, "Buchanan Aide Takes Leave Under Fire," *The New York Times*, February 16, 1996.

27. Rousas J. Rushdoony, *This Independent Republic: Studies in the Nature and Meaning of American History,* Thoburn Press, 1978. p. viii.

28. Howard Phillips, "Contemporary Politics" Part 3, Fall 1992. American Vision.

29. For a discussion of these parties, see James Ridgeway, *Blood In The Face*, Thunder's Mouth Press, 1990.

30. Howard Phillips, *The Next Four Years: A Vision Of Victory*, Legacy Communications. p. xiii.

31. Howard Phillips, "Contemporary Politics," Parts 1 & 2 speech to a conference hosted by the Reconstructionist groups American Vision, and the Institute for Christian Economics, says Grant helped USTP get on the ballot in 1992. Grant who was also a featured speaker at

the founding conference of USTP, signed a 1994 "Open Letter to Pro-Life Republicans," which attacked the GOP as "evil." "We are supporting the U.S. Taxpayers Party," wrote Grant et al, *"because it's right* [Emphasis in the original] No wavering, no waffling, no mumbling, no juggling, no mixed signals, just the truth." Co-signers were Randall Terry, Julie Makimaa, Howard Phillips, and columnist Joseph Sobran.

32.   Crawford, op. cit., p. 271.

33.   Gary North, *Backward Christian Soldiers: An Action Manual for Christian Reconstruction*, Institute for Christian Economics, 1984. p. 23

34.   Ibid., pp. 26-27.

35.   Howard Phillips, Friends of Chalcedon, letter, September 1989.

36.   Joseph L. Conn, "Pyramid Scheme: Republican Party Leader Must Strike A Deal With The Religious Right, Or National Affairs Briefing Salesman Ed McAteer And His Friends Just Might Do Business Elsewhere In 1996," *Church & State,* March 1996.

37.   For accounts of the 1996 USTP convention, see Frederick Clarkson, "Out on the Fringe," *In These Times*, September 16, 1996; Sasha Abramsky, "When God Laughs, It's Not Funny," *The Progressive*, October, 1996

38.   House & Ice, op. cit., p. 37.

39.   Gary North, "Reconstructionist Renewal and Charismatic Renewal," *Christian Reconstruction*, May/June 1988.

40.   Gary North, *Backward Christian Soldiers: An Action Manual for Christian Reconstruction*, Institute for Christian Economics, 1984. p. 150. This book is dedicated to Gen. Albion Knight, a longtime member of the board of the U.S. chapter of the World-Anti-Communist League, and the 1992 vice-presidential candidate of the U.S. Taxpayers Party.

41.   Bill Moyers, "God And Politics: On Earth As It Is In Heaven," PBS, December 23, 1987.

42.   Cantor, op. cit., p. 120.

43.   Frederick Clarkson, "The Second Coming: The Politics of Washington for Jesus '88," *Washington City Paper,* April 29, 1988.

44.   Beth Spring, "Pat Robertson In Michigan: Vying for Evangelical Voters," *Christianity Today*, September 5, 1986.

45.   NBC Nightly News, April 5, 1988.

46.   North, *Backward*, op. cit., pp. 220-221.

47.   Garry Wills, *Under God*, op. cit., p. 194. See also Anson Shupe, "The Reconstructionist Movement on the New Christian Right," *The*

Christian Century, October 4, 1989.

48. Gary DeMar, letter to *Christianity Today*, August 17, 1992. Respond-
     ing to an interview with Robertson in *Christianity Today*, June 22,
     1992. Gary North, impatient with what he calls the theological schiz-
     ophrenia of most of the pre-millennial world, is now saying that any
     politically active Christian is an operational post-millenialist.

49. Cantor, op. cit., pp. 25; 125.

50. Clapp, op. cit.

51. Dan Moraine, "Bankrolling Their Beliefs: Politics: In Quietly Fund-
     ing Think Tanks and Tax-Exempt Lobby Groups Two Millionaires
     Are Advancing Their Agendas," *The Los Angeles Times,* July 8,
     1996.

52. Jane Glenn Haas, "The Salvation of H.F. Ahmanson Jr.," *Orange
     County Register*, July 7, 1985. See also, Don Lattin, "Christian
     Right's New Political Push, *San Francisco Chronicle*, May 12, 1992.

53. Russ Bellant, *The Coors Connection: How Coors Family Philan-
     thropy Undermines Democratic Pluralism.* South End Press, 1990.
     See also, Dan Moraine, "2 Wealthy Conservatives Use Think Tanks
     To Push Goals," *Los Angeles Times*, Home Edition, July 8, 1996,
     which reports that Ahmanson provides about $30,000 a year for
     National Empowerment Television.

54. Ralph Frammolino, "Ahmanson Heir Bankrolls Religious Right's
     Agenda," *The Los Angeles Times,* October 10, 1992.

55. John Jacobs, "Fighting Bill," *Sacramento Bee,* January 9, 1994.

56. Tracey Jeffreys-Renault & Jerry Sloan, *Without Justice for All: A
     Report on the Christian Right in Sacramento and Beyond,* Planned
     Parenthood of the Sacramento Valley, 1993. p. 31.

57. Moraine, op. cit.

58. Ibid.

59. Dan Moraine and Carl Ingram, *The Los Angeles Times*, November
     24, 1995.

60. Sloan, op. cit.

61. Moraine, op. cit.

62. Sloan, op. cit.

63. Moraine, op. cit.

64. Sloan op. cit., pp. 30-31.

65. Moraine, op. cit.

66. Ibid.

67. Eric Bailey, "Hurtt Gets Closer Scrutiny in 32nd Senate Seat Race,"
     The Los Angeles Times, January 25, 1993.

68. Ron Nissimov, "Wayne Johnson: A Conservative Consultant with

Ties to the Religious Right," *California Journal,* January 1993.

69. Richardson, who produced a video for the Reconstructionist Plymouth Rock Foundation, was described as "probably the nation's outstanding Christian State legislator. After 20 years of fighting for Biblical principles in the CA State Senate. *The Correspondent,* July 1988.

70. Moraine, op. cit.

71. Wayne C. Johnson, "Practical Politics in a Lawless Age," speech at Third Annual Northwest Conference for Christian Reconstruction, May 14, 1983. (audiotape)

72. Peter Applebome, "County's Anti-Gay Move Surprises Only a Few," *The New York Times,* August 28, 1993.

73. Joseph Morecraft, "Biblical Role of Civil Government," Biblical World View & Christian Education Conference, August 31, 1993.

74. Ibid.

75. See W.B Reeves, *Hidden Agenda: The Influence of Religious Extremism on the Politics of Cobb County, Georgia,* Neighbors Network, 1994.

76. Kathey Alexander and Gayle White, "Focus on 'American Vision': Reconstructionists Advance a 'Radical' Christian Belief that Includes Support for Cobb's Anti-Gay Resolution," *The Atlanta Journal-Constitution,* July 5, 1994.

77. Reeves, op. cit., p. 7. Gordon Wysong's brothers are also involved in far-right politics. Harvey Wysong was the Georgia State Director of the Fully Informed Jury Association. Charlie Wysong heads the anti-abortion group, the American Rights Coalition in Chattanooga, Tennessee.

78. See editorial, "Theocracy in America: A Bad Prescription from Dr. Hotze," *Church & State,* February, 1993.

79. Reeves, ibid., p. 6. For more on Hotze see Frederick Clarkson, "The Great Right Hope," *The Freedom Writer,* February 1993.

80. Quoted in Joe Conn, "The Reconstructionist Connection," *Church & State,* March 1996.

81. Titus acknowledged his influence from the podium, and Phillips thanked "my wise counselor, the great R.J. Rushdoony" in his book *The Next Four Years: A Vision of Victory,* Legacy Communications, 1992. p. xiii.

82. The platform states that Supreme Court decisions are binding only on the parties before the court and do not provide "a political rule for the nation. *Roe v. Wade* is illegitimate, contrary to the law of the nation's charter and constitution. It must be resisted by all civil government officials, federal, state and local, and by all branches of the

government, legislative, executive and judicial." *U.S. Taxpayers Party Platform – 1996.* p. 3.

83. Larry Pratt, *Safeguarding Liberty: The Constitution & Citizen Militias*, Legacy Communications and Gun Owners Foundation, 1995. p. ix.
84. North, *Backward,* op. cit., p. 261.
85. North, *Political Polytheism*, op. cit., p. 601.
86. Robert Boston, "Failed Crusade," *Church & State*, November 1994.
87. See for example, "Books Not Bricks," *The Body Politic*, October 1993.
88. Robert L. Thoburn, *The Children Trap,* Biblical Blueprint Series, Dominion Press, Thomas Nelson Publishers, 1986. pp. 171-172.
89. Ibid., pp. 159-161.
90. Robert L. Thoburn, *The Christian and Politics*, Thoburn Press, 1986. p. 124.
91. Pratt, op. cit., p. 138.
92. Bill Moyers, "God and Politics: On Earth As It Is In Heaven," PBS Broadcast, December 23, 1987.
93. Cantor, op. cit., p. 122.
94. Christopher Klicka, *The Right Choice: The Incredible Failure of Public Education and the Rising Hope of Home Schooling,* Noble Publishing Associates, Gresham, OR,1992. p. 109.
95. Ibid., p. 6.
96. Ibid., p. 177.
97. Ibid., p. 383.
98. Dana Hawkins, "Homeschool Battles," *U.S. News & World Report*, February 12, 1996.
99. Op. cit., p. 286.
100. Gary North, "Comprehensive Redemption: A Theology of Social Action," *Journal of Christian Reconstruction*, Summer, 1981.
101. Rushdoony, op. cit., pp. 542-544.
102. Ibid., p. 566.
103. Gary North, *When Justice Is Aborted: Biblical Standards For Non-Violent Resistance,* Dominion Press, 1989. p. 116.
104. Robert Boston, "Operation Precinct," *Church & State*, July/August 1994.
105. Frederick Clarkson, "Inside the Covert Coalition," *Church & State*, November 1992.
106. Joe Conason, "Christian Coalition Enters New York City," *The Freedom Writer*, May/June 1992.

Chapter 6: The Devil in the Details: How the Christian Right's Vision of Political and Religious Opponents as Satanic May

Lead to Religious Warfare

1. Chuck & Donna McIlhenny, *When the Wicked Seize a City: A Grim look at the Future and a Warning to the Church,* Huntington House Publishers, 1993. p. 231.

2. Ibid., p. 127.

3. Ibid., p. 148.

4. Joseph L. Conn, "Bully Pulpit: Baptist Preacher Rick Scarborough Has Driven The Infidels From Pearland, Texas, And He Wants Your Town To Be Next," *Church & State*, May 1996.

5. Don Lattin, "'God's Green Beret' Plans to Assault S.F. Demons," *San Francisco Chronicle*, September 1, 1990. See also Chip Johnson, "The Devil You Say? San Francisco Faces Halloween Exorcism," *The Wall Street Journal*, October 30, 1990; and Don Lattin and David Tuller, "6,500 Christians Attend S.F. 'Exorcism', Gays, Pagans Rally Outside Auditorium," *San Francisco Chronicle*, November 1, 1990.

6. Steve Baldwin, campaign speech, June 20, 1991. Audiotape.

7. Frederick Clarkson, "The Christian Coalition: On The Road To Victory?", *Church & State*, January 1992.

8. Gary North and David Chilton, "Apologetics and Strategy," *Tactics of Christian Resistance*, Geneva Divinity School Press, Tyler, Texas, 1983. p. 107.

9. Skipp Porteous, "The World According to Pat Robertson: The Rev. Pat Robertson Has Mounted a Battle of Biblical Proportions to Rescue America from Satanic Forces," *Reform Judaism*, Spring 1993.

10. Pat Robertson, *The New World Order: It Will Change The Way You Live*, Word Publishing 1991. p. 37.

11. Ibid., p. 253.

12. Randall A. Terry, *Why Does A Nice Guy Like Me Keep Getting Thrown In Jail?*, Huntington House Publishers and Resistance Press, 1993. p. 33.

13. Karen Branan and Frederick Clarkson, "Extremism In Sheep's Clothing: A Special Report on Human Life International," *Front Lines Research*, June 1994.

14. "HLI President Urges Prayer To Combat 'Forces Of Darkness' At Cairo," *The Wanderer,* August 25, 1994.

15. Joseph Lapsley Foreman, *Shattering The Darkness: The Crisis of the Cross in the Church Today*, The Cooling Spring Press, 1992. p. 26.

16. Rousas John Rushdoony, *Institutes of Biblical Law*, Presbyterian and Reformed Publishing, 1973, p. 776.

17. Gary North, *When Justice Is Aborted: Biblical Standards for Non-*

Violent Resistance, Dominion Press 1989. p. 20.

18. Gary North, *Unconditional Surrender: God's Program for Victory*, Institute for Christian Economics, 1991. p. 121.

19. North, op. cit.

20. Robertson, op. cit., p. 235.

21. Ibid., p., 254.

22. Ibid., p. 218-219.

23. Ibid., p. 227.

24. David Cantor, *The Religious Right and the Assault on Tolerance, & Pluralism in America,* Anti-Defamation League, 1994, p. 26.

25. Ibid., p. 24.

26. Dr. Lester Sumrall, *Demonology & Deliverance: Principalities & Powers,* LeSEA Publishing Company, 1993.

27. Ibid., p. 103.

28. Ibid., p. 131.

29. Ibid., p. 65.

30. Ibid., p. 63.

31. Ibid., p. 89.

32. Ibid., p. 51.

33. Ibid., p. 112.

34. Gary North, *Conspiracy: A Biblical View*, Dominion Press, 1986. p. 15.

35. Chuck & Donna McIlhenny, op. cit., p. 232.

36. R.J. Rushdoony, *The Nature of the American System*, The Craig Press, Presbyterian and Reformed Publishing Company, p. 156.

37. Seymour Martin Lipset and Earl Raab, *The Politics of Unreason: Right-Wing Extremism in America 1790-1970,* Harper & Row, 1970. p. 42.

38. Gary North, *Political Polytheism: The Myth of Pluralism, Institute for Christian Economics*, 1991. p. 567.

39. Steve Brunsman, "Masonic Campaign Counters Baptist Claims," *The Houston Post*, February 20, 1993.

40. Pat Robertson, fundraising letter for the Christian Coalition of Iowa, 1992.

41. For a discussion of this film see Frederick Clarkson, "The Anti-Gay Nineties," *The Freedom Writer,* March-April 1993; reprinted in Frederick Clarkson and Skipp Porteous, *Challenging the Christian Right: The Activists Handbook,* Institute for First Amendment Studies, 1992, p. 83; see also Laura Flanders, "Hate on Tape: The Video Strategy of the Fundamentalist Right," *Extra!,* June 1993; reprinted in Chip Berlet, ed., *Eyes Right: Challenging the Right-Wing Backlash, South End Press*, 1995. p. 105.

42.   Stanley Montieth, *AIDS, The Unnecessary Epidemic: America Under Siege*, Covenant House Books, 1991. p. 383. The publisher is Reconstructionist, Dalmar D. Dennis, who is also a member of the National Council of the John Birch Society.

43.   Branan and Clarkson, op. cit. See also "Stanley Montieth Replies," *Front Lines Research*, November 1994.

44.   Michael Lind, "Rev. Robertson's Grand International Conspiracy Theory," *The New York Review of Books*, February 2, 1995.

45.   Ibid., p. 25.

46.   Rousas John Rushdoony, *Law and Society: Institutes of Biblical Law*, Vol. II, Ross House Books, 1986. p. 167.

47.   Robert Boettcher, *Gifts of Deceit: Sun Myung Moon, Tongsun Park and the Korean Scandal,* Holt, Rinehart & Winston, 1980. p. 344.

48.   Steve Hassan, *Combatting Cult Mind Control*, Park Street Press, 1988. p. 25

49.   Ibid., pp. 26-29. An account of Hassan's experiences also appears in Boettcher, op. cit., pp. 179-180.

50.   Robertson, op. cit., p. 228.

51.   Sara Diamond, *Roads to Dominion: Right-Wing Movements and Political Power in the United States,* The Guilford Press, 1995. p. 238. See also Kate Cornell, "The Covert Tactics and the Overt Agenda of the New Christian Right," *Covert Action Quarterly*, Winter 1992-93.

52.   Robertson, op. cit., p. 168.

53.   Quoted in Cornell, op. cit.

54.   Skipp Porteous, "The World According to Pat Robertson: The Rev. Pat Robertson has mounted a battle of biblical proportions to rescue America from Satanic forces," *Reform Judaism*, Spring 1993.

55.   Ibid.

56.   Robertson, op. cit., p. 254.

57.   *Army of God*, circa late 1970s. Updated 1992. pp. ii; See also Anne Bower, "Army of God: Still On The March," *The Body Politic*, December 1995.

Chapter 7: Bombings, Assassinations, and Theocratic Revolution: Vigilantes Enforce God's Law

1.   Mimi Hall, "Suspicious Fire Sparks New Fears at Clinics, *USA Today*, August 11, 1994; Allie Shah, "Brainerd Fire Destroys Planned Parenthood Clinics, Other Businesses," *Star-Tribune*, August 11, 1994.

2.   Jeff Cohen and Norman Solomon, *Through the Media Looking Glass: Decoding Media Bias and Blather in the News,* Common

Courage Press, 1995. p. 54.

3. *Newsday*, July 31, 1994.
4. Gary North, *When Justice Is Aborted*, Dominion Press, 1989. p. 65. "God's law sanctions every kind of protest, including violent revolution if lower magistrates approve."
5. Paul Hill, "Should We Defend Born and Unborn Children With Force?" Defensive Action, 1993. A shortened version of this paper, which skirts the issue of militias and revolution. appeared in *Life Advocate* magazine, August 1993.
6. Gary North, *Christian Reconstruction: What It Is, What It Isn't*, Institute for Christian Economics, 1991. p. xiv.
7. Kathy Sawyer, "Turning from Weapon 'Of the Spirit' to the Shotgun," *The Washington Post,* August 7, 1994.
8. Paul J. Hill, fundraising letter, October 1993.
9. Associated Press, July 31, 1994.
10. Greg L. Bahnsen, *No Other Standard: Theonomy and Its Critics*, Institute for Christian Economics, 1991. pp. 62-64.
11. Rousas John Rushdoony, *Christianity and the State*, Ross House Books, 1986. p. 7. See also Billy Falling, *The Political Mission of the Church*, Christian Voters League, 1990. p. 46.
12. See Chapter 8 for further discussion of the humanism issue.
13. Fred Bayles, "Abortion Foes Stand by Support of 'Justifiable Homicide," Associated Press, August 10, 1994. See "Defensive Action" September 6, 1993.
14. Lapsley Forman, *Shattering the Darkness, The Crisis of the Cross in the Church Today*, Cooling Spring Press, 1992. p. 188.
15. Lorrie Denise Booker, "City Wins Order Barring Abortion Protesters' Tactics," *The Atlanta Constitution*, March 29, 1990.
16. Frederick Clarkson, "Pretenders To The Throne," *St. Louis Journalism Review*, September, 1990.
17. *Regent University Graduate Catalog*, 1994-1996. p. 127.
18. Bill Kaczor, "Religious Law Institute Offers to Help Hill; Robertson Group Wants Out," Associated Press, August 2, 1994. Hill was later acquitted of the noise violation, but convicted on the trespassing charge.
19. Ibid.
20. An ad in *Life Advocate* magazine offered "a copy of Michael Hirsh's doctoral thesis on the defense of Michael Griffin" to those who contributed $20 or more to the legal defense of Shelly Shannon, who was ultimately convicted of the attempted murder of abortion provider Dr. George Tiller.

21. Michael Hirsh, "Use of Force In Defense of Another: An Argument for Michael Griffin," *Regent University Law Review*, Spring 1994. pp. 120-121. (suppressed).

22. Ibid. p. 168. Hirsh is aware that a defense attorney resorting to "Biblical Truth" in a judicial proceeding is unlikely to be tolerated, let alone prevail. But interestingly, in bemoaning the fate of his beliefs, he invokes "Yale law professor Stephen Carter [who, in his book *The Culture of Disbelief*] recently warned against modern society's improper prejudice against 'God talk.'

23. See for example, Eric Lipton, "Law Review Cancels Abortion Article," *The Washington Post*, August 23, 1994.

24. Matthew Bowers, "Abortion Paper's Author Fired: CBN-based Law Center Differed With His Defense of Clinic Killings, *The Virginian-Pilot*, November 1, 1994.

25. "Abortion Foe Files Appeal, Cites 'Orwellian' Probation," Associated Press, February 19, 1995.

26. Frank J. Murray, "Florida Justices Hear Plea For Abortion-Clinic Killer," *The Washington Times*, June 1, 1996. Other attorneys involved in Hill's appeal were Vincent F. Heuser and Roger J. Frechette. See also, "Pro-Life Forces Defend Murderer of Abortion Doctor," *Church & State*, July/August 1996.

27. For information on HLI see Frederick Clarkson and Karen Branan, "Extremism in Sheep's Clothing," *Front Lines Research*, June 1994. Sandi DuBowski, Human Life International: Promoting Uncivilization," *Front Lines Research*, May 1995, and Steve Askin, *A New Rite: Conservative Catholic Organizations and Their Allies*, Catholics for Free Choice, 1994.

28. International Anti-Abortion Research Project: Preliminary Report, *Political Environments*, Summer 1995.

29. Keith A. Fournier, "Is Planned Parenthood Killing Abortionists?", *Culture Wars*, May 1995.

30. Hirsh, op. cit., p. 117.

31. Dallas Blanchard, *Religious Violence and Abortion: The Gideon Project*, University Press of Florida. p. 196

32. The ACLU Washington office was firebombed on the Fourth of July, 1984.

33. Jim Naughton, "The Faces of 2 Antiabortionists: A 'Pretty Normal Life' Contrasts With Confrontational Stands," *The Washington Post*, December 3, 1991.

34. Michael Bray, "The Ethics of Operation Rescue," presented at the 42nd National Conference of the Evangelical Theological Society,

November 15-17, 1990, New Orleans Baptist Seminary, New Orleans, Louisiana.

35. Ibid.

36. Michael Bray and Michael Colvin, *Capitol Area Christian News*, December 1993.

37. Michael Bray, *A Time to Kill*, Advocates for Life Publications, Portland, OR, p. 118.

38. Ibid., pp. 124-125.

39. Ibid., p. 164, 169.

40. Ibid., pp. 169-171.

41. Ibid., pp. 140-143.

42. Gary North, *When Justice Is Aborted: Biblical Standards for Non-Violent Resistance*, Dominion Press, 1989. pp. 128-129.

43. Ibid., pp. 116-117.

44. Ibid., pp. 91-93.

45. Ibid., p. 131.

46. Ibid., p. 159.

47. Jonathan Hutson, "Operation Rescue Founder Predicts Armed Conflict," *Front Lines Research*. May 1995.

48. Chip Berlet, "Freemason and other Conspiracy Theories and their Relationship to Armed Militias, the Patriot Movement, and the Christian Right," Political Research Associates, February 5, 1996.

49. Michael Bray, *A Time to Kill*, Advocates for Life Publications, 1994. pp. 110 - 112.

50. Marion Manuel, "To Kill Abortionists?", *The Atlanta Journal-Constitution*, August 28, 1994.

51. Laurie Goodstein, "Suspended Priest Preaches 'New Theology' of Antiabortion Homicide," *The Washington Post*, August 5, 1994.

52. John Goetz, "Missionaries' Leader Calls for Armed Militias," *Front Lines Research,* August 1994.

53. Melinda Liu, "Inside the Anti-Abortion Underground," *Newsweek*, August 29, 1994.

54. *Field Manual: Principles Justifying the Arming and Organizing of a Militia*, The Free Militia, 1994. Section 1. p. 40.

55. Jo Mannies, "Sinister Militia Ties Called a 'Leap In Logic,'" *St. Louis Post Dispatch*, June 7, 1995.

56. Tom Bates, "Pro-Life Movement Echoes Crisis of '60's Anti-War Fight: Militancy Splinters Abortion Foes," *Rocky Mountain News*, November 28, 1994.

57. Bill Smith, "Prosecute for Abortions, Group Says," *St. Louis Post*

Dispatch, August 5, 1995,

58. *Unholy Alliance,* Public Policy Institute, Planned Parenthood Federation of America, 1995. Jan Legnito, producer.

59. Beth Hawkins, "Patriot Games," *Metro Times*, October 12, 1994.

60. Sandi DuBowski, "Storming Wombs and Waco: How the Anti-Abortion and Militia Movements Converge," *Front Lines Research*, October, 1996

61. John K. Wiley, "Judge Rules Probable Cause to Detain Men Arrested in Robberies," Associated Press, October 16, 1996

62. James Ridgeway, *Blood In The Face: The KuKlux Klan, Aryan Nations, Nazi Skinheads, and the Rise of a New White Culture*, Thunder Mouth Press,1990

63. Nicholas K. Geranios, "Fourth Man Sought; Home Search Finds Cache of Weapons, Bomb Making Materials," Assoicated Press, October 10, 1996.

64. Mimi Hall, "After Conviction, Still Fears of Clinic Violence," *USA Today*, March 7, 1994.

65. Amy Pagnozzi, "Deadly Acts Defended with Rational Words," *Daily News*, December 31, 1994.

66. "A Time to Kill," "The 5th Estate," Canadian Broadcasting Company, December 13, 1994. Julian Sher, producer, Howard Goldenthal, associate producer.

67. Anne Bower, "Army of God: Still Marching," *The Body Politic*, December 1995. See also, Anne Bower, "Shelly Shannon: A Soldier In The Army Of God," *The Body Politic*, December 1995.

68. David Chilton, "Juries: Bulwark Against Tyranny," *Sacramento Union*, March 17, 1991.

69. IRS Form 990, annual filings for the Carthage Foundation.

70. Phil Kuntz, "Citizen Scaife: Heir Turned Publisher Uses Financial Largess to Fuel Conservatism," *The Wall Street Journal,* October 12, 1995. Karen Rothmyer, "Citizen Scaife," *Columbia Journalism Review*, July/August, 1981.

71. Stephen Adler, "Jurors Should Reject Laws They Don't Like, Activist Group Argues," *The Wall Street Journal*, January 4, 1991.

72. "A Well Hung Jury," Mainstream Voters Project, *Bulletin!,* March 1996; Sara Bongiorni, "Baldwin Bill Dead In Water: Juries Would Have Been Allowed To Ignore Law," *Daily Transcript*, April 16, 1996.

73. Gary North and David Chilton, "Apologetics and Strategy," in *Tactics of Christian Resistance*, Geneva Divinity School Press, Tyler, Texas, 1983. p. 135.

74. DeMar, *Ruler of The Nations*, op. cit., pp. 218-219. DeMar also writes

on page 41, that "individuals, schools, churches, business establishments, and civil governments must choose the law of God as the standard for decision-making. Since the individual is not free to break the law, the courts are not free to judge on any other basis of law-order than that set forth in the Bible."

75. Mike Colvin, "The Jury System: A Grand Institution Now In Decay," *Capitol Area Christian News*, March 1994.

76. Rousas John Rushdoony, *The Institutes of Biblical Law,* Presbyterian and Reformed Publishing Company, 1973. p. 510.

77. Rev. David C. Trosch, "Jurors Who Can Morally Lie," *Life Advocate*, December 1994.

78. James Coates, *Armed and Dangerous: The Rise of the Survivalist Right,* Hill and Wang, 1987. p. 119.

79. Associated Press, "Who Are the Freemen?", April 3, 1996.

Chapter 8: The Fight for the Framework: Resetting the Terms of Debate

1. Stephen L. Carter, *The Culture of Disbelief: How American Law and Politics Trivialize Religious Devotion*, Basic Books, 1993.

2. Thanks to the White House, the book figured into national news stories and was reviewed or discussed by a large number of both popular and professional periodicals. See for example, Kenneth L. Woodward, "Making Room for Religion," *Newsweek,* September 20, 1993; James Carroll, "God's Patriots," *The Atlantic Monthly*, December, 1993; Winston Davis, "Translating God-Talk: Church, State and the Practice of Civility," *Christian Century*, April 20, 1994; Paul Reidinger, "Keeping the Faith," *ABA Journal*, October 1993; Dr. Robert S. Alley, "The Culture of Disbelief: Trivial Pursuit," *Church & State*, December, 1993. Robert J. Lipschutz and Steven K. Green, "The Culture of Disbelief: A Review," *Georgia State Bar Journal*, Summer, 1994.

3. James Davison Hunter, *Culture Wars: The Struggle to Define America*, Basic Books, 1991. p. 34.

4. James Davison Hunter, *Before the Shooting Begins: Searching for Democracy in America's Culture War*, The Free Press, 1994. p. viii.

5. Ibid., pp. 4-5.

6. McIlhenny, p. 49; McIlhenny refers to Rushdoony as a "friend" on page 73.

7. McIlhenny, p. 59.

8. McIlhenny, p. 68.

9. Hunter, *Culture*, p. 112.

10. Hunter, *Culture*, pp. 109-110.

11. Hunter, Culture, p. 262.

12. Hunter, *Culture*, p. 151.

13. Hunter, *Culture*, pp. 315-316.

14. Ana Puga, "'Newcomers Preach Violence," *The Boston Globe*, October 30, 1994.

15. For example, according to statistics from the National Abortion Federation and the Center for Reproductive Law and Policy, in 1992 there were: 16 arsons; 1 bombing; 13 attempted arsons or bombings; 57 chemical attacks; 26 clinic invasions; 116 incidents of vandalism; 6 cases of assault and battery; and 83 clinic blockades. See *Pro-Choice Idea*, August 1993. Pro-Choice Resource Center, Mamaroneck, NY.

16. Hunter, *Before,* p. vii.

17. *News Release*, National Abortion Federation.

18. Hunter, *Culture*, p. 316.

19. McIlhenny, op. cit., p. 19.

20. "Anti-Gay Violence, Victimization & Defamation in 1989. National Gay & Lesbian Task Force, 1989. p. 6-7

21. Ibid., p. 19. In signing the Act, Mr. Bush stated: "The faster we can find out about these hideous crimes the faster we can track down the bigots who commit them... Enacting this law today, helps us move towards our dream, a society blind to prejudice, a society open to all."

22. Hunter, *Culture,* pp. 191-192.

23. "Anti-Gay/Lesbian Violence, Victimization & Defamation in 1990," National Gay & Lesbian Task Force Policy Institute, 1990. p. 4.

24. Hunter, *Before,* p. 78.

25. Hunter, *Before,* p. 78. The anti-abortion *Human Life Review* jumped at the chance to quote Hunter's misinformed slam on Planned Parenthood's tax status. Colleen Boland, "The Culture War: Will the Shooting Really Begin?", *The Human Life Review*, Fall, 1994. p. 54.

26. *Service Report*, Planned Parenthood Federation of America, 1993. Planned Parenthood Federation America (PPFA) is comprised of 163 separately incorporated affiliates, which administer about 950 women's health centers. PPFA affiliates are multi-service agencies that feature family planning, often including abortion, HIV and cancer screening, and pre-natal care. In 1992, for example, PPFA provided contraceptive services to nearly 2 million people; HIV screening to 130,000, and abortions for about 131,000. In that year, 63 affiliates, or just over 1/3 performed abortions, which constituted about 8 percent of all abortions in the U.S.

27. Mark Crutcher, *Firestorm: A Guerrilla Strategy for a Pro-Life*

America, Life Dynamics, July 1992. For a discussion of this strategy, see Barbara Rochelle, "Praying for Plaintiffs: Legal Attacks on Legal Access to Abortion," *Front Lines Research,* February 1995.

28. Hunter, *Before*, p. 264.
29. Editorial, *The Washington Times*, February, 28, 1991.
30. Hunter, *Before*, pp. 87-89.
31. Hunter, *Before*, p. 264.
32. Hunter, *Before*, p. 85.
33. Hunter, *Before,* p. 264. Additionally, in neither the chapter nor the notes, does he mention that two similar studies which he also discusses, were also sponsored by anti-abortion groups for purposes of strategic research, (page 265). However, in an earlier version of this chapter which appeared two years before in *First Things* (see note 36 below), he does disclose that the Tarrance study "was commissioned by the Family Research Council, a division of Focus on the Family," and the Wirthlin study "was commissioned by the National Conference of Catholic Bishops."
34. Hunter, *Before,* p. 156.
35. Richard John Neuhaus, "Combat Ready," *National Review*, May 2, 1994.
36. James Davison Hunter, "What Americans Really Think About Abortion," *First Things*: *A Monthly Journal of Religion and Public Life*, June/July 1992. p. 14; 16.
37. Leon Howell, "Funding The War of Ideas," *Christian Century*, July 19, 1995. Neuhaus' own organization, the Institute on Religion and Public Life, which publishes *First Things*, is also largely funded by the same group of conservative foundations.
38. Leon Howell, "Old Wine, New Bottles: A Short History of the IRD," *Christianity & Crisis*, March 21, 1983; See also Leon Howell, "Funding The War of Ideas," *Christian Century*, July 19, 1995; Leon Howell, *Funding The War Of Ideas: A Report to United Church of Christ, Board for Homeland Ministries,* October 1995, Cleveland, OH.
39. Hunter, *Culture*, p. 261.
40. Hunter, *Culture,* pp. 380-381. Hunter also wrote a piece for Neuhaus' journal *This World* based on his testimony.
41. Deposition of James Davison Hunter, Douglas T. Smith et al., v. Board of School Commissioners of Mobile County, et al., (consolidated with Douglas T. Smith, et al, v. Fob James, Governor of Alabama, et al. August 25, 1986. p. 13, 16.
42. Ibid., p. 57.

43.   Transcript of proceedings, Volume I, October 6, 1986 to October 7, 1986. pp. 298-299.

44.   Ibid., p. 300.

45.   Ibid., p. 368.

46.   Ibid., pp. 341-342

47.   Judge Brevard Hand, Decision, March 4, 1987, amended March 10,1987. One who was nevertheless influenced by the case was Stephen Carter, op. cit., p. 171-172. Carter thinks the judge "might have been on to something important" because, he argues, that even if secular humanism is not a religion it is an "educational philosophy" or even an "ideology." Carter thus internalizes the main point of the Christian Right.

48.   Interestingly, Hunter's views under oath anticipate his views in *Culture Wars*. "The dogma of humanism as a meaning system is the hostility to theistic dogma... in sociological terms dogma would be defined as an position over which there is no debate. There is no compromise." Ibid., p. 269.

49.   United States Court Of Appeals For The Eleventh Circuit, 827 F.2d 684; 1987 U.S. App. LEXIS 11526; 103 A.L.R. Fed. 517, August 26, 1987. Undeterred, Hunter adapted one of his background papers into an article "America's Fourth Faith: A Sociological Perspective on Secular Humanism." *This World*, #19, 1987. pp. 101-110. Once again, with the help of Neuhaus, Hunter made no mention of the origins of the piece, nor even the case itself. Interestingly, Neuhaus previously published an excerpt from Brevard Hand's decision, see W. Brevard Hand, "Humanism A Religion?", *This World*, #17, 1987. pp. 110-114.

50.   Hunter, *Before*, p. viii.

51.   James Davison Hunter, "Before the Shooting Begins," *Columbia Journalism Review*, July/August, 1993.

52.   David Earle Anderson, "Cultural Battles, Moral Visions," *Christianity and Crisis*, June 22, 1992.

53.   Hunter, *Culture*, 131-132. Anti-abortion leader Harold O.J. Brown in a review for *Christianity Today* found *Before the Shooting Begins* so "persuasive" that it left him wondering about the viability of democracy or if it is even "the right thing." He was particularly disturbed by Hunter's comparisons of the issue of slavery prior to the U.S. Civil War, to the seemingly irreconcilable camps on the abortion issue. Brown is chairman of the anti-abortion Christian Action Council, based in Falls Church, Virginia. See Harold O.J. Brown, "Abortion and the Failure of Democracy," *Christianity Today*, August 15, 1994.

54. Charles B. Sanford, *The Religious Life of Thomas Jefferson*, University Press of Virginia, 1984. p. 28.

55. Ibid.

56. Sanford Levinson, "The Multicultures of Belief and Disbelief," *Michigan Law Review*, May 1984. p. 1873.

57. *Federal News Service*, February 3, 1994.

58. Michael Kinsley, "Martyr Complex," *The New Republic,* September 13, 1993.

59. Robert S. Alley, "Disputing the Charge of a Cultural Conspiracy, *Free Inquiry*, Winter 1993/94.

60. Robert S. Alley, "The Culture of Disbelief: Trivial Pursuit," *Church & State*, December 1993.

61. Daniel Miller, "Hamp Free-lancer Digs Into Coalition Strategy," *Union-News,* (Springfield, MA) July 31, 1996.

62. Jay Alan Sekulow, "The Culture of Disbelief: A Review," *Georgia State Bar Journal,* Summer 1994. It is important to note that the (often fallacious) anecdotes about suppression of religious expression told by the likes of Pat Robertson in support of the same claim as Carter's are routinely conflated into crises of Biblical proportions. One story from the "persecution" lore of the Christian Right, on how a Tennessee student was supposedly give a zero on a report because it happened to be about Jesus Christ, was debunked by Robert Boston, "Anatomy of a Smear," *Church & State*, January 1996.

63. Carter, op. cit., p. 266.

64. Carter, op. cit., p. 229.

65. Carter, op. cit., p. 57.

66. Pamela Maraldo, Address to the Southern Regional Meeting, Planned Parenthood Federation of America, 1994.

67. Ralph Reed, *Active Faith*, The Free Press, 1996. p. 200.

68. Ibid., p. 82.

69. Carter, op. cit., p. 24.

70. Frank S. Mead, *Handbook of Denominations in the United States*, Ninth Edition, 1990. Abingdon Press. p. 113; 239.

71. Ibid., p. 58.

72. Ibid., pp. 25-26.

73. Sun Myung Moon, "Leaders Building World Peace," *Unification News*, September 1992.

74. John Judis, "Rev. Moon's Rising Political Influence: His Empire Is Spending Big Money To Try To Win Favor With Conservatives," *U.S. News and World Report*, March 27, 1989.

75. See for example, Steve Hassan, *Combating Cult Mind Control*, Park

Street Press, 1988; see also Flo Conway and Jim Seigelman, *Snapping: America's Epidemic of Sudden Personality Change*, Second Edition, Stillpoint Press, 1995.

76. Carter, op. cit., p. 11.

77. Carter, op. cit., p. 96.

78. Carter, op. cit., p. 93.

79. Carter, op. cit., pp. 86-89.

80. See for example, Barton's book *To Pray or Not to Pray*, (1988) and The Myth of Separation, (1992), WallBuilder Press, Aledo, TX. Both books were in wide circulation in Christian Right circles prior to the publication of *The Culture of Disbelief.*

81. Carter, op. cit., p. 90.

82. Carter, op. cit., p. 267.

83. Carter, op. cit., p. 19.

84. Carter, p. 15. "And through all of this trivializing rhetoric runs the subtle but unmistakable message: pray if you like; worship if you must, but whatever you do, do not on any account take your religion seriously. That rhetoric, and that message, are the subjects of this book. This book is not about law, but about attitudes—the attitude that we as a political society hold toward religion."

85. Carter, p. 15. He agrees, with the Christian Right on "broad parental rights to exempt children from educational programs on religious grounds and participation by parochial schools in private school voucher programs…"

86. I hope that this essay will encourage people to seek out better information and analysis about the Christian Right — and to demand better than they usually get from the media. Personally I recommend the books and articles of knowledgeable writers like Russ Bellant, Chip Berlet, Robert Boston, Joe Conn, Sara Diamond, Jean Hardisty, Skipp Porteous, and Lenny Zeskind, among others who have studied this and related movements for many years. Their work is cited throughout the text, notes and resources section of this book. The Christian Right would be far less powerful today, if writers like these had received half of the media and scholarly attention accorded Hunter and Carter.

87. Hunter, *Culture*, p. 64.

Chapter 9: Promise Keepers: The Death of Feminism?

1. Frederick Clarkson, "Righteous Brothers: Are The Promise Keepers Renewing Family Values Or Advancing The Agenda Of The Christian Right?, *In These Times*, August 5, 1996. Many of the references to the Syracuse rally are also discussed in this article.

2. Norman Solomon, "Mass Media Are Boosting Promise Keepers," *Media Beat*, Creators Syndicate, August 3, 1996.

3. Ralph Reed, *Active Faith*, The Free Press, 1996. p. 95.

4. Billy Bruce, Full Gospel Business Men's Group Splits," *Charisma*, September 1996.

5. John D. Spaulding, "Bonding In The Bleachers: A Visit To The Promise Keepers," *The Christian Century*, March 6, 1996.

6. Hans Johnson, "Broken Promise?", *Church & State*, May 1995.

7. Dr. Tony Evans, "Spiritual Purity," *Seven Promises of a Promise Keeper*, Focus on the Family, 1994. p. 79-80.

8. Lee Quinby, "The Gendered Year 2000," paper presented at "The Millenium Cusp: Western Cultures at 1000, 1500, 2000 and Beyond." Tremont Temple, Boston, MA, October, 16, 1996.

9. Suzanne Pharr, "Seeking the Promise of Equality," *Sojourner: The Women's Forum*, September 1996.

10. Evans, op.cit., p. 79.

11. Peggy Leslie, "Unity In Diversity Typifies Promise Keepers," *Southern California Christian Times*, August 1996.

12. John D. Spaulding, "Bonding In The Bleachers: A Visit To the Promise Keepers," *The Christian Century*, March 6, 1996.

13. Jeff Hooten, "Making Their Voices Heard;" and Jeff Hooten, "Breaking Down Walls: Promise Keepers Is Fostering Brotherly Love In Stadiums Across The U.S., *Citize*n, May 27, 1996

14. Interview with the author, July 1996.

15. Hooten, op. cit.

16. For a discussion of CNP, see Russ Bellant, "The Council for National Policy: Stealth Leadership Of The Radical Right," *Front Lines Research*, August 1994. See also Skipp Porteous, "Reshaping America: CNP Instrument Of Government Shutdown," *Freedom Writer*, January/February 1996.

17. Russ Bellant, *The Religious Right in Michigan Politics*, Americans for Religious Liberty, 1996, p. 12.

18. Ralph Reed, *Active Faith*, The Free Press, 1996. p. 69. For a further discussion of Reed's book, see Frederick Clarkson, "Whitewashing the Christian Right, *In These Times*, August 5, 1996.

19. Ibid., pp. 67-68

20. Ibid., p. 68.

21. Ibid., p. 69.

22. Ibid., p. 63.

23. Jane Glenn Haas and Marilyn Kalfus, "Guided By A Wealth of Convictions: Howard Ahmanson Is Out To Make A Difference In The

World, $10 Million At A Time," *The Orange County Register*, June 30, 1996.

24. Alfred Ross, Lee Cokorinos, *Promise Keepers: The Third Wave of the American Religious Right*, Sterling Research Associates, November 1996, p. 17-18.

25. John Swomley, "Promises We *Don't* Want Kept," *The Humanist*, January/February, 1996.

26. *PK 1996 Break Down The Walls Men's Conferences*. p. 5

27. Bill McCartney, "A Call To Unity," *Seven Promises of a Promise Keeper*, Focus on the Family, 1994. p. 164.

28. Russ Bellant, "Promise Keepers: Christian Soldiers for Theocracy," anthologized in *Eyes Right! Challenging the Right Wing Backlash*, South End Press, 1996. p. 84. See also, Russ Bellant, "Mania In The Stadia: The Origins And Goals Of Promise Keepers," *Front Lines Research*, May 1995. *see also* Russ Bellant, *The Religious Right in Michigan Politics*, Americans for Religious Liberty, 1996,

29. Introduction, Chapter 2, *Seven Promises of a Promise Keeper*, Focus on the Family, 1994. p. 45.

30. Quoted in Russ Bellant, "Promise Keepers: Christian Soldiers for Theocracy," in *Eyes Right! Challenging the Right Wing Backlash*, Chip Berlet, ed. South End Press, 1995, p. 83.

31. Bellant, op. cit., p. 83.

32. Bill Bright, *The Coming Revival: America's Call To Fast, Pray and Seek God's Face*, New Life Publications, 1995. p. 61.

33. Ibid., p. 56

34. Ibid., p. 57.

35. Ibid., p. 57.

36. Ibid., p. 56.

37. Ibid., pp. 58-59.

38. Nancy Novosad, "God Squad: The Promise Keepers Fight For a Man's World," *The Progressive*, August 1996.

39. Hans Johnson, op. cit.

40. Bellant, op. cit., p. 83.

41 Alfred Ross and Lee Cokorinos, op. cit., p. 5-7. The U.S. Navy in Pat Robertson's home town, Virginia Beach, VA, planned to sponsor a PK "Wake-Up Call" rally until the Anti-Defamation League complained that such sponsorship violated the separation of church and state. The Navy withdrew, but the show went on anyway, sponsored by the Military Ministries of Campus Crusade for Christ. Toward Tradition, a right-wing Jewish group whose main purpose seems to be to serve as apologists for the Christian Right, accused

the ADL of "Christian bashing." Julia Duin, "Jewish Groups Fight Over Christian Rally," *The Washington Times*, November 21, 1996.

42   Pat Robertson, *The New World Order: It Will Change The Way You Live*, Word Publishing, 1991 p. 254.

43.   Bob Gorman, "Participants Will Be Told: Get Spiritual House In Order," *The Post Standard*, June 7, 1996.

44.   Novosad, op. cit.

45.   Lee Quinby, "Movement Preaches Inequality Of Women, Power for Men," *The* (Syracuse) *Post-Standard*, June 7, 1996.

Chapter 10: Defending Democracy: Rethink the Strategy

1.   Gary North and David Chilton, "Apologetics and Strategy," *Tactics of Christian Resistance*, Geneva Divinity School Press, Tyler, Texas, 1983. p.101.

2.   See discussion of the origins of the Rutherford Institute in Chapter 4.

3.   Gary North, *Conspiracy: A Biblical View*, Dominion Press, 1986. p. 141.

4.   These points are discussed in more detail in Frederick Clarkson and Skipp Porteous, *Challenging the Christian Right: The Activists Handbook*, Institute for First Amendments Studies, 1993.

5.   Leonard Zeskind, "Armed and Dangerous: The NRA, Militias and White Supremacists are Fostering a Network of Right Warriors," *Rolling Stone*, November 2, 1995.

6.   Gary DeMar, *Ruler of the Nations: Biblical Principles for Government,* Dominion Press, 1987. p. 218.

7.   Michael Bray, *A Time to Kill*, Advocates for Life Publications, 1994. pp. 171-172.

8.   See discussion of Hirsh and ACLJ chief Keith Fournier in chapter 7.

9.   Rob Boston, "Pat Robertson and Church-State Separation: A Track Record of Deception," *Church & State*, April 1996.

10.   William Saletan, "Sin Of Omission," *Mother Jones*, May/June 1996.

11.   Ibid.

12.   Chip Berlet, ed., *Eyes Right! Challenging the Right Wing Backlash*, South End Press, 1995. pp. 316-324. The full text is published in this book and is separately available from Political Research Associates. See Resources Section.

Index

About the Author

Frederick Clarkson is a widely published journalist, author, and lecturer, who specializes in the Radical Right. He was the first to expose the Christian Coalition's plans to take over the Republican Party, and his ground-breaking articles on the Christian Right are frequently years ahead of the pack. He was the first to expose how elements of the Christian Right were encouraging the formation of citizen "militias," almost five years before the Oklahoma City bombing propelled the militia movement into public consciousness (*Mother Jones* Nov./Dec. 1990). Clarkson has also written extensively about the empire of televangelist Pat Robertson.

He is the co-author of *Challenging the Christian Right: The Activist's Handbook*, (Institute for First Amendment Studies, 1993), for which he and his co-author were named among the "Ten Media Heroes of 1992" by the Institute for Alternative Journalism, which described them as "especially brave at taking on powerful institutions and persistent about getting stories out...journalists and activists who persevere in fighting censorship and protecting the First Amendment," and "understanding the Christian Right's recent strategy of stealth politics early on, and for doggedly tracking its activities across the U.S."

His work on the Unification Church of Sun Myung Moon is recognized internationally. He has served as a consultant to documentaries and news features on Moon's organization for, among others, CBS News, PBS, and German and Japanese television. He is the founding editor of *Front Lines Research*, a bi-monthly journal on the Radical Right, published by the Public Policy Institute, of Planned Parenthood Federation of America. Front Lines Research has quickly established itself as an authoritative source of information and analysis for the pro-choice community and the media. Thus Mr. Clarkson is frequently called and quoted by major media outlets, including *The New York Times, The Washington Post, USA Today, The Boston Globe*, and *The San Francisco Examiner*. He has also appeared on numerous local and national radio talk-shows and news programs, notable NPR's Morning Edition. He also co-hosted live coverage of U.S. Senate hearings on the "militia movement" for Pacifica National News. His television appearances include FOX-TV, CNN, NewsTalk and the CBS Evening News.